De Palma on De Palma

De Palma on De Palma

Conversations with
Samuel Blumenfeld
and Laurent Vachaud

Afterword by Bruce Joel Rubin

Sticking Place Books
New York

© Sticking Place Books 2024
Translation by Paul Cronin

The original French edition of this book was published in 2001 by Calmann-Lévy.
An updated edition was published in 2019 by Carlotta.

Designed by Goran Tovilovic

www.stickingplacebooks.com

All rights reserved.
No part of this book may be reproduced, stored in or introduced into a retrieval system, or transmitted, in any form or by any means (electronic, mechanical, photocopying, recording or otherwise) without the written permission of the publishers, except in the case of brief quotations embodied in critical articles or reviews.

ISBN 978-1-942782-35-3

CONTENTS

In Search of Brian De Palma	1
Introduction to the Second Edition	9
Filmography	13
Chapter One Early Years – Short Films	21
Chapter Two *Murder a la Mod* – *Greetings* – *Hi, Mom* – *Dionysus in 69* – *Get to Know Your Rabbit*	35
Chapter Three *Sisters* – *Phantom of the Paradise* – *Obsession*	49
Chapter Four *Carrie* – *The Fury*	75
Chapter Five *Home Movies* – *Dressed to Kill* – *Blow Out*	99
Chapter Six *Scarface* – *Body Double*	125

Chapter Seven
*Wise Guys – The Untouchables – Casualties of War –
The Bonfire of the Vanities – Raising Cain* 149

Chapter Eight
*Carlito's Way – Mission: Impossible – Snake Eyes –
Mission to Mars* 191

Chapter Nine
Femme Fatale – The Black Dahlia – Redacted – Passion 239

Afterword by Bruce Joel Rubin 295

Index 299

IN SEARCH OF BRIAN DE PALMA

"You are something of a paradox."

This is how arms dealer Max greets the secret agent played by Tom Cruise in one of the most remarkable scenes in Brian De Palma's *Mission: Impossible*.

Rarely has dialogue in a Hollywood blockbuster so captured the personality of its director, for if any filmmaker is a master in the art of cultivating paradox, it's De Palma. As part of the generation of the American New Wave in the Seventies, which helped save Hollywood from the rise of television, De Palma thwarted the expectations of critics and audiences – more so than his contemporaries Martin Scorsese, Steven Spielberg, George Lucas, Francis Coppola and William Friedkin. "I don't cater to the public, why should I cater to the critics?" he declared at the start of his career in an interview with *Film Comment*. His lack of diplomacy and constant challenging of conventions have forever condemned him to the margins of the Hollywood system.

It is certainly true that De Palma is a man of complexities. Though celebrated thanks to his huge-budget films starring the biggest of names, he remains a pure product of Sixties counterculture, rebellious towards the establishment, forever drawn to experimentation. A millionaire and an A-list director who competes for the most ambitious projects, he's the only one of his peers who hasn't built an empire or production company. In spite of being judged in his home country as a shameless Hitchcock plagiarist, he is nonetheless celebrated in France as a major artist, pushing the medium of film and the potential of the camera to its limits. Whatever their genre and however successful, De Palma's films always exude a euphoric love of cinema, the kind of exultation so seldom seen in contemporary American movies.

It also seems to us – and this is yet another paradox in contrast to De Palma's public image – that he is a filmmaker whose work is very much autobiographical. Through satires like *Greetings*, the thrillers *Sisters* and *Dressed to Kill*, and the film noir *Carlito's Way*, De Palma paints not so much an image of America as a picture of himself and those around him. If there is one theme that recurs in his films, it's the "family plot," instigated by manipulative parents and antagonistic siblings. Even in a film as baroque as *The Fury* – critically reviled upon its release and yet one of his great successes – adults manipulate children to make them serve their own interests. As always with De Palma, the children revolt. A recurring theme such as this seems surely to have been inspired by real-life experiences.

This is how *De Palma on De Palma* came about. Asking him to sit for the longest interview he has ever agreed to wasn't so much about learning the secrets of the craft of a master of suspense; it was more about listening to a man, who for thirty-five years has hidden behind a mask, undergo a process of self-analysis.

Before undertaking this project we spent considerable time wondering why no one had ever bothered to speak at length with De Palma. The answer was obvious. Simply put, De Palma himself. Laurent Bouzereau, one of his most fervent enthusiasts, wrote in his fascinating study *The De Palma Cut* that the filmmaker had been too often trashed by critics to trust them any longer, even when it came to his most fervent admirers. If no one was interested in Brian De Palma, the feeling was most definitely mutual.

So creating this book was no easy task, for De Palma or for us. First contact is always crucial. Taking advantage of his visit to Paris for the release of *Carlito's Way* in 1993, we found ourselves – like every journalist who came to interview him that day – confronted by De Palma's camcorder and having to state our names and the name of the publication we wrote for. He seemed amused when we asked him, in turn, to introduce himself by speaking into our tape recorder. He patiently answered questions while ordering cappuccinos he didn't drink. The ease with which De Palma linked *Carlito's Way* to episodes in his personal life was fascinating. He even went so far as to confide to us at the end of the interview that he couldn't think of anyone to spend the holidays with.

The brevity of this first meeting frustrated us, but at the same time, we were convinced that De Palma would be open to the idea of a book. Another indication that he might be interested was that in 1991, after the American release of *The Bonfire of the Vanities*, Julie Salamon's *The Devil's Candy*, a book about that film's troubled production, was published. More than any interview, it shed light on De Palma's complex personality. He had allowed a *Wall Street Journal* reporter to observe every aspect of the making of the film, from beginning to end, even if it meant alienating Hollywood executives. The endeavour speaks volumes about De Palma's masochistic tendencies. He remains one of the few filmmakers to have done everything possible to make his sponsors look like idiots, by documenting proof of their incompetence and capriciousness.

In 1994, we set out to contact De Palma again – but how exactly? He had neither a production company nor an assistant. Through Anne Lara, the press agent for Columbia Pictures in Paris, and Michael Wilson, we procured a New York address. We sent a letter, then a second one, but neither yielded a response. Then we remembered that De Palma was friendly with French filmmaker Régis Wargnier (it was after seeing Wargnier's *Indochine* that De Palma hired Patrick Doyle to compose the music for *Carlito's Way*). Interested in our project, and despite being busy with the preparation of his own film, *A French Woman*, Wargnier promised to have a word with De Palma about it.

Several months later, just when we were about to give up, Wargnier called to tell us that De Palma was coming to Paris. He had started pre-production on *Mission: Impossible* and was auditioning French actors in a Parisian hotel, where he agreed to meet us. We weren't sure if he had already said yes to the book or was simply looking to chat with us. Hordes of journalists lined the corridors of the hotel that day. In a nearby suite Tom Cruise, star and producer of *Mission: Impossible*, was doing press for *Interview with the Vampire*. De Palma was staying on the same floor under an assumed name. He ordered cappuccinos (which, once again, he didn't drink) and neglected to offer us even a glass of water.

In order to convince him to work with us, we showed him several books similar to the kind we were proposing. He insisted that he had only one hour, but this second conversation ended up lasting three, including a tape recorder malfunction, which much irritated De Palma. Another interruption came when Jean Reno showed up to audition for the role of Krieger in *Mission: Impossible*. De Palma disappeared with him for five minutes – all it took for Reno to be hired for the film. De Palma returned, but by that point his mind was clearly elsewhere, so we suggested that we stop for the day. When we asked when we might meet again, he answered, tersely, "Tomorrow I'll be in London," but didn't provide us with an address or fax number.

A week later De Palma was back in Paris, checked in at the Ritz under the name Bruce Barton, the first names of his two brothers. He couldn't decide who he wanted to cast as Claire in *Mission: Impossible* and wanted to film new tests with Tom Cruise and Emmanuelle Béart, who ultimately got the role.

Wargnier secured another meeting for us. This time De Palma's enthusiasm surprised and delighted us. Perhaps he saw our questions as a kind of intellectual challenge that pushed him to think about his films in new ways. He was relaxed, and reminded us of a patient happy to talk to his psychiatrist during the session but who would never address him outside the office. According to Michael Caine, the greatest compliment De Palma gave the actors in *Dressed to Kill* was, "That's the take we're printing." That day, luckily, De Palma was happy enough to show us digital storyboards for the Eurostar sequence in *Mission: Impossible*.

Despite an agreement that we would record fifteen hours of interviews before the filming of *Mission: Impossible* began, we ended up not seeing De Palma again until the end of the shoot – a full year later. In the meantime, there wasn't much communication between us. Pinewood, the British studio where *Mission: Impossible* was filmed, apparently hadn't been forwarding our messages, and we eventually learned from Ned Rosen, De Palma's assistant on the film, that production had been difficult. In July 1995, we got back in touch with De Palma through one of his friends in London, and a meeting was scheduled for the following month. In the South Kensington house where he lived during the film's production were large trunks full of personal belongings, suggesting that he was very ready to leave. Our interviews resumed from where we had left off, but De Palma's thoughts were elsewhere and he looked tired. His responses were punctuated with yawns, and he thanked us for keeping him awake. We were disappointed because there wasn't much we could do with the material we had recorded. A new interview was scheduled for the following day, and De Palma – having just seen a first cut of *Mission: Impossible* and convinced, rightly, of the film's commercial potential – was at the top of his game. Perhaps this wasn't the best time to ask him about *The Bonfire of the Vanities*, one of his most painful failures, but that's what we did. Talking about his adaptation of Tom Wolfe's bestseller nearly put De Palma to sleep. When we insisted on scheduling another interview, De Palma raised his eyebrows, as if he were trapped in an unending nightmare. But it was, in fact, about to end – because the following day De Palma disappeared.

We read in *Variety* that Paramount was going to produce *Snake Eyes*, a thriller written by De Palma and David Koepp. In October 1997, we contacted Jay Cocks, the screenwriter of Martin Scorsese's *The Age of Innocence* and a long-time friend of De Palma's. He promised to talk to De Palma about our project, at which point things progressed at speed. De Palma sent us a brief email confirming that he wanted to finish the book.

Despite this reassuring email and three months of silence, we didn't back down. Endless schemes to remind De Palma about our project and impress on him its urgency were set in motion, including one that involved us pretending to be a big fan of his from Switzerland, heartbroken that there was no book of interviews with him. We were astonished when De Palma immediately replied without suspecting that he was talking to the same two Frenchmen who had been tracking him for two years. Official contact resumed shortly thereafter. Several appointments were scheduled between April and October 1998 at his home in New York, then in Paris, where De Palma was promoting *Snake Eyes*. When those meetings were suddenly cancelled, we again lost hope, but later discovered that De Palma was going through a difficult time, including the successive deaths of his brother Bruce and mother Vivienne.

Thanks to De Palma's personal assistant, we were able to maintain contact with him and eventually, for a whole week, spend several hours a day with him at his New York home on lower Fifth Avenue – an extremely simple apartment where he has lived for twenty-five years – during which time we threatened to abandon the book if we weren't able to complete it by the end of the year. De Palma was aloof, and we noticed an espresso machine reserved for his use only, but he was alert and open, answering our questions – even the most personal ones – without batting an eyelid. He also listened without irritation to our reservations about *The Untouchables* and *Wise Guys*. This routine continued every day between 5 and 9pm, after his writing sessions with Jay Cocks on the script for *Nazi Gold* (which remains unproduced). Before we returned to Paris, De Palma showed us *Dionysus in 69* and *Murder a la Mod*, two of his rarest films, on video tape.

The considerable amount of time required to transcribe and edit these interviews and the sudden start of production of a new De Palma film, *Mission to Mars*, in April 1999, forced us to postpone publication of this book. We decided to wait for the March 2000 release of the film to talk to him, in Paris, about his first foray into science fiction. Exhausted by post-production on *Mission to Mars*, he admitted that he had come to France, the country that has always been enthusiastic about his films, for some time off. He was, in fact, thinking about a project he could shoot there, and during the 2000 Cannes Film Festival, where *Mission to Mars* was screened out of competition, De Palma handed out a script he had written during his Parisian interlude. His presence in Cannes and his prolonged stay in France seemed as surreal as his latest film. The man we had been desperately tracking for six years was now everywhere: newspapers, television, the Internet, in book and DVD stores, on the Promenade de la Croisette and in movie theatres, where he saw several films a day. We also noted that he hadn't lost his sense of humour: while taking part in a conference on the future of cinema organised by *Le Monde* and the Cannes Film Festival, he explained (to Brazilian filmmaker Walter Salles) that he would only be considered a real film director the day he had led a production company into financial ruin.

On a more serious note, the year 2000 marked a turning point in De Palma's career, and he acknowledged to the head of an American studio he met at the Deauville festival that turning sixty had profoundly affected him. Add to this the scars left by the consecutive losses of his older brother Bruce and mother in 1997 and 1998. One can certainly understand that De Palma –

whose entire body of work was born of a need to prove to his mother that he was as talented as Bruce – was deeply disoriented by their absence. This idea that his films were made in hopes of gaining some recognition from his family is exemplified by *Mission to Mars*, a film about rebirth and the longing for a new sense of serenity, in which a man travels into space to fill the void left by the disappearance of his loved one. France isn't Mars, but it's where Brian De Palma decided to lick his wounds and shoot his new film, *Femme Fatale*, with Antonio Banderas and Rebecca Romijn-Stamos – surely an important turning point in his future work.

Samuel Blumenfeld and Laurent Vachaud

INTRODUCTION TO THE SECOND EDITION

The previous edition of this book ended with *Mission to Mars*, Brian De Palma's first and only attempt at a science fiction blockbuster. When the film was released in March 2000, De Palma was still generally held in high esteem. Solicited by Hollywood studios and celebrated by European critics, he was clearly equally capable – when given the opportunity – of taking side roads and making less fine-tuned, more esoteric films. *Femme Fatale*, for example, made for producer Tarak Ben Ammar in Paris with a collection of French technicians and actors, is an important stage of his unique career path and demonstrates his affinity for experimentation. Nevertheless, his main focus has always been America, and a return to Hollywood would have been a logical next step.

The fifteen years that have passed since then have largely offset this state of affairs. Although De Palma still divides his time between the United States and Europe, he hasn't directed another film for an American studio or even shot an entire production in the United States. His last four films were all made abroad: *Femme Fatale* in Paris, *The Black Dahlia* in Sofia (the Los Angeles of the 1940s was reconstructed in the Bulgarian capital, an economic necessity but also imbued with symbolic significance – as if Hollywood has become alienated from its own imagery), *Redacted* in Jordan and *Passion* in Berlin.

There are several reasons for this shift. De Palma's frequent commercial failures since *Snake Eyes* gradually meant that he was removed from any list of go-to directors. Moreover, he has little time for a system that is increasingly focused on special effects and franchises aimed at teenage audiences. We still recall the bewilderment on De Palma's face, in 2008, when *Redacted* was released and he was handed the script of *Wolfman* (eventually directed by Joe Johnston, in 2010, with Benicio Del Toro and Anthony Hopkins). How was such an offer even conceivable? Clearly most Hollywood producers had no idea who he was.

Fiercely independent, he preferred to devote himself to personal projects that he could take charge of himself – though this was done at the risk of exile and the constraints of smaller budgets. The fact is that De Palma always worked best in the United States, with the resources Hollywood offered him, including American stars, whose celebrity he took pleasure in desecrating. *Femme Fatale*, *The Black Dahlia*, *Redacted* and *Passion* were all distinguished projects, films over which he had almost full control. But despite their excellence and *Redacted*'s Silver Lion at the Venice Film Festival in 2008, critics and audiences weren't much impressed, and future projects began to look increasingly difficult to finance. *Passion*, his latest, was released five years ago, an unusually long gap for De Palma.

As a result, as we prepared the update of this book, De Palma was less busy than ever, though paradoxically he has never seemed more serene. He isn't bitter or regretful, but instead rather lucid when it comes to his career and enthusiasms about films he hopes to make and which will be more experimental than ever. Those big star-studded productions? Been there, done that, he says. He claims to be too old and unpopular to return to that world, and his focus is now turned entirely towards new modes of digital expression and the storytelling they might inspire.

He also repeated a sentiment we had often heard him say during our first interviews: "No director makes his best films after sixty." De Palma, willingly accepting that his best work is behind him, has no problem describing his own career in similar terms to those of John Ford and Alfred Hitchcock. After all, like many filmmakers of his generation, he has nothing left to prove, and his career includes at least a dozen films that will go down in history. His work is regularly seen in cinemas and on television, and in the case of *Sisters* and *Carrie* has inspired mediocre remakes. De Palma has also gained recognition from a new generation of directors, as indicated by Noah Baumbach and Jake Paltrow's 2015 documentary about him.

These days, many of De Palma's colleagues are experimenting with television. It's an option he considered briefly, but television, as he sees it, is in the hands of producers and writers, and a director as visually oriented as De Palma will never truly flourish in the medium.

He's different – more honest, more subversive, as confirmed by the films he has made since *Mission to Mars*, which bear his trademark but don't fit into any traditional career profile.

Another detail that surprised us during these new interviews is the way in which De Palma talks about Hitchcock. He often brought up *Family Plot*, the English director's final film, as the example to be avoided at all costs. For him, *Family Plot* is an excess, an adulteration of an otherwise impeccable filmography. De Palma is clearly anxious about botching his final exit while also fully conscious of its inevitability. Hence the concern, before hanging up his gloves for good, to release at least one *Frenzy*. Here is De Palma referring to Hitchcock's impressive 1972 return to form after the disappointments of *Torn Curtain* and *Topaz*. In this light, we consider *Passion* a rebound to his Hitchcockian thrillers of the Eighties.

There are other, more personal reasons for his career slowdown. De Palma has plenty of money – certainly compared to the generations of directors who preceded him – which he would rather spend on his two daughters, Lolita and Piper. By prioritising the personal over the professional, he distinguishes himself once again from the New Hollywood group, of which he has always been the black sheep. Martin Scorsese, Steven Spielberg and Francis Coppola have spent the latter part of their careers being honored or presiding over festival juries, including at Cannes, but De Palma has never been a member of that club.

Today, paradoxically, he is more liberated and less cut off from the world than they are. The central character of *Citizen Kane*, the demiurge who exercises his power from behind closed doors, keeping his distance, has always haunted his films, from *Phantom of the Paradise* to *Scarface*. At the same time, it's an image that terrifies De Palma. More than once he has told us how isolation represents death for the artist – hence his fierce desire to keep his distance from anything that might draw him into this kind of cul-de-sac.

His friends have all become Howard Hughes-like characters. Francis Coppola is the head of a food empire. George Lucas turned the *Star Wars* universe into a multinational corporation which he sold to Disney for $4 billion. Steven Spielberg is one of the elder statesmen of Hollywood. Martin Scorsese, walled up in his New York office, has built an empire on cinephilia. But De Palma has created nothing but movies. If he is as wary as ever of the corrupting power of money, he doesn't look at the world from afar. He is part of it. Of all the New Hollywood filmmakers, he is the only one to have made a film about the war in Iraq and expressed interest in new forms of film narrative, which are reasons enough for the new edition of this book.

Samuel Blumenfeld and Laurent Vachaud
June 2017

FILMOGRAPHY

SHORTS AND DOCUMENTARIES

1960
Icarus
Director: Brian De Palma
Screenplay: Brian De Palma
Cinematography: Brian De Palma
Editor: Brian De Palma

1961
660124: The Story of an IBM Card
Director: Brian De Palma
Screenplay: Brian De Palma
Cinematography: Brian De Palma
Editor: Brian De Palma

1962
Woton's Wake
Director: Brian De Palma
Screenplay: Brian De Palma
Cinematography: Brian De Palma
Editor: Brian De Palma

1962
Mod [unfinished]
Director: Brian De Palma

1964
Jennifer
Director: Brian De Palma
Screenplay: Bruce Rubin
Cinematography: Brian De Palma
Editor: Brian De Palma

1966
The Responsive Eye
Director: Brian De Palma
Screenplay: Brian De Palma
Cinematography: Brian De Palma
Editor: Brian De Palma

1966
Show Me a Strong Town and I'll Show You a Strong Bank
Director: Brian De Palma
Screenplay: Brian De Palma
Editor: Brian De Palma

1969
To Bridge This Gap
Director: Brian De Palma
Screenplay: Brian De Palma
Editor: Brian De Palma

FEATURES

1968
Murder a la Mod
Director: Brian De Palma
Screenplay: Brian De Palma
Cinematography: Bruce Torbet
Editor: Brian De Palma
Music: John Herbert McDowell, William Finley

1968
Greetings
Director: Brian De Palma
Screenplay: Charles Hirsch, Brian De Palma
Cinematography: Robert Fiore
Editor: Brian De Palma
Music: Eric Kaz, Steven Soles, Artie Traum

1969
The Wedding Party [filmed in 1963]
Director: Brian De Palma, Wilford Leach, Cynthia Munroe
Screenplay: Brian De Palma, Wilford Leach, Cynthia Munroe
Cinematography: Peter Powell
Editor: Brian De Palma, Wilford Leach, Cynthia Munroe
Music: John Herbert McDowell

1969
Dionysus in 69
Director: Brian De Palma, Robert Fiore, Bruce Rubin
Screenplay: Euripides, William Arrowsmith
Cinematography: Robert Fiore, Brian De Palma
Editor: Bruce Rubin

1970
Hi, Mom!
Director: Brian De Palma
Screenplay: Brian De Palma
Cinematography: Robert Elfstrom
Editor: Paul Hirsch
Music: Eric Kaz

1972
Get to Know Your Rabbit
Director: Brian De Palma
Screenplay: Jordan Crittenden
Cinematography: John A. Alonzo
Editor: Frank J. Urioste, Peter Colbert
Music: Jack Elliott, Allyn Ferguson

1972
Sisters
Director: Brian De Palma
Screenplay: Brian De Palma, Louisa Rose
Cinematography: Gregory Sandor
Editor: Paul Hirsch
Music: Bernard Herrmann

1974
Phantom of the Paradise
Director: Brian De Palma
Screenplay: Brian De Palma
Cinematography: Larry Pizer
Editor: Paul Hirsch
Music: Paul Williams

1976
Obsession
Director: Brian De Palma
Screenplay: Paul Schrader
Cinematography: Vilmos Zsigmond
Editor: Paul Hirsch
Music: Bernard Herrmann

1976
Carrie
Director: Brian De Palma
Screenplay: Lawrence D. Cohen
Cinematography: Mario Tosi
Editor: Paul Hirsch
Music: Pino Donaggio

1978
The Fury
Director: Brian De Palma
Screenplay: John Farris
Cinematography: Richard H. Kline
Editor: Paul Hirsch
Music: John Williams

1979
Home Movies
Director: Brian De Palma
Screenplay: Kim Ambler, Dana Edelman, Robert Harders, Stephen Le May, Charlie Loventhal, Gloria Norris
Cinematography: James L. Carter
Editor: Corky O'Hara
Music: Pino Donaggio

1980
Dressed to Kill
Director: Brian De Palma
Screenplay: Brian De Palma
Cinematography: Ralf D. Bode
Editor: Jerry Greenberg
Music: Pino Donaggio

1981
Blow Out
Director: Brian De Palma
Screenplay: Brian De Palma
Cinematography: Vilmos Zsigmond
Editor: Paul Hirsch
Music: Pino Donaggio

1983
Scarface
Director: Brian De Palma
Screenplay: Oliver Stone
Cinematography: John A. Alonzo
Editors: Jerry Greenberg, David Ray
Music: Giorgio Moroder

1984
Body Double
Director: Brian De Palma
Screenplay: Brian De Palma, Robert J. Avrech
Cinematography: Stephen H. Burum
Editors: Jerry Greenberg, Bill Pankow
Music: Pino Donaggio

1986
Wise Guys
Director: Brian De Palma
Screenplay: George Gallo, Norman Steinberg
Cinematography: Fred Schuler
Editor: Jerry Greenberg
Music: Ira Newborn

1987
The Untouchables
Director: Brian De Palma
Screenplay: David Mamet
Cinematography: Stephen H. Burum
Editors: Jerry Greenberg, Bill Pankow
Music: Ennio Morricone

1989
Casualties of War
Director: Brian De Palma
Screenplay: David Rabe
Cinematography: Stephen H. Burum
Editor: Bill Pankow
Music: Ennio Morricone

1990
The Bonfire of the Vanities
Director: Brian De Palma
Screenplay: Michael Cristofer
Cinematography: Vilmos Zsigmond
Editors: Bill Pankow, David Ray
Music: Dave Grusin

1992
Raising Cain
Director: Brian De Palma
Screenplay: Brian De Palma
Cinematography: Stephen H. Burum
Editors: Robert Dalva, Paul Hirsch, Bonnie Koehler
Music: Pino Donaggio

1993
Carlito's Way
Director: Brian De Palma
Screenplay: David Koepp
Cinematography: Stephen H. Burum
Editors: Bill Pankow, Kristina Boden
Music: Patrick Doyle

1996
Mission: Impossible
Director: Brian De Palma
Screenplay: David Koepp, Robert Towne
Cinematography: Stephen H. Burum
Editor: Paul Hirsch
Music: Danny Elfman

1998
Snake Eyes
Director: Brian De Palma
Screenplay: David Koepp
Cinematography: Stephen H. Burum
Editor: Bill Pankow
Music: Ryuichi Sakamoto

2000
Mission to Mars
Director: Brian De Palma
Screenplay: Jim Thomas, John Thomas, Graham Yost
Cinematography: Stephen H. Burum
Editor: Paul Hirsch
Music: Ennio Morricone

2002
Femme Fatale
Director: Brian De Palma
Screenplay: Brian De Palma
Cinematography: Thierry Arbogast
Editor: Bill Pankow
Music: Ryuichi Sakamoto

2006
The Black Dahlia
Director: Brian De Palma
Screenplay: Josh Friedman
Cinematography: Vilmos Zsigmond
Editor: Bill Pankow
Music: Mark Isham

2007
Redacted
Director: Brian De Palma
Screenplay: Brian De Palma
Cinematography: Jonathon Cliff
Editor: Bill Pankow

2012
Passion
Director: Brian De Palma
Screenplay: Brian De Palma
Cinematography: José Luis Alcaine
Editor: François Gédigier
Music: Pino Donaggio

2019
Domino
Director: Brian De Palma
Screenplay: Petter Skavlan
Cinematography: José Luis Alcaine
Editor: Bill Pankow
Music: Pino Donaggio

CHAPTER ONE

EARLY YEARS – SHORT FILMS

One of the first things we discovered about you was that your father was a surgeon and that when you were a teenager you would watch him work. Critics have deduced that this might explain your taste for blood.

My father was an orthopedic surgeon, a big shot in his field. He ran a medical journal and wrote books that were translated all over the world. He was a real workaholic and spent all day at the hospital. When I was seventeen, I went to see him do an amputation. I'll never forget it. I was wearing a gown and stood right next to him at the operating table. He sawed off the patient's leg, then handed it to me.

Is your father still alive?

He's retired, and spends his time writing novels. He's finished two. I read the first one, *The Anatomist*, the story of a necrophiliac killer. It wasn't bad. He likes writing books, but doesn't publish them.

Your grandparents are Italian, yet of all the Italian-American filmmakers working today, you're probably the one who has represented this community the least in your films.

I never felt Italian-American, at least not like Martin Scorsese, who married an Italian woman and lived his whole life in that world. Although Italian and Catholic, my parents baptised me in a Presbyterian church.

How do you explain that?

I was born in 1940 in Newark, New Jersey, a working-class area. When I was five, my father was appointed professor at Jefferson Medical College in Philadelphia, so we moved there from New Jersey. My parents wanted to fit in, so my mother became active in the Philadelphia scene and sent my brothers and me to our local Presbyterian church. From then on we were brought up like any other middle-class Protestants.

So you had a religious education.

Yes and no. I never liked going to services; they didn't interest me at all. But for twelve years I went to a Quaker school, the Friends' Central School, where Quaker philosophy was often discussed. That's probably where my strong sense of moral order comes from. But I was always fascinated by Catholic imagery, which I found terrifying and really quite violent. It's been a constant source of inspiration for me.

How would you describe your family?

Very strange. I realised the other day that I never knew the birthdays of my brothers, Bruce and Barton, or my parents. I guess that's why it's so important to me that my two daughters' birthdays are celebrated as they should be. As a kid I don't remember my birthday, or anyone else's birthday, being celebrated at home. I once called my mom and asked her if she knew what day it was. She didn't. How could she have forgotten her own son's birthday? After those kinds of childhood experiences, it isn't surprising that I see families as places where people manipulate and destroy each other. I can't talk about "living in the bosom of a family" because I never experienced such a thing.

What kind of child were you?

I was the youngest of three brothers, so no one paid me much attention. My parents didn't get along and I spent a lot of time alone, trying to avoid family squabbles. My childhood was a lot like the Beach Boys song "In My Room." During the summer, while everyone else was at the beach, I was inside reading, for hours at a time. My brothers and I grew up in a competitive atmosphere – it was always all about who could be the best. That all ended once we left home, but when I think back on it that competition only existed because our parents were there to foster it. I'll give you another example. Bart, Bruce and I were science fiction fans, but it never occurred to us to share our magazines. We each had our own collection. When a new issue of a sci-fi magazine came out, I would buy my own copy and Bruce and Bart would buy theirs. When the magazine arrived the three of us would be in our little rooms, each with the same collection on our shelves. I've always wondered how our parents could have let that happen.

Your older brother, Bruce, was their favourite son.

Bruce was considered a genius by my parents. I remember coming home from school one day and my mother saying, "Don't make any noise! Bruce is thinking." They literally treated him like a god, which had tragic repercussions. Once he was on his own he never fit in anywhere and could never connect with anyone, because he had been somehow drained of all humanity. He had such a high opinion of himself that he ended up losing his mind and moving to an island in New Zealand, where he lived cut off from the world. That didn't stop him from having many admirers who religiously revered everything he wrote. He died in 1997. I hadn't seen him or spoken to him for about fifteen years.

He was a physicist.

Yes. He had gone to MIT [Massachusetts Institute of Technology] and became an inventor. He developed several strange contraptions, like an "anti-gravity" machine and another that generates energy indefinitely. Don't ask me how it works, but I've been assured that it does.

You were a techie yourself in your youth.

I dreamed of becoming a physicist. When I was in high school I built a computer and entered a number of competitions. I won several prizes, locally and even nationally.

Was it a way of challenging Bruce on his own turf?

For sure. I actually won first prize in a contest where he came in third. I still remember the name of the project I presented: "On the Application of Cybernetics to the Solution of Differential Equations." But it didn't mean much to my parents. Whatever happened, Bruce was always the family genius and I was his imitator. It wasn't until I became famous that my mother began to acknowledge me. She loved to visit me in California and brag about her film director son, which always made me uncomfortable. My father, on the other hand, was never interested in my work. Not long ago I was watching a documentary about that genius Leonard Bernstein, whose father insisted that he join the family business. He could never understand why his son would devote himself so completely to music. When I think about it, that kind of attitude must completely condition your existence. It seems incredible to me, even today, that my father took no notice of what I did for a living. But I've come to terms with it. If he's not interested in me, too bad for him.

Is your mother still alive?

She died in 1998, four or five months after Bruce. She and my father had been separated since 1958.

Did their separation affect you?

To be honest, I was the one who provoked it. Their marriage had been on the rocks for a while, but my mother never had the willpower to leave my father. One day, when she was home alone with me, she swallowed a whole bottle of barbiturates. I took her to the hospital and called my father, who promised me that nothing like this would ever happen again. He thought she must have caught him with another woman, and when she came home from the hospital my mother did in fact tell me that my father was cheating on her with one of his nurses. Since she had always described him as being a bit depraved, I believed her right away. But the truth – and I didn't understand this until much later – is that he was a workaholic who did all he could to ignore his marital problems. He spent most of his time at the hospital, and one day met someone there. In the end it was all very banal, though at the time I didn't understand it. To me, this woman was the odd one out, and my mission was to help my mother get a divorce by providing her with proof of my father's infidelity, which I put my heart and soul into.

As you can imagine, this was a very intense time in my life. For the first time, I was doing something that Bruce was unable to do. My brothers had never known how to deal with the situation, but I had a plan. My father had stayed in our house during the summer of 1958. I lived with him during the week and on weekends stayed with my mother, who was at our second house by the ocean. I knew that my father had started seeing his mistress again. On Friday nights, before I left, I would tap his phone using a tape recorder my mother had given me for Christmas. I did this all summer, to no end. Then I followed him with my camera in hopes of catching him with his mistress, but again I got nowhere. Finally I realised that the best way to proceed was to catch them in the act, so I broke into his office one night and found him and his mistress together. My parents separated soon after but didn't divorce until much later. The irony is that they both started new lives and were very happy. My mother married another doctor and my father married his mistress, who he's still with today. My parents were both people meant to be with someone – just not each other.

How do you look back on your behaviour at that time?

If I went to such extremes it was because my mother manipulated me. She knew that I resolved crises by taking action – unlike my brothers – and played into it. In the end, these events allowed me to resolve my Oedipus complex. As I pushed my father aside, my mother became mine and mine alone. But life with her was a nightmare, and I gradually came to appreciate my father's point of view and understand why he left her. Years later he opened up to me a little. I say a little because he's not the kind of person who easily expresses his feelings, and he really had to work at it to talk to me. But until then my brothers and I had heard only my mother's point of view. She spoke of dad as an outsider, conspiring against us. "He's the bad guy," she would say. "You guys are on my side. Make him feel guilty." It wasn't until I became a father that I was able to see how my mother had instilled all these ideas in us. My father was awkward with his children, for sure, and still is, but the reason things got so out of hand back then was because my mother distorted everything. Much later I also realised that our family had dissolved because of me. When I made the divorce possible, our home was wrecked forever. My mother moved into her own apartment, my father stayed in town at his office, and my brothers each went their own way. There no longer was a place where we could all meet up together, even once a year.

You remained close to your brother Barton.

We've become close, but that wasn't the case when we were kids. Bart is a painter who lives in Menlo Park, near San Francisco. He taught art history at a small school in California near Stanford. He got the job right after graduating and still lives there. He retired in 1997. He's a very good watercolourist. The portrait of Geneviève Bujold in *Obsession* is one of his, and he also took the photos of Geneviève and Cliff Robertson that you see during the opening credits. My parents' devotion to my older brother heavily affected Bart, who constructed his personality by systematically taking the opposite view to Bruce's. Bruce was a scientist, Bart became an artist. Bruce never took much care of his body, Bart was a real athlete. Bruce was very cerebral, Bart was very physical. Bruce was a bit chubby, Bart was skinny. Bruce was neat, Bart was very messy. But he never wanted to take on Bruce on his own turf. He took another direction, whereas from the start I was ready for a shootout with Bruce. That never went away. I always thought the reason I was so strong, so resilient, was because I survived the awful fights I had with my parents and Bruce. I can't imagine tougher opponents than those three.

You said that reading was a childhood escape. What were your favourite books?

I remember really loving Frank L. Baum – *The Wizard of Oz* and all the Oz books.

How do you explain that The Wizard of Oz *had such an impact on filmmakers of your generation? Steven Spielberg, John Boorman, David Lynch and Martin Scorsese have all at one time or another been obsessed with the story.*

I have no idea. I imagine that this wonderful world "over the rainbow" fascinated us. I was a big reader of science fiction as a child. I'll never forget Alfred Bester's *The Demolished Man*. I also loved *Sirens of Titan* by Kurt Vonnegut, and Stendhal, especially *The Red and the Black*. Russian novelists fascinated me, and I liked English novels from the end of the nineteenth century – Oscar Wilde, Conan Doyle, H.G. Wells, Robert Louis Stevenson. I read other things besides novels, including lots of essays.

Have you ever been tempted to become a writer?

No, though I've always loved hanging out in bookstores, and as a kid used to rummage through shelves. I would choose something at random – a book on cyberspace, or ants, or Borneo. Bookstores are like big libraries to me. There's nothing better than aimlessly wandering around them. I also like strolling through cities. I record everything I see in my head, things that might later serve as inspiration for a story or script. Walking is a real stimulation for me, which is why I'm so miserable in Los Angeles, where the only way to get around is in a car. On top of that there aren't many bookstores. I think that in eight months of being there I always went to the same three. Most of the bookstores there are big chains. They look like supermarkets and only carry bestselling novels – nothing like the wide variety of books you find in English or French bookstores.

Was cinema an escape?

More like a Saturday night distraction. I used to go with my girlfriend but the interest ended there. I had seen a few Michael

Powell movies on TV – *The Red Shoes* and *The Thief of Baghdad* – which made a big impression on me, but I was much more interested in electronics and making computers.

What about theatre?

Same thing. I had been in shows in high school but it wasn't until I got to New York, when I went to Columbia University, that I really got interested in that kind of thing. I remember *Vertigo* coming out at Radio City Music Hall in New York the fall of my freshman year. It wasn't my first Hitchcock – I had seen other films by him on television and even some, like *To Catch a Thief*, in the theatre. But my discovery of *Vertigo* in VistaVision is a moment I'll never forget. Everyone made a big deal about the 1995 restoration, but for me it was a disappointment because they didn't show the film in its original format. At college I was surrounded by people who talked about theatre and film day and night. They went to see everything that was trendy, like François Truffaut, Jean-Luc Godard, Federico Fellini, Luchino Visconti. There were several film clubs, which were really eye-opening for me. It was 1958, at the beginning of the New Wave in France. I enrolled as a physics major but ended up getting a liberal arts degree, in 1962.

Which directors made an impression on you?

Godard, much more than Truffaut. I was fascinated by the spontaneity of his films, the way he let his actors do what they wanted and how he filmed them. *Greetings* is inspired by Godard and the documentaries of Robert Drew, D.A. Pennebaker and Richard Leacock, all of whom were making important films at the time.

You said in the mid-Sixties that you wanted to become the American Godard.

Many of us, including Jim McBride, wanted to make that dream come true. We were referring to Godard's 1959 to 1965 period; nobody wanted to be like later Godard! The problem with such an innovative director is that once you've figured out what he's doing, you don't want to watch his films anymore. I find it very difficult to watch Godard's films today; they do nothing for me. It's even difficult for me to watch Hitchcock films nowadays because there's nothing for me to discover. But the first time was magical. Generally speaking, what connects you to a work of art is the emotion it evokes, which varies depending on your age and experience. More abstract works of art may intrigue you intellectually, even teach you something, but you aren't ever going to really connect with them, which is why we keep coming back to films that speak to us. The truly great works of art manage to both move us *and* make us think.

Did John Cassavetes' early films have an influence on you?

Not as much as they did on Martin Scorsese. Cassavetes' films are character studies. Only the characters matter to him. My films are more visually inspired; I wasn't interested in characters at the time. I was making comedies, left-wing films that reflected the times we were living in. The form was what got me going, not the characters. My favourite directors were Hitchcock, Powell and Pressburger, David Lean, Luchino Visconti, Tony Richardson, Karel Reisz, John Schlesinger, the Free Cinema directors in Britain – the Europeans, essentially. It was Martin Scorsese, who I met in 1964 when he was a student at New York University, who helped me discover and appreciate American directors. He idolised them and knew every one of their films by heart. Of all of us, Marty is the real archivist. His collection of films is enormous and his influence on me has been considerable, even when it comes to foreign films. By the time we met he already knew all about Michelangelo Antonioni, whose work he had seen on television long before I did.

What were your first experiences with a movie camera?

In my second year of college I acted in several plays put together by students. At the same time some of them were making their first short films. Since I was very keen on technique – spying on my father with a camera in my pocket taught me a lot about photography – one of these guys, Eugene Marner, asked me to be a cameraman on his film. To really understand what happened next, you have to know that at Columbia the big annual show, a musical put on by students, is called the Varsity Show. A script competition is held each year, and a committee, the Columbia Players, decide which play will be staged. In 1959, two works were in the running. One was by Steve Rossen, Robert Rossen's son. The other was by Terrence McNally, who later became a successful playwright. No one could decide between the two. Although I wasn't a member of the committee – I didn't become one until much later – I went to one of their meetings anyway, just before Christmas vacation. The atmosphere was explosive. It must have been about one o'clock in the morning and no one could decide which was the best script. At one point everyone turned to me and said, "Let him decide." So I voted for McNally's very funny *A Little Bit Different,* about a film crew that ends up in Africa. Cannibals eat characters inspired by famous Americans of the period. Being rather naive, I didn't know that the Varsity Show elections were based on deals between students, like, "I'll vote for your play if you give me the lead or the director." Eugene Marner had made such a deal with Steve Rossen, whose play he wanted to direct, and here I was screwing up his plan by voting for someone else.

I'll always remember the night we went to shoot Marner's short film. It was two in the morning, we were on 110th Street. I had set up the camera and lights; there wasn't a soul around. I was shooting undercover because we didn't have a permit. All of a sudden Marner's girlfriend, Charlene Settrena, starts yelling at me. "You two-faced asshole! Didn't you know that Gene was supposed to direct Steve's play?" I said I didn't. "Did you vote for McNally?" she asked. "Yes," I said. "His was the best." And she completely lost it! I can still picture her, a very dark-haired girl, of Sicilian origin. I was dating her sister, Pamela. Finally Charlene said, "We're out of here!" – and they all left. My director, my girlfriend Pamela, abandoned me in the middle of 110th Street with the camera and the actor. Determined as I am, I decided to make the movie myself, which is how *Icarus,* my first short film, came about.

What's it about?

It's a mythological story that makes fun of our very programmed modern lives. The god Pan arrives in New York and emerges from the subway and begins to wreak havoc on everyone's overly regimented existence. The visual idea I had was a metaphorical one, with everyone walking on wires and Pan trying to make them lose their balance. When he causes a young girl to fall, she loses her mind. It was a kind of precursor to *Dionysus in 69*, which I made nine years later. My second short, *660214: The Story of an IBM Card*, starred Jared Martin, who I shared a room with as a student, and Christina Callaghan, an actress from Sarah Lawrence, a liberal arts college in Bronxville attended mainly by girls. This time it was a two-character film – three, if you count Death. I was very influenced by Ingmar Bergman. The protagonist was a painter who lets himself wither away. It's also about determinism, hence the IBM card, which kind of symbolised that. I don't really remember anything else. It was pretty pretentious.

The war in Vietnam began while you were at Columbia.

For people like me, the war was bullshit. You can see it in my films from that era. We were all asking ourselves, "What the hell are we doing over there? Why do people want to go?" Kennedy and Johnson were trying to convince us that the war made sense, but it made absolutely no sense to me, so we were looking for any way to get out of going. Some people persuaded their doctor to give them a letter, others got the hell out of the country, some got married and started a family – anything to avoid the draft. Those who did go were either poor or black, or guys like Oliver Stone, who were desperate for the experience of war. But no one in their right mind, except hardcore patriots, went to Vietnam. I was an uninformed patriot, you might say, and the more I learned about the war, the stronger my position became.

How did you escape the draft?

I tried everything. I pretended to be a homosexual, I imbibed any number of things to induce the allergies I was prone to, I smoked cigarettes until I was coughing and wheezing like a madman, I had a doctor's certificate stating that I was practically allergic to the air. I eventually found myself in front of a shrink. I looked him straight in the eye and told him I wanted to become a communist and that communism was the best path forward. They thought I was crazy and sent me home. I used all of that when I made my third feature, *Greetings*, which reflected what we were all going through.

Your third short film, Woton's Wake, *which you made when you were at Columbia, won several awards.*

It's a kind of satirical pastiche of films that were being released at the time, based on the myth of Pygmalion. The hero is an artist, played by William Finley, who makes sculptures out of anything he can find. One of them transforms into a pretty girl and he chases her with a blow torch, trying to force her to turn back into a statue. Some sequences were obviously inspired by Bergman's *Seventh Seal*, others by Fellini's *8½* and *King Kong*. The film was quite successful. I entered it into a competition, the Cinema 16 Independent Film contest, which Amos Vogel organised, where all kinds of experimental shorts were screened. I submitted all my films, but none of them won anything until *Woton's Wake*, which was awarded the grand prize and the Rosenthal Foundation prize for the best short film made by a person under 25. Martin Scorsese won the same prize.

Around this time you met Wilford Leach, who played an important role in your career.

When I joined the Columbia Players I began an ongoing collaboration between students from Columbia and Sarah Lawrence. We would put on plays together. Columbia didn't really back me on this project, so I ended up spending more time at Sarah Lawrence, where Wilford Leach was a professor of drama. He was interested in film and helped me get a scholarship to Sarah Lawrence so that I could continue studying. Leach saw something in me, and I learned a lot from him. I ended up spending two wonderful years in the theatre department, from 1962 to 1964, and graduated with an MA.

While you were at Sarah Lawrence you made your first feature film, The Wedding Party. *Wilford Leach co-directed it with you and Cynthia Munroe.*

Contrary to what I've often read, Cynthia wasn't my girlfriend, though I sure would have liked her to be! We were both students in Wilford's Sarah Lawrence class. She came from a very wealthy family and had a real talent for writing. Along with other students at Sarah Lawrence, we wanted to make a sketch comedy movie about love in America, in the spirit of [the 1962 French anthology film] *Love at Twenty*. Cynthia and I had each written a sketch, and other directors, including John Hancock and Ulu Grosbard, worked with us on the project for a year, at which point everyone had to find some money so we could produce it. I raised $10,000 and Cynthia put her own money in, but no one else could raise anything and the project stalled. The script for Cynthia's sketch was based on my best friend Jared Martin's wedding at his country house in New Jersey, where William Finley and I were groomsmen. The three main characters were based on Jared, William and me. I thought the script she wrote based on this story was much better than mine, so I suggested we focus on only one story – hers – and make it into a feature film. I knew she had the means to finance the production. It should by now be clear that I was prepared to go to any length to make a film. I've always known that finding money was a key part of the director's job. I'm always telling students that if they can't find money to make films, they should do something else with their life. Cynthia fully financed *The Wedding Party*, which ended up costing $100,000.

How did you find the actors?

Charlie Pfluger, who played the groom, was a student at Columbia. Jill Clayburgh, the bride, was a classmate at Sarah Lawrence. Robert De Niro, who plays one of the witnesses, came to an open casting session that William Finley and I held in a Greenwich Village loft. He did a scene and started improvising with William. He was already very impressive, and at 21 wasn't even old enough to sign his contract. It was his first film.

One of the influences of The Wedding Party *seems to be silent movies.*

And Richard Lester. There's a lot of speeding up and slowing down, very quick editing effects and jump cuts. Again, our influences were the French New Wave and the Angry Young Men of British Free Cinema – everything that was trendy in the Sixties. I was in charge of shooting and editing. Leach, who had much more experience than me, directed the actors. We shot on Shelter Island and in Pennsylvania with Peter Powell, a documentary cameraman. The filming took over a year. We started in December of '64, continued through the summer of '65, and shot for another two or three weeks a bit later on. It took me a long time to edit the film, in the little studio where I lived. We finally released it in theatres ourselves in 1966, in the midst of making my third feature, *Greetings*.

CHAPTER TWO

MURDER A LA MOD – GREETINGS – HI, MOM – DIONYSUS IN 69 – GET TO KNOW YOUR RABBIT

When you were at college you began to distance yourself from your conservative upbringing. You were such a rebel that at one point you even spent a night in prison. It's the first thing you have in common with Alfred Hitchcock.

Yes, except that I was twenty-three when it happened, and Hitchcock was still a kid.

What did happen exactly?

It's funny, because I recently tried to use the story as the starting point for a film. I was living through a very complicated love affair at the time. One night, after realising that the girl didn't love me anymore, I started drinking, one thing led to another, and I ended up playing poker and lost all my money. When I went out into the street I wondered how I was going to get home. I saw a motorcycle, which I stole, and started running red lights.

A cop caught up with me but I knocked him down and took off. He shot at me, I ended up at the police station, and the next day my mother and older brother bailed me out. The most traumatic part was discovering just how self-destructive I could be when things didn't go my way. Everyone feels suicidal at some point, but in my case I know exactly how to go about it, believe me. From then on I was extremely conscious of my limitations and never did anything like that again. I would find myself in pretty dire situations where I was in over my head, but because I had learned to control myself, I emerged unscathed. I know exactly how much pressure I can handle before I go overboard.

What did you do when you graduated from Sarah Lawrence?

With a friend of mine, Kenny Burrows, I started a small company that produced documentaries and industrial films. The idea was to make enough money to finance a feature film. We got two commissions: *To Bridge This Gap*, about social housing for black people in New Orleans, which was made for the NAACP [National Association for the Advancement of Colored People] and *Show Me a Strong Town and I'll Show You a Strong Bank*, which we made for the Treasury Department. We filmed an inspector who made surprise visits to banks. He would show up unannounced and they would open all the doors for him, especially because we were filming. That experience later gave me the idea for a screenplay, *Nazi Gold*, which I wrote with Jay Cocks and was planning to direct in 1999 after *Snake Eyes*, in which the characters rob a Swiss bank while making a commercial for the bank. They steal Nazi gold that was confiscated from Jews during World War II. Kenny and I also made *The Responsive Eye* for the opening of the Op Art exhibition at the Museum of Modern Art in New York, where there were all kinds of eccentric people hanging around. That film won several awards.

You also made a film called Mod. *What can you tell us about it?*

It's a documentary about rock music. I went to England to film bands like The Who and The Animals, and was even on The Rolling Stones' first American tour. It should have been a feature but the film never left the lab because we didn't have any money.

We don't know much about your second feature film, Murder a la Mod, *which you made in 1967.*

It was screened at the Gate Theater on Second Avenue in New York. Kenny Burrows and I were able to finance it with the money we earned from our commissions, and also with the help of a co-producer who specialised in erotic films. We convinced him that *Murder a la Mod* would be full of naked girls. The budget for the film was $50,000. We put up half and the producer put up the rest. You can imagine his shock when he saw the film. He was expecting to see pretty much anything but that! We distributed it ourselves, as a double feature with Paul Bartel's short *The Secret Cinema*. It ran for a couple of weeks.

Murder a la Mod *shows the murder of an actress filmed in three different ways.*

The first part is filmed like a soap opera, from the point of view of a girl murdered with an ice pick. The second, Hitchcockian segment starts again from the beginning, and the third takes the point of view of the deaf and dumb psychopath, played by William Finley. It's a very strange and very funny high-speed burlesque film. You can see some of *Murder a la Mod* in the scene from *Blow Out* when Dennis Franz is watching TV in his room while waiting for Nancy Allen. It was the first time I realised how differently audiences respond to a story depending on the style of filmmaking. I used the same device in *Greetings*, my next film, where once again there were three main characters and three different styles.

Greetings came out of a frustrating period. After graduating from Sarah Lawrence, I was handed a grant from Universal. Two years later I was selected by the studio to be part of a group of young talent that was expected to come up with ideas for films. I remember suggesting a story about the Charlie Starkweather case, which later inspired Terrence Malick's *Badlands*. It was all rather frustrating because it turned out that the studio wasn't actually interested in our projects. One day Charles Hirsch, who was working for the studio in New York, said to me, "Look, I'm going to try to get some money and we're going to make a movie without them." At that point I had made only two feature films. That's how *Greetings* came about. We shot it in a two-week frenzy on a budget of about $20,000, which we raised in cash. It paid for the film stock and nothing else. We started shooting in 16mm but after a week realised that everything was blurry because of a defective camera, so we started over, this time in 35mm. The film reflects what we were obsessed with in the Sixties: girls. We were in the middle of a sexual revolution. Everyone was trying to avoid the draft so they wouldn't have to go to Vietnam. And of course there was the Kennedy assassination. I mixed in my obsession with voyeurism, as personified by De Niro's character. We found a distributor and the film was a big hit. It made about $3 million at the box office.

Were some scenes improvised?

Yes, like the one between Bob De Niro and Allen Garfield outside the museum. You can see Bob losing his concentration and Al making him laugh. The funny thing is that Al wasn't even supposed to be in that scene. The actor I had been rehearsing with stood us up at the last minute so I called Al.

One of the most impressive sequences in Greetings *is when the character played by Gerrit Graham uses the naked body of a girl to explain the path of the bullets that killed President Kennedy.*

That was a very Sixties thing to do; there were naked girls in every movie at the time. I had read every book on the assassination. People think I'm obsessed with it, but it's actually not the assassination I'm interested in, it's the subsequent investigation. What the Kennedy investigation taught me, and what I later used in several of my films, is that the more you investigate something, the less you learn. I stopped reading books on the subject the day I heard that Kennedy's remains vanished from the hospital. For thirty-three minutes no one knew where his body was. It sounds crazy, but these things sometimes happen. All it took was for it to be put in an elevator and for no one to be there to receive it when the doors opened. Complete carelessness, but when it comes to such an elaborate investigation, no one wants to believe in negligence. It's the perfect starting point for a conspiracy. I don't actually believe in conspiracies, even though my films are full of them. They're just starting points for stories.

Where were you the day of John Kennedy's assassination?

Walking around Bronxville with my girlfriend, Jill Clayburgh. I think it was our first date. We heard the news while passing a television store.

What are your thoughts about the Sixties today?

Politically, they marked the beginning of the age of suspicion, the moment when we came to realise that our leaders were lying to us. And yet, for a long time, the Kennedys symbolised a kind of political golden age for our country. They embodied the spirit of Camelot. But it was too good to be true, and today we see how often they lied to us. It was made worse by the fact that they succeeded Eisenhower – the man from D-Day! – who we trusted so blindly. Starting with Kennedy, the lie entered the White House, and now, as we approach a new millennium, the country has reached a kind of point of no return when it comes to cynicism. When President Clinton lies on live television about oral sex in the Oval Office, you have to wonder if we can get any more cynical. I've always felt that the personality of the President reflects the mood of the entire country. *Greetings* won the Silver Bear at the Berlin Film Festival. Along with my two awards at the Avoriaz film festival for *Phantom of the Paradise* and *Carrie*, it's the only award I've ever received.

Your next film, Dionysus in 69, *is an adaptation of Euripides'* Bacchae *by the Performance Group, a New York theatre troupe. What made you want to film their show?*

William Finley, who was part of the troupe, suggested I come see them at the Performance Garage, an avant-garde theatre in Greenwich Village. I was so amazed by what I saw that I immediately decided to make a film of it.

Who was the director?

Richard Schechner, whose productions were very trendy. This was the era of street theatre and Happenings. The actors played half-naked in a kind of trance; they were inspired by the ceremonial birth rituals of primitive tribes. That was the Sixties!

Believe me, you really missed out. *Dionysus in 69* was unlike anything I had ever seen. The lifestyles of the performers were radically different from mine, but I was fascinated by what they were doing. The show was performed as much in the auditorium, amidst the audience, as it was on stage. I made the film because I wanted to know more about Schechner's way of working, but also to try to capture the incredible electricity in the room during a performance. That's how I came up with the idea of shooting in split screen, with one camera on the audience and another on the actors. We filmed two performances, me following the flow of the play and the actors' movements, the other cameraman, Bob Fiore, capturing audience reactions. In the movie the screen is divided in two. On the left side you see what I shot, on the right what Fiore was filming. It's amazing that we didn't catch each other in shot.

There isn't much editing.

My love of long takes was born out of *Dionysus in 69*. Some shots in that film are eight minutes long, and almost every film I've made since has a long take in it. After all, it's the best way of catching lightning in a bottle. That's how Orson Welles put it. Anyone who has made documentaries knows what he means. You capture on film something that happens only once and will never happen again. If you manage to commit to film an important moment in its entirety, you'll have something really powerful and organic that can never be recreated with editing, because when you glue two shots together you might create some new emotion, but you're doing so in an artificial, manipulative way. You turn the image into a lie.

If you really want to film something authentic, there's no other way to do it than let the camera roll and allow the actors to create the emotions themselves. That's why stage performances – with emotions playing out in front of you live – are sometimes so impressive. It's the opposite of what happens in movies when you think you can recreate everything artificially, like in animation. But nothing could be further from the truth, which is why so many of today's films are emotionally empty. The editing is frantic and the shots last only a few seconds each, but in the end they express nothing. When I was making *Dionysus in 69* I knew I was part of a unique moment that would never be repeated. I *had* to be there. That's what cinema is: being in the right place at the right time, overcoming problems, and ultimately catching that lightning in a bottle.

Was Dionysus in 69 *shown in the United States?*

It was released in a New York theatre in 1970 but didn't play for long. The Performance Group broke up soon after that and I lost track of them. But in their heyday they were a real team. I'll never forget them.

Did you use actors from the Performance Group in any of your films?

Besides William Finley, who was in *The Wedding Party*, *Murder a la Mod*, *Sister*s, *Phantom of the Paradise* and *The Fury*, I cast William Shepherd in *Phantom*, when Swan gets stabbed. He choreographed the final sequence.

In Euripides' Bacchae, *a messenger speaks of women dismembering Pentheus' body. His mother also takes part in the ritual. They take it a step further by devouring him. Your obsession with sacrifice, which you deal with again and again in your films, seems to have begun with* Dionysus in 69. *There are images of a woman with her hands covered in blood in* Sisters, Phantom of the Paradise, Carrie, The Fury, Dressed to Kill, Casualties of War, *even* Snake Eyes.

Very possibly, yes.

Hi, Mom! *is your only sequel. Robert De Niro plays Jon Rubin, his peeping tom character from* Greetings, *once again.*

I originally developed the script for producer Martin Ransohoff, who I had a contract with. The first drafts of *Phantom of the Paradise* and *Sisters* were also written under that agreement. My intention with *Hi, Mom!* was to make a film even weirder than *Greetings*. Once again I had three characters and three different ways of filming. First there was the story of the housewife who filmed her everyday life, like a diary, with a small 8mm sound camera, and then there was the part about the revolutionaries. The "Be Black, Baby" Happening was inspired by new kinds of theatre that were going around in which the performers harangued audience members. The black members of those troupes – and there were a lot of them – were the most unforgiving. That part of the film was shot in a cinéma vérité style, almost like *Dionysus*. And finally, there was the section about the voyeur Jon Rubin, who makes porn movies for producer Joe Banner, a character inspired by the co-producer of *Murder a la Mod*.

Hi, Mom! can be translated into French as "Salut maman."

It's what people always say [to the camera] when they're on television. From that point of view, *Hi, Mom!* was prophetic because now more than ever everyone's dream is to be on TV. It's the ultimate American fantasy.

What do you think of television today?

I don't pay any attention to the content; it's the formal aspects that interest me. These days you can't help but notice that on American television the edges of the screen are increasingly covered in brand names, which is just one more form of advertising. The size of the frame shrinks because of all the rubbish embedded in the image. As if it wasn't enough to watch commercials between programmes all day long… Now there's also advertising *during* the programmes! And I'm not talking about home shopping, where the host presents the products directly to the camera. It's the same on the Internet, where there are all kinds of sidebars. Television fascinates me as an advertising space. It's one big billboard. They're always coming up with new ways of getting us to buy things.

Look at what happened with newspapers. It used to be that you could easily distinguish between news and advertising. The articles were obviously the core of the paper and the rest was advertising. No longer. These days *everything* is advertising: the news, the programmes, everything, twenty-four hours a day. And for good reason. American consumers eat it up, and it makes a lot of money for a lot of people. The first time I was on TV it was to promote *Greetings*, when I was invited to talk about the revolutionary spirit of the times. During commercial breaks the host promoted a brand of aspirin. That's when it hit me. I realised that to this guy I was no more than aspirin, a product he was selling to the public. Ever since, this idea has shown up, again and again, in my films.

Jon Rubin is reminiscent of Travis Bickle in Taxi Driver, *another character played by De Niro.*

There are certainly similarities between the two, especially when Rubin plays the cop in "Be Black, Baby" and rehearses in front of a ladder. At one point he even says something like "You talkin' to me?" – just like in *Taxi Driver*.

And he's as obsessed with black people as Bickle is.

Paul Schrader, the author of *Taxi Driver*, must have seen *Hi, Mom!*

Your early films are very different from the ones you make today. What did you learn from them and do you often watch them?

I don't watch them very often. But the way I direct actors was influenced by documentaries I made or saw in the Sixties. Those films set a new standard for realism, whether it was the way people talked or simply how they looked at the world. They helped us understand what reality really was, which we then set about trying to recreate in our films, and from that starting point acting became more naturalistic. The ideas in all my films have their roots in the Sixties. From a certain point of view, my first features give a fairly accurate indication of how society was evolving. They were thirty years ahead of their time.

Of your films from this period, which do you like the most?

Dionysus in 69 is quite faithful to my original conception. *Hi, Mom!* too. *Greetings* is more exuberant, full of energy and life. It reminds me of an old rock'n'roll song. Technically my recent work is better, but in terms of spontaneity, nothing comes close to the first few films.

Hollywood came calling after the success of Greetings. *In 1970, Warner Bros. asked you to direct* Get to Know Your Rabbit.

It was my first job offer from a studio. The end result wasn't great, which is a shame because I always liked the idea. As I said earlier, while I was promoting *Greetings*, I came to understand just how much the revolutionary spirit of the times had been co-opted by capitalism. Capitalism always neutralises protest. It smothers it with riches, turning it inside out, forcing it to fall into line. Look at what's happened with piercing and tattoos. That's what *Get to Know Your Rabbit* is all about. A guy who quits his job and becomes a magician and dancer is so successful that he himself is transformed into a trend-setter and a product. People dress like him, copy his magic tricks, and emulate his lifestyle. He finds himself head of the company he's created in spite of himself, before managing to escape again. I'm obsessed with the idea that the system always pulls you back in. It's one of capitalism's hidden strengths.

Who is Tommy Smothers, star of Get to Know Your Rabbit?

One of the two Smothers Brothers, comic singers who had their moment of glory on a popular American television show at the end of the Sixties. They were fond of controversy, and had a guest on their show who was a little too politically inflammatory for CBS, so eventually the network fired them. The brothers retaliated by taking CBS to court for breach of contract. Tommy was tangled up in that lawsuit when he started working with me. At the beginning of the shoot everything was fine between us, but little by little he became angrier and angrier at the establishment and had it in for everyone on the set, including me. From then on things were difficult between us, and at one point he disappeared for a few days. Nobody knew where he was.

We finally finished the film but it turned out that many scenes with Tommy didn't work. I wanted to re-shoot some of them but the studio objected and fired me. Warner Bros. supervised the final cut and shut me out of the process. The cast included Allen Garfield, an old friend of mine, Katharine Ross, and of course Orson Welles, who played the master magician. I fought with the studio because they insisted on hiring Gig Young, who had just won an Oscar for *They Shoot Horses, Don't They?* But I hung on and got Welles. I contacted him myself, much to everyone's displeasure. It was an unforgettable experience. Welles was a born storyteller with extraordinary talents; his personality was magical. He was and still is one of my idols. One day he asked me which accent I wanted him to have in the film, and then, as he moved his finger over a map of the United States, from one region to the next, his accent changed. He was doing the film for the money and insisted that we write his lines on pieces of cardboard so he would be able to refer to them at any time. Eventually he learned it all by heart. He paid a lot of attention to the other actors, who loved being around him. When he wasn't working he usually sat around reading a book. He didn't want to be bothered with questions like, "Orson, tell me about how you did the opening shot of *Touch of Evil*."

For you, Welles symbolises the artist broken by the system.

He is, for filmmakers, the most significant such example. I know a lot about his life and work. Having talked to many people who worked with him, including Bernard Herrmann, and having worked inside the Hollywood system myself, I have an understanding of the problems he encountered and the traps he fell into. Orson became successful too quickly and too soon. He might have been able to make movies from scratch, but he still needed the toys that Hollywood had to offer and that enabled him to maximise his talent, which is what happened when he made *Citizen Kane*. He was given everything he needed for that film and the results are extraordinary. The tragedy is that he was never again allowed to play with the big electric train set and spent the rest of his career struggling. His films were recut behind his back and he had to scrape together money left and right just to get them made. Unlike Hitchcock, who mastered the system perfectly, Orson Welles thought he could do everything himself. When you've been told your whole life that you're a genius, that's what you end up believing. It's a danger we all face, and it's why Welles' life is an example for the rest of us who unfortunately tend to be called geniuses. There's no director more deserving of that description than Orson Welles. I've never known a more fascinating or cultured man. Yet even he needed help.

Did you stay in touch with him?

No. He worked on the film for a month and I never saw him again.

Did he ever watch any of your films?

I don't think so. He didn't go to the movies anymore.

Get to Know Your Rabbit *was produced by Warner Bros., where much later you made* The Bonfire of the Vanities, *your biggest commercial failure.*

All of us, with the exception of Steven Spielberg, started at Warner Bros. George Lucas with *THX 1138*, Francis Coppola with *Finian's Rainbow*, Martin Scorsese with François Reichenbach's *Medicine Ball Caravan*, which he edited, and me with *Get to Know Your Rabbit*. We all met at Warner Bros. in the Seventies when we were all working on films that turned into big failures for the studio. That's what connected us. Francis Coppola's case is especially representative, because after he directed *Finian's Rainbow* and produced *THX 1138* for Warner Bros., the studio told him, "OK, your contract is up. Give us our money back." Overnight, Francis' company, Zoetrope, found itself owing several hundred thousand dollars to Warner Bros. He was broke and agreed to make *The Godfather* to pay off his debts. Let's not talk about the disaster of *Medicine Ball Caravan* that Scorsese was working on. Things got better for him after that. He made two successful films for Warner Bros., *Mean Streets* and *Goodfellas*. I was less fortunate.

Under what circumstances were you fired?

Martin Scorsese and I had gone to a party at producer Fred Weintraub's house. Ted Ashley, who ran the studio, was there, as well as Fred and eighty-three Warner Bros. secretaries. It was a party for the girls. [*laughs*] Scorsese and I were both under contract with Warner Bros.; we were two rookies who were in the big league for a night. It was the Seventies – I don't need to tell you that there were a lot of drugs and pills going around. That wasn't our thing at all, so we were really bored.

Everyone was so insincere – "You're wonderful!" and "You're the greatest!" – so we just started making fun of them. We shut ourselves in a room and began shouting at each other: "You idiot! Where did you find such a stupid suit? Look at those shoes! Don't tell me you actually bought them!" And so on. We were mocking them and their fake politeness. We were laughing so hard that, little by little, everyone else joined us in the room and watched us play our little game. Finally, who shows up with a big smile on his face? That's right – Ted Ashley! Dead silence. No one dared say anything. We were all working for him, don't forget. Everyone shut up, except me. I looked him straight in the eyes and said, "Your suit is absolutely grotesque! But we love you, Ted, don't we Marty? Everybody loves Ted!" Ashley smiled and walked out. The next week I was fired. I no longer existed. It was John Calley, the second-in-command at Warner Bros., who got rid of me. Those guys never forget; you can't make fun of them. You work for them, making the films they want you to make. That's how it works. It reminds me of that bit in John O'Hara's book *Appointment in Samara* when the hero, without really knowing why, throws a glass of liquor in his boss' face. The contempt you have for these people grows and grows. One day you can't hold back any longer and it explodes. That's what happened to me. And I was punished for it with four or five years of hell.

Did you go back to New York after that?

Yes. Martin Ransohoff asked me to direct a film called *Fuzz*, which was eventually made in 1972 by Richard A. Colla. It wasn't a good time for me. The release of *Get to Know Your Rabbit* had been put on hold and *Fuzz* was the only offer I had. I hired Burt Reynolds for the lead, but Ransohoff, who wanted to do a kind of *M*A*S*H* set in a New York police station, was going to cast Raquel Welch and Yul Brynner. I worked for a while on the script with Ransohoff and the writer and started casting, but just the idea of having Raquel Welch and Yul Brynner… I was sure it was going to be a disaster. It was all so absurd. And to make matters worse, my love life was very complicated at the time. I really just didn't want anything to do with *Fuzz*.

I still remember the day; it was December 9th. "I have to get out of here," I said to myself. I had done my time in New York and just turned down the only offer I had. It was time for me to start over, so I got on the first plane to California, not really knowing what I could do there. Jennifer Salt, who was living on the West Coast with another actress, Margot Kidder, suggested I move in with them. I started dating Margot and my life completely changed. I had the idea of putting Jennifer and Margot together in the same movie. The script, which became *Sisters*, came together pretty quickly. I remember giving the two leads to Jennifer and Margot as a Christmas present when we lived together in their beach house. From that point on it was just one thing after another. I was back on track.

CHAPTER THREE

SISTERS – PHANTOM OF THE PARADISE – OBSESSION

Your parents taught you to be very competitive at a young age, pushing you to always be better than the best. For a long time your brother Bruce was your reference point, but when you became a director, it seems that Hitchcock became your antagonist. He was the unrivalled god you had to surpass in order to thrive.

That's true.

Was your relationship with Hitchcock strictly competitive?

You could look at it that way, but Hitchcock first and foremost is the master of cinematic grammar, and if you have any interest in form, which I do, who else to turn to but him? When it comes to that kind of thing, nobody has ever come up with anything as important as Hitchcock.

What about Stanley Kubrick?

No. Whenever he came up with a way of filming people, Stanley repeated it over and over again, whether it was the zooms of *Barry Lyndon* or the dolly shots of *The Shining*. That said, his kind of formal rigour was extremely effective. Stanley had a big influence on me, especially his use of silence in *2001: A Space Odyssey*. I also like the way he expanded time in *Barry Lyndon* so it seemed as if everything was happening in slow motion – the camera movement, the performances. You feel as if you're experiencing time in a completely new way, as if you're actually back in the eighteenth century. It's impressive stuff. But I would be so bored making a Stanley Kubrick film; I couldn't work under such strictures. I like to exploit every element of cinematographic language and every resource the camera has to offer. For every scene, I look for the shot or camera movement that best communicates the information I want to convey.

Are there any rules you follow?

Very few, but when characters are sitting and speaking important dialogue I usually don't move the camera. Faces and reactions are what I focus on, because that's what audiences want to see. On the other hand, when I want to convey the frenzy of a particular action, the camera moves. I switch from one device to the other; depending on what I'm shooting. Hitchcock didn't do it any differently.

Sisters is your first "Hitchcockian" film. Many filmmakers have been inspired by Hitchcock, but none of their films have been as closely connected with his as yours.

Because, unlike me, who really understands what he was doing and how great it is, they don't think like him. French critics have endlessly analysed his work, so they all think they know Hitchcock, but most people haven't watched his films closely enough, and anything they have to say about them is superficial. They're always talking about the usual clichés and don't try to understand what's *really* happening on screen. Because I understand why Hitchcock chose one shot over another, I can measure the true extent of his genius. I see the purity, the precision of his cinematographic language.

When someone brings up Hitchcock every time someone takes a shower in one of my films or a woman is killed, I say, "Really?" If the journalist insists, I ask what they *really* mean by a comment like that. I've watched so many of his films, analysed his technique and reused some of his ideas, so I'm more capable than anyone of knowing whether or not what I'm doing is inspired by Hitchcock. I can't handle these comparisons anymore; most of the time they aren't in the least relevant. If you knew how many critics can't actually see what they're looking at! Hitchcock was subjected to this himself early in his career. Nobody understood his genius for filmmaking, his science of storytelling and editing.

There are, however, big differences between you and Hitchcock.

So many! The stories I tell are mostly very different from his. He had a Victorian sensibility and a lingering guilt, which stemmed from his Catholic upbringing. I don't have those kind of hangups. I learned Hitchcock's vocabulary, but also developed a lot of other techniques on my own. I use slow motion a lot, for example. I challenge you to find a slow motion shot in a Hitchcock film, or a split-screen shot. Everyone always criticises me for those things, but it's just a way of building a vocabulary and then filling in the blanks.

The idea of an innocent man wrongly accused appears in several Hitchcock films. With you, on the other hand, no one is ever innocent. In a film like Carrie, *every character is guilty of something.*

It's possible. I've never thought about it in those terms. On the other hand, I'm aware of my interest in outsiders, people excluded from the establishment, and for good reason: I'm one of them. I've spent many years working within a system for which I don't have much respect. I feel the same way about studio executives and critics.

How did you go about writing the script for Sisters?

I was inspired by a photo of two Russian Siamese twins, Masha and Dasha, published in *Life* magazine. You see it in the film when Margot and her Siamese sister are shown connected at the waist.

It was such a powerful image that I reproduced the caption: "The older they become, the more precarious is their psychological balance." I read everything I could on the subject, especially about Chang and Eng, the first Siamese twins. That kickstarted the film for me and I wrote the script with a friend, Louisa Rose. I also had a split-screen image in my head that I knew I wanted to include. On one side is a wounded man using his own blood to write something on a window, on the other is a neighbour across the street watching him. I was really into split screen at the time. I had just edited *Dionysus in 69* using the technique and was always thinking in terms of counterpoint and image juxtaposition.

I also came up with the scene where the psychopath, Danielle, goes home with a man and kills him. I wanted to make the audience believe that there were two sisters before the revelation that actually there's just one of them, and I wanted to explore the idea of a mad doctor who uses his patient as a guinea pig. I think I got the idea from the scene in Michael Powell's film *Peeping Tom*, where the father throws spiders in his son's bed in order to film the fear on his face. I love the idea of the son continuing his father's research.

The character of a mad doctor appears in several of your films.

Yes, and in that sense Dr. Breton in *Sisters* foreshadows Michael Caine's character in *Dressed to Kill* and John Lithgow's in *Raising Cain*. All these evil megalomaniacs who think they're gods and end up doing evil were actually inspired by my brother Bruce.

Sisters *opens with a scene that purposely misdirects the audience. We think Margot Kidder is blind, when in fact she's participating in a game show called* Peeping Toms. *You use this false beginning conceit in* Blow Out, Body Double, Mission: Impossible *and* Mission to Mars.

That's right, because unlike Jean-Luc Godard, who insists that cinema is truth twenty-four times a second, I see it as a lie twenty-four times a second.

Do you like the TV show Candid Camera?

Sure. It turns audiences into voyeurs. I've heard it said that *Candid Camera* is a good teaching tool for filmmakers, but I don't need a TV show like that to study human behaviour. I can just ride the subway or take a walk.

If your talent for satire shines through in the opening scene of Sisters, *you also know how to create something much more menacing. This becomes clear as soon as we see William Finley sitting in the audience during the show, even though he doesn't do anything in particular. He eventually leaves, but strangely enough the shot of his empty chair doubles our anxiety, as if it's letting us know that something awful is about to happen. You use this idea again in* Snake Eyes, *when Gary Sinise gets up from his seat to follow the redhead, just before the assassination of the secretary of defense.*

That's right.

Another example of a scene that mixes horror and comedy is when Danielle and Breton hide Philip's body in the sofa.

That scene was a real challenge. When I was writing the script for him, Martin Ransohoff told me it wasn't believable. No one was going to believe that a guy could be folded into a sofa. That's why I did the scene in one shot, to say to him, "You don't think so? Well, look!" We really did put Lisle Wilson in the sofa, which we then closed up on him.

Why did you make Grace, the journalist played by Jennifer Salt, so aggressive?

It certainly wasn't to settle any score with journalists, because at the time I was on rather good terms with the critics. I knew quite a few of them, Jay Cocks in particular, who wrote for *Time* and was one of my best friends. I also knew Pauline Kael and Richard Schickel very well; I would often run into them at screenings when I accompanied Jay. So I didn't intentionally make Grace such a bitch. What mattered to me was that she was witness to a murder. The fact that she's a journalist is secondary.

One of the best scenes in the film is when Breton brainwashes Grace. She inhabits Dominique and relives the operation that separated the Siamese twins. You film her nightmare in black and white, documentary-style, like the cinéma vérité film about Dominique that Grace watches.

That scene is really a testimony to the extensive research I'd done. Thanks to Jay Cocks I was able to access the *Time* archives and even film in their offices. I shot the dream sequence, with Jennifer looking straight into the camera, myself. The room was so small that I could only see her performance with my eye glued to the viewfinder.

The aesthetics of the cinéma vérité *film that Grace watches are reminiscent of Tod Browning's* Freaks. *Was that film meaningful to you?*

Of course, yes.

What do you remember about the shoot?

Good memories. Margot was my girlfriend, Jennifer had studied with me at Sarah Lawrence, and I had shared a dorm room with William Finley when I was in college. We were a real community. I lived with Margot on Fifth Avenue. We took the ferry every morning to Staten Island where all the exteriors were shot. The apartment scenes were filmed in a studio, in a set we built in New York. I still remember the last shot, with Charles Durning climbing the telephone pole. The sun was coming up, the sky was getting bluer and bluer; it was a real race against the clock. Chris Soldo, my assistant director, was running around like crazy. He was eighteen years old at the time and it was his first film. We must have worked twenty-four hours non-stop to finish filming *Sisters*. Our big problem was with the technicians' union because the production didn't comply with their rules, so they asked us to stop working for three days, but I managed to make an arrangement with them.

Ed Pressman, the producer of Sisters, *played an important role in American cinema of the Seventies.*

He produced *Phantom of the Paradise* and Terrence Malick's first film, *Badlands*. I met Ed when I was in Los Angeles. Martin Ransohoff had refused to do *Sisters* and I had just bought the script back from him. Ed read it and immediately wanted to do it. He managed to raise enough money, a couple of hundred thousand dollars, to get the film started, and continued to raise money during filming. The budget eventually came to $600,000.

The film's credits state: "A Pressman-Williams production." Who is Williams?

Paul Williams. He was associated with Ed. He was a director who made two films, *The Revolutionary* and *Out of it*, with Jon Voight.

Is this the Paul Williams who plays Swan in Phantom of the Paradise?

No, that's little Paul. There's a little and a big Paul Williams. Ed's partner was the big one. Ed's parents owned Pressman Toys, a toy company, and had an office on 23rd Street and Broadway. That's where Pressman-Wiliams had their headquarters. I was working in their offices after the catastrophe of *Get to Know Your Rabbit*, and Paul Williams was still a director working at Warner Bros. His film *Dealing*, adapted from Michael Crichton's first novel, which he wrote with his brother Douglas when they were students at Harvard, was a disaster.

Sisters *was your first collaboration with Bernard Herrmann. Was it your idea to have him do the music?*

My editor Paul Hirsch and I prepared a provisional score for the film, which included many of Herrmann's most famous themes, so naturally we asked ourselves, "Whatever happened to this guy? Is he even alive?" Ed Pressman had an uncle who knew Herrmann's brother, who was a dentist. Bernard himself lived in London. I called him up and he came over. I remember the scene as if it were yesterday. He came out of the elevator with his cane, his eyes glued to the floor, sporting shaggy hair. He was sweating, fresh off the plane. I remember saying to him, "Hello, Mr. Herrmann, it's an honour to meet you," to which he replied, "Where's the screening room?" He was quite direct when you first met him. He came into the room, we sat down, and the film started. The first thing we heard was a piece of music borrowed from *Psycho*, the screeching violins that you hear during the murder in the shower. When he heard that, Bernard started shouting, "Stop! Take that music off!" Hirsch and I were terrified. "Mr. Herrmann," I stammered. "I'm very sorry." "How can I watch your film," he said, "with the music from *Psycho* ringing in my ears?" He got up from his seat, went into the projection booth, and shut off the music himself. Later, I explained to him that I wasn't planning to add music to the title sequence with the fetus. "But you need a theme," he said. "You have to let the audience know right away what kind of movie they're watching. Nothing happens in your film for twenty-five minutes!" "Nothing happened in the first twenty-five minutes of *Psycho* either," I replied. Then he exploded. "Hitchcock can afford to keep the audience waiting! BUT YOU ARE NOT HITCHCOCK!"

Later I learned that Hitchcock had done the same thing with *Psycho*. He didn't want music in the Janet Leigh shower scene, only sound effects. But if we remember one thing from *Psycho* today it's the music, which is the most brilliant soundtrack in the history of cinema. Hitchcock told the unfortunate Benny, "No music during the shower sequence." Me saying "no music during the credits" must have brought back bad memories.

You have your own version of Psycho's *screeching violins in* Carrie, *every time her powers are triggered.*

Those are sound effects. I hope Benny forgives me.

Around the time of Sisters *you met George Litto, who played a considerable role in your career.*

He was an important person in my life. I met him after I took Martin Ransohoff's advice when he told me I should get an agent, so I contacted Robbie Lantz, the archetypal highbrow East Coast agent who handled big stars like Liz Taylor. He was a little distant with me, which put me off, but in the end he negotiated my contracts with Ransohoff. Once *Sisters* came along, I decided to find another agent, and through Waldo Salt, Jennifer's father, I heard about George Litto, who represented a bunch of blacklisted writers at the time. Litto was also negotiating Robert Altman's contracts. I first met him when I was in California with Ed Pressman. He was an outsider, a Sicilian, very brilliant but kept to himself. I liked him right away. We hit it off and I asked him to become my agent. I've never regretted it. If he believes in you, Litto will defend you tooth and nail. He's also an honest guy who does all it takes and goes wherever necessary to make sure his clients are paid for their work.

Phantom of the Paradise, which won the Grand Prix at Avoriaz in 1975, is your only musical film to date. What do you remember about the experience?

Those were good times. The idea for the film came to me after hearing a Muzak version of a Beatles song in an elevator. I thought it would be interesting to take a great song and cover it in all sorts of different musical genres: Beach Boys style, hard rock, rockabilly… Then I combined three classic stories – *The Phantom of the Opera*, *The Picture of Dorian Gray* and *Faust*.

As with Hi, Mom! *and* Sisters, *you developed* Phantom of the Paradise *for producer Martin Ransohoff.*

Yes, and when I realised he would never produce it, I bought the rights back and sold them to Ed Pressman. I wrote the first draft of the script with Louisa Rose, who had helped me on *Sisters*. Once again Ed loved the script, and we immediately hired Paul Williams to write the music. Since he can also act, I thought it would be a good idea to cast him as Swan. Paul has a very particular look; he's very small, rather strange, but interesting. He has a very dark sense of humour, which was perfect for Swan. He's very good at writing commercial pop, but he's also open-minded, meaning he can adapt to different styles. Three years after *Phantom of the Paradise* he and Barbra Streisand won the Oscar for "Evergreen," the song that features in the remake of *A Star is Born*. Before that he wrote the music and songs for Alan Parker's *Bugsy Malone*, which I liked a lot.

Where did you find the other actors?

William Finley, who plays Winslow, was in *Sisters*, and a lot of the technical crew also worked on that film. I spotted Jessica Harper in an off-Broadway play. She was from Sarah Lawrence like me and had an incredible voice, and I thought she would be good for the role of Phoenix. The Juicy Fruits were a group of improvisers. They formed a real band in Los Angeles soon after, The Groundhogs. William Finley knew one of the members.

Jessica Harper later acted in Suspiria *by Dario Argento, a filmmaker you're often compared to.*

I saw *Suspiria* but don't remember much about it.

Where did the name Swan come from?

I don't remember. Initially I called his record company Swan Song Records, but the name was already registered and the rights holders threatened us with a lawsuit. We had to remove all mentions of the name from the film and replace them with Death Records, though I've been told that there are still some hints of Swan Song Records here and there.

This is the first of your films to thematise a pact with the Devil.

Yes. Remember that rock standard "Sold My Soul to Rock 'n' Roll"?

William Friedkin, the director of The Exorcist, *claims to believe in the Devil. Do you?*

Let's just say that I believe in good and evil, though my understanding of evil has nothing to do with mythology or religion. As far as I'm concerned the Devil is quite real and you don't need to make *The Exorcist* to evoke him. Just head over to Hollywood and you'll find studio executives who are exclusively interested in making money and would love nothing more than to buy your soul. I've known quite a few of these people.

Why did you choose to open Phantom of the Paradise *with a prologue in which the camera zooms in on the Death Records logo while a voiceover introduces Swan?*

That's actually Rod Serling, creator of the TV series *The Twilight Zone*, speaking the prologue text. Why the prologue? It was important that audiences understand as quickly as possible that the film is a mixture of three genres: horror, musical and comedy. The prologue is dark and disturbing and lets us know that this is a horror film. Then we cut to the opening sequence with The Juicy Fruits singing, which introduces the musical and the comedy. It's not an easy combination to pull off.

The audition scene, where Swan watches from behind the mirror, reminds us of the moment in Michael Powell's The Red Shoes *when Anton Walbrook watches the show from his dressing room.*

You're right to make the connection. The scene was inspired by Powell's film.

Why did Michael Powell's films have such an influence on you and Martin Scorsese? It seems strange at first because…

…the films we make are so different. Yes. But I like a lot of films that are in no way similar to those I make myself. Like Marty, I discovered Powell's films on television. For me, *The Red Shoes* is the perfect movie; I can replay it frame by frame in my head. That's pretty rare. Everything works wonderfully; it's very innovative, very moving. It's the greatest film I know about artistic creation. That's why it touched us so much. Ballet as metaphor for *all* artistic work.

The theme of the double, as represented by positive and negative characters, is present throughout your work. The protagonist often sees in the antagonist a reflection of the monster he could have become. This is particularly true of Swan and Winslow in Phantom of the Paradise.

It's true. I'm also aware that my characters create a reality for themselves that everyone else has to conform to. In fact, I do the same thing when I make a film. Tony Montana in *Scarface*, Meserve in *Casualties of War* and Swan in *Phantom* – they're all surrounded by a fawning entourage, people who reflect back to them the distorted image of the world in which they imagine themselves to live. Sherman McCoy, the hero of *The Bonfire of the Vanities*, is also part of this family. He lives in a protected world and considers himself a Master of the Universe. But when his car hits that kid in the Bronx and the media goes wild, he realises that there's another reality out there, a very different one, which he didn't know even existed. Swan was inspired by Howard Hughes. He has absolute control over the universe in which he evolves. I often see similar cases of rich people who end up isolating themselves and evolving in an opaque, dehumanised universe, founded on the most corrupt values. Another character who fascinates me is Hugh Hefner, founder of *Playboy*. If he decides to get up at six in the evening, then that's when the day will start for everyone around him. I also like demiurges like Walt Disney, who built his own world, Disneyland.

The final scene of Phantom of the Paradise *is extraordinary. It reminds us of the atmosphere of* Dionysus in 69.

You're exactly right; the scene was inspired by Richard Schechner's productions. I asked William Shepherd, who was in *Dionysus in 69*, to do the choreography. He makes a brief appearance, just before Swan's murder. I shot the scene as if it were a documentary. As soon as the band starts to play, the audience reacts and gets on stage to mingle with the musicians, like in *Dionysus in 69*.

Where did you shoot the film?

The interiors were filmed in Los Angeles. For the auditorium we found an old movie theatre in Dallas, where most of the shooting took place. The exteriors of Swan's house were filmed around Central Park, in New York, and the scene where Swan takes Phoenix to the roof of his house and says, "Look down" was shot near City Hall. In fact, that was the last shot we filmed. *Phantom of the Paradise* was very enjoyable to make. I love musicals; they're a lot of fun to shoot. All the music is pre-recorded. Ours was very over-the-top.

The sets and costumes of Phantom of the Paradise *are very original. Who had the idea of the bird-head mask worn by the phantom?*

I always had in mind an image of a 45rpm vinyl press that would disfigure him, hence the idea of the mask that he would then wear to hide himself. Why a bird mask? Jack Fisk, the art director, must have had the idea. He also designed the Death Records logo, which I found very funny.

How did you meet Fisk?

Through Ed Pressman. Jack did the sets for Terrence Malick's *Badlands*, which Ed produced, and afterwards Jack worked on *Carrie*. He's married to Sissy Spacek, who also worked on *Phantom* as a set designer.

Fisk later became a director.

Yes. His first film, *Raggedy Man*, starred Sissy and Eric Roberts. He did two or three more after that.

How was the release of Phantom of the Paradise *in the US?*

Big. It only cost $1,200,000 to make and we sold it for $2 million to the distributor, 20th Century Fox. But we weren't legally covered. We hadn't asked for any permissions, so we were landed with a bunch of lawsuits. Universal accused us of plagiarising *The Phantom of the Opera*, which they owned the rights to. The film was originally called *Phantom* but the authors of the comic book with the same title forced us to change the title. This all came down on us as we were finalising our deal with the studio.

The Fox people told us we had better settle all the lawsuits or they would reduce or even cancel their offer. We ended up paying Universal $500,000. Fox's offer, meanwhile, dropped to $1,500,000, which we were forced to accept. So we went from the mindset of, "Wow, how amazing we are for selling our little independent film for two million dollars!" to "Holy mackerel! How are we going to get out of all these damn lawsuits?" I don't need to tell you that all of this made me a copyright infringement specialist. We probably would have won our case against Universal, but we didn't have time to go to court.

Fox loved the film, and their president Alan Ladd Jr. acquired the rights and made a big deal of releasing the film. It did well in Los Angeles but badly in New York and the rest of the country. A big disappointment. I remember the night of the release, William Finley and I went to check out the theatres in New York, but there was hardly anyone there. In France and Canada, on the other hand, it was a hit. In Winnipeg they still organise the "Phantompalooza," where cast members are invited. They show up in costume and chat with audiences. Don't ask me why the film did well in Winnipeg; I have no idea. And then, five or six years after the film came out, I was in Paris and someone came up to me and said, "You want to come and see this. Your movie is still playing in theatres here." I said, "Are you kidding me?" He said, "No, I'm not,' and he took me to see it. The theatre was packed. I remember thinking, "Go figure." The soundtrack continues to sell very well in Europe. So the film was a hit in some countries and an absolute flop in others. For me it was a disappointment. I really thought it would be a hit.

Did you already know Paul Schrader, the screenwriter of Obsession, *your next film?*

I met Schrader around 1972 at a press screening of Robert Mulligan's *The Other* in New York. When I was in Hollywood looking for a distributor for *Sisters*, Schrader saw the film and wrote a dense, well-argued review of it. We met once or twice after that and exchanged ideas, then one day he gave me a script he had written called *Taxi Driver*. I remember reading it over Christmas vacation. I was living with Margot Kidder and Jennifer Salt at the time. I read it to them one morning and thought, "This is amazing," but I didn't exactly know what to do with it. I didn't want to direct it myself; it was much too dark for me. But it was, nonetheless, an absolutely remarkable script, so I gave it to Julia and Michael Phillips, the producers who lived next door to us, and that's how *Taxi Driver* got started.

Years later, when the film was in production, the Phillipses did me a big favour by giving me a percentage of the profits, which was very generous of them. In the end I made $150,000, which was a lot of money back then. In interviews Schrader said that I wanted to do *Taxi Driver*, that he didn't want me to do it, and that I was upset when the project ended up being made by Scorsese. That's not how I remember it at all. Schrader often rewrites history in his own way. If he gave me the script it was obviously because he wanted me to direct it. Scorsese wasn't around at the time. In fact, I don't think Schrader even knew who Scorsese was.

Schrader immediately struck me as utterly unrestrained, full of repressed violence, almost suicidal. He didn't have "I'm going to kill myself" tattooed on his forehead, but he kept saying that one day he was going to blow his brains out. He would joke about it while talking insistently about things like his Calvinist upbringing. It was part of an act he developed to make himself look good. He had been raised as a Calvinist, that's for sure, but he would go on about it endlessly. It was like a refrain with him: "Hey, I'm the self-destructive guy with the weird religious upbringing." Schrader was in awe of his older brother Leonard. I think that's what brought us together. Like Bruce, Leonard was considered the genius in the Schrader family, the real intellectual. Paul wasn't considered quite so talented. Although they wrote several scripts together, the Schrader brothers had a contentious relationship. I don't think they speak to each other these days.

Schrader became a director. What do you think of his films?

He's improving, but he's still a way from being good. He's a brilliant scriptwriter but not the greatest of filmmakers, and not quite equipped to direct his own scripts. When they're given to Martin Scorsese or to me, his stories really take off. When he films them himself, they're heavy and overly intellectual because he lacks perspective. What I really like about his films are the ideas he's working with, not the way he brings them to life. *Light Sleeper* is by far the best film of his films to date.

Obsession *is inspired by Hitchcock, but in a different way than* Sisters, *since it's quite openly a variation on Hitchcock's* Vertigo.

That's right. That's exactly what Schrader and I said to each other when we came up with the idea for the film: what kinds of *Vertigo* variations can we come up with? Understand that *Vertigo* is based on the most brilliant idea in cinema. A man, James Stewart, falls in love with an illusion, Kim Novak, created from scratch by a manipulator, Tom Helmore – which is precisely what happens when you watch a film. You fall in love with an illusion created by the director. It's a really great idea, and if you know anything about the movie business you know that you should never meet the actors you love because they never live up to your expectations. The characters they play are merely mirages created by a director. This is also one of the reasons why I never wanted to meet Hitchcock, because I didn't want the image I had of this masterful filmmaker to clash with the reality of an over-the-hill director.

Do you know if Hitchcock was aware of Obsession?

I read in a book that he did see it, yes, and apparently he wasn't much impressed. He thought it was too similar to *Vertigo*. The idea is the same for sure, but to be honest I think my story is better. *Vertigo* is full of holes. There's no logic to it.

What if James Stewart hadn't jumped in the water to save Kim Novak?

For example, yes. Or what if when he came down from the bell tower the first time, he went to look at the girl's body and thought, "But that's not Kim Novak…" *Obsession* has a better plot. There's this suggestion of incest, which makes the ending even better. It's so much stronger than *Vertigo*'s incoherent ending, where the nun comes in to ring the bells, which really is a cheap effect. "Boo! Scare me!" In any case, it's definitely not the most appropriate climax for a film like that. The fact that she dies twice in front of him is of course completely devastating, unbelievable. But surely they could have found something better. Even when I first saw the movie it bothered me.

How was the writing of the Obsession *screenplay?*

I was at Scorsese's house because he had asked me to help him edit *Mean Streets*. At the time, Marty was spending a lot of time with Schrader. They were trying to put *Taxi Driver* together and also planning an adaptation of Dostoyevsky's *The Gambler*. I remember Marty setting up a screening for us of the old Fox version, with Gregory Peck. At the time Schrader didn't have a penny to his name. He had written the script for *The Yakuza* with his brother and it was up for auction. Two buyers were interested. The bids were going up – I'm talking about hundreds of thousands of dollars. Schrader, who was always showing off, was very pleased with himself. He and I ended up making a bet over cards, which I won. He didn't have the $200 he owed, of course, so I said, "Take me to dinner." We went to Musso & Frank's and started talking about *Vertigo*, which had recently been screened at the LA County Museum in an unforgettable, beautiful VistaVision print. I hadn't seen it in years. Over dinner, Schrader and I laid the groundwork for a story that used the same idea, then I went home that night and wrote it down. It was probably four or five pages long. Then Schrader came back to see me out at the beach and we talked. We decided to write a script and try to get the thing up and running as quickly as possible. Schrader said he would write it on his own if I would give him full credit for the story. "That's not fair," I said. "We came up with the idea together. You and I came up with the concept." We argued, and in the end he gave in, but he held out for a long time before going off and writing the screenplay. That's his style. Once he has an idea he's relentless and will wear you down by any means necessary. The credits list both of us as authors of the original story.

The original title was *Déjà Vu*, but we figured no one would understand what that meant. I gave the script to my agent, George Litto, who was making his debut as a producer. It took him a long time to get the financing together, which came from odd places. A law firm in Cincinatti put money into the film and then deducted it from their taxes. Once we had Cliff Robertson and Geneviève Bujold, the deal came together.

Did you cast them?

Yes. I had seen Geneviève in a film with Richard Burton, *Anne of a Thousand Days*. It was a stroke of luck that she accepted because she was represented by John Ptak, a very tough agent. We didn't have a lot of money, so the problem was finding inexpensive actors. I saw a lot of people before I settled on Cliff Robertson. I wasn't wildly happy with him. He's a bit stiff for my taste, but I couldn't afford anyone else.

Who would you ideally have liked to have play Courtland?

It needed the James Stewart of its day, whoever that was. Richard Burton had this romantic, obsessive side but I couldn't afford him. Hitchcock could afford the biggest stars. He was at the pinnacle of his career when he made *Vertigo*.

Kim Novak wasn't his first choice for the role of Madeleine.

That's right. He wanted Vera Miles but she got pregnant and he was forced to cast Kim Novak. The first time I saw *Vertigo* I was most impressed with Jimmy Stewart and Barbara Bel Geddes. Kim Novak didn't make much of an impression, but the more often I saw the film, the more extraordinary I found her performance. She's an enigma, really very mysterious. You can't tell what she's thinking, which is very much in line with the script. It's interesting how opinions can shift over the years.

Was it deliberate on your part to start the plot of Obsession *in 1959, one year after the release of* Vertigo?

That's an interesting observation, but actually the answer is no. I did it that way to fit the timeline. I don't know if you know this but in Schrader's original script there was a third act, set in the future. He never forgave me for rewriting the ending. In his version Amy gets on a plane and vanishes into thin air, and Courtland never hears from her again. Twenty years later he returns to Florence and finds Amy cloistered in a convent, half mad. Nobody knows what happened to her, and she doesn't remember anything. Finally she's hypnotised and the kidnapping is replayed to induce a psychological shock in her. This time Courtland brings the money, she cries out "Daddy! Daddy!" and we understand that she's his daughter.

When we were getting the financing together, we realised that we didn't have nearly enough money to shoot this third part of the story. Bernard Herrmann, who I was talking to about the music, told me to throw it out. "It'll never work," he said. "The story shouldn't go on that long." And he was right. The film naturally ended at the end of act two. My idea was that Geneviève's character is writing a letter before attempting suicide. She would be brought back, her father would meet her at the airport, and that's when she would cry out for her daddy.

For us, the key scene in Obsession *is when Courtland first sees Sandra at San Miniato Basilica in Florence. After discovering a painting underneath the one she is restoring, she asks Courtland if it should be preserved or destroyed. This could be you saying, "This movie reminds you of* Vertigo, *but it's not* Vertigo. *Should we watch it with Hitchcock in mind or forget all references and take it for what it is?"*

People always said that all I was doing was stealing from Hitchcock, but that's such an ignorant way of looking at things. Artists have always been inspired by what comes before them, and if Hitchcock had such a fantastic idea, why can't I adapt it in my own way? That's what Shakespeare did. Why should I be afraid of being influenced by Hitchcock? I'm very proud of *Obsession*.

Why did you shoot in Florence?

Because I know the city well. I went there in 1959 on a scooter that I rented in Rome. I travelled all the way back to Paris and on the way visited all the towns up in the hills and spent time in the art galleries.

According to Steven C. Smith, Herrmann's biographer, Hitchcock thought of shooting Vertigo *in New Orleans.*

Really? That would have been a good idea.

Bernard Herrmann was annoyed at him for moving the action to San Francisco.

I didn't know that. That's interesting. I always set my stories in places I know. That's why *Snake Eyes* is set in Atlantic City. I think that it's important for a director to know all about where he makes his films and the people who live there. I shot documentaries in New Orleans and knew every corner of the place.

The character of a child wanting to avenge her mother is reminiscent of you trying to help your mother get a divorce from your father.

Absolutely, which is why Geneviève's character is the most powerful in the film. Unlike Hitchcock, who identified with the voyeur played by Jimmy Stewart in *Vertigo*, I identify with the vengeful child.

The sequence where John Lithgow takes Sandra/Amy back to the airport is another very strong moment. In flashbacks you have Bujold play her character as a child. It's a bold move.

I was able to do that because Geneviève has the face of a child. I don't think a child could have played that scene any more convincingly.

In the final shot of the film the camera swirls around the actors to the point of vertigo. It's one of your favourite moves.

It wasn't easy to do. We had to run at full speed around the actors, pay attention to Cliff's and Geneviève's performances, and not get our feet caught in the cables. It was also hard for Cliff and Geneviève, who had never done anything like that before. "We're not going to be able to do many takes," I told the crew just before shooting. "The actors are going to run to each other and Geneviève is going to explode with emotion. We have to be ready to capture it the first time." We got it the first time, that night, in the airport. Once again we caught that lightning in a bottle and captured it on film.

Amy becomes a little girl again right in front of our eyes.

It moves me even today.

But a devastating ending. Robertson has to express both the joy of having found his daughter and the horror of having slept with her. There is no redemption for the hero, just like in Blow Out.

Exactly, yes.

Would you describe Obsession *as a romance?*

Yes, perhaps a tragic romance. We tend to forget that true romanticism is tragic. Those stories always end badly. Look at Powell and Pressburger's *The Red Shoes*. It doesn't get any more romantic than that! No truly great love story ends well. That's what makes it beautiful, the fact that it never completely comes true. *Obsession* is about a man who falls in love with his daughter and sleeps with her. At the end of the film we're left wondering what's going to happen to them.

You never make it explicit that Courtland is sleeping with Amy.

I shot a scene but Columbia refused to distribute the film if I included it. As it stands, you can believe that Courtland dreams that he takes the girl home and marries her, which is a very kitschy sequence. But the truth is that he went to bed with her. It wasn't a fantasy.

You often say that your Gothic sensibility doesn't come from your readings, yet it's impossible not to think of Edgar Allan Poe when watching Obsession. *The whole passage where Cliff Robertson goes to visit the mausoleum of his wife and daughter conveys the same emotion as Poe's poem "Annabel Lee."*

It's interesting you think that because I don't know much of Poe's work. I've obviously seen the movies based on his books but I haven't read many of them. He's someone who fascinates me even though I know very little about his life. I'm sure I know the poem you're referring to, but it's not something I've studied closely. I've never read Poe's short stories.

You must know his poem The Raven.

I know what it's about and I've seen the film Roger Corman made of it, which is a whole other thing. I know Nathaniel Hawthorne better than I know Poe. I remember studying Hawthorne's *The Scarlet Letter* and a few other classics. I think that's where my Gothic sensibility comes from.

You shot Obsession *between* Phantom of the Paradise *and* Carrie, *two very baroque films which use split screen. There's nothing like that in* Obsession.

After experimenting with *Sisters* and *Phantom*, I wanted a more classical style for *Obsession*. I was still learning. With *Sisters* and *Obsession* I was processing Hitchcock. I had *Vertigo* in mind – those long walks filmed from James Stewart's point of view, when he tails her through the city. That's what I was hoping to reference.

Obsession *is the first film you shot with two collaborators with whom you worked for many years: director of photography Vilmos Zsigmond and actor John Lithgow. How did you meet them?*

Vilmos had worked with Steven Spielberg on *The Sugarland Express*, but it's through George Litto that I heard about him for the first time. Vilmos had also shot films for Robert Altman, who Litto represented. I don't remember exactly when we met for the first time, but we got along right away. Vilmos has a very *mitteleuropa* sense of humour; he's one of those people with whom I immediately felt on the same wavelength. He's very bright and intellectual, and very practical at the same time, always investigating the latest techniques. I get along well with that kind of technical mind because I have one myself. On my first film I did everything myself – camera, sound, everything. Technicians love working with me because I know *exactly* what I want.

Vilmos and I spent the day and a good part of the night walking around the square in Florence where we were going to film Geneviève and Cliff's night walk. We were tearing our hair out for the best locations to shoot when all of a sudden it dawned on us. Why not put the camera behind Michelangelo's David? We'll film the famous statue from behind. And that's what we did. As for John Lithgow, I first saw him on stage in a play at Princeton University. William Finley pointed him out to me. I recommended him to Paul Williams when he was making *Dealing* with Barbara Hershey.

Like most of your work, the music in Obsession *plays an important role. We're thinking in particular of the sequence on the steamboat when Michael Courtland brings the ransom money. The tension is created largely by music.*

I remember that when we recorded the piece that accompanies that sequence, Benny was conducting the orchestra himself but wasn't going fast enough, which explains why at certain moments the music isn't quite synchronised with the action. The negative had already been cut so there was no way to readjust the shot. We were recording when Bernard suddenly got into an argument with the orchestra because he didn't like the sound of the horns, at which point the brass section let it be known that they had never dealt with such a bad conductor and left the studio. Fortunately a friend of Benny's, Laurie Johnson, was there with us. He caught up with the musicians and convinced them to go back to work, this time under his direction. Benny wasn't happy, but the fact is that he was no longer able to conduct; he wasn't well enough. Laurie took over, but the way the film was edited he couldn't drive the horns fast enough to get the music where he wanted it. We fixed it a little bit in the mix to make it fit, but if you look at the film you might notice some mismatch here and there between sound and image.

Obsession was one of Herrmann's favourite films.

I'll always remember the first time he saw it, without music. By the end of the film he was almost in tears. "Brian," he said, "this is a wonderful movie. I know because I can hear the music." He meant that he could hear it in his head as he watched the images. His score, which he composed in record time, was so much better than I imagined.

Did he see the finished film?

No. He died just after recording the music for *Taxi Driver*, in 1975, on Christmas eve.

You're a connoisseur of film music.

Yes. When I go to see a film I always pay attention to the music. That's why I like to go to festivals so much, to Montreal for example. I see a lot of foreign films, which means I get to listen to music written by composers I'm unfamiliar with. I also listen to a lot of CDs; I'm always sniffing out new music. There's a Blockbuster record store near my place in New York and I'm in there all the time, going through albums, one by one. When I find one I like I record it and might use it as a temp music track. But it's rare to be surprised by a soundtrack. It's as if composers are getting lazier, even though it's the best job in the world. It's so much fun. You watch a movie, write a score, and six weeks later you're done.

Has a collaboration with a composer ever gone wrong?

The music written by the first composer hired on *Mission Impossible* wasn't working for me, so I politely told him his services were no longer required. I'm not too crazy about the music in *Wise Guys*, but overall I've been pretty lucky. I was always able to choose my composers. I work closely with them and don't stop until I get what I want. What I don't do is leave them to their own devices.

You're a great admirer of David Lean, yet you've never worked with Maurice Jarre.

Actually, I'm not a big fan of Jarre. The greatest French film composer in my opinion was Georges Delerue. A real giant. It's one of my big regrets not to have worked with him. His score for Godard's *Le Mépris* is probably one of the most beautiful in the history of film.

What other composers would you like to work with?

I like Eric Serra, especially his score for Luc Besson's brilliant *Nikita*, which I love. I also liked the music for *Léon*. James Horner is also good, especially the music he wrote for the Tom Clancy movie, *Patriot Games*. I also like his score for *Brainstorm*. He's one of the best in America today. There aren't many others that interest me – perhaps that guy who wrote the music for *Chinatown*, Jerry Goldsmith. Dave Grusin – I used him for *The Bonfire of the Vanities* and liked what he did. Then there's John Williams. I loved the score he wrote for *The Fury*. I'd love to work with him again, but we've never been able to get our schedules together.

You obviously have a musical mind. Did you ever think of becoming a musician when you were young?

I have no musical talent to speak of, but when editing I'm good at choosing things from old soundtracks that best fit my images. I do all kinds of experiments so I can see what works and what doesn't.

Do you play music on the set during shooting, to help the actors?

Sometimes. I played melancholic music when we shot the scene in *Carlito's Way* where Carlito is shot on the train platform.

You often use opera.

I love opera. I put some in *The Untouchables*, and even more ironically in *The Bonfire of the Vanities*, with the most ridiculous staging ever imagined for Mozart's *Don Giovanni*. In France a few years ago some directors were asked to make films based on famous operas – *Don Giovanni*, *Carmen*. I couldn't see the point. What's much more interesting is using opera as a cinematic device. I've always wanted to set a scene in a suspense film at an opera performance, where someone's being murdered, but I had to drop it because *The Godfather Part III* did that very thing so well. The great composers of today don't work in film; they're writing rock'n'roll or Broadway musicals, which have very different foundations than film.

What about the use of classical music in film?

That's what Stanley Kubrick is so good at. When he was editing *2001: A Space Odyssey* he used Strauss waltzes as a temp score, and then, when he couldn't find a composer to come up with anything better, he just kept them in the film. On the other hand, it's awkward when he uses Béla Bartók in a horror movie. The problem with classical music is that nine times out of ten the audience knows the piece you're using, which means they have a head start on your images. They can guess what direction things are moving in. Audiences know when a crescendo or a break in tone is coming. That's a problem in a horror movie, where the goal is to take the viewer by surprise. I was thinking about this the other night while watching *The Shining* on TV. You remember the scene where the camera follows the kid on his tricycle and we hear Bartok's "Music for Strings, Percussion and Celesta"? That bothered me because the moment the kid stops in front of the room to turn the door handle, I knew that we were about to hear the bong. I know that piece by heart; it's one of my favourites.

So you're in favour of music written specifically for a film?

It's important for a director to find the right composer. Look at Hitchcock. The power of many of his films came from Bernard Herrmann's music. *Psycho* wouldn't be *Psycho* without his score. Bernard was going to write the score for *Carrie*, and when he died I looked around for a new composer. I had seen a film by Nicolas Roeg called *Don't Look Now* and loved the music, by Pino Donaggio. He lived in Venice. I met him and we immediately hit it off. He did *Home Movies*, *Dressed to Kill*, *Blow Out*, *Body Double* and *Raising Cain*. He's a real charmer. He doesn't speak English very well, so before each job I make a tape for him, full of the kind of music I'm looking for. I put a lot of Herrmann's pieces on the tape I gave him for *Dressed to Kill*, and for *Blow Out* too. I love everything he's done for my films, but I don't know if I would hire him again. I think I got a little tired of his music. Not that it was bad; it just doesn't excite me anymore when I hear it under my images. There's no surprise anymore. It's like when you always work with the same writer or cinematographer, in the end all your films end up looking the same. At a certain point you have to look elsewhere.

CHAPTER FOUR

CARRIE – THE FURY

What is it that first connects to you to a book or screenplay?

The visual potential of a story always comes first. Images have to appear in my mind when I read a script, and I want to be able to understand immediately how to film them. It could be a split screen, like in *Sisters*, or the long slow-motion scene at the dance in *Carrie*, or Gillian's escape in *The Fury*. More and more, my films are structured around three or four big visual scenes, which for me encapsulate the whole film. My job is to create transitions between these scenes and maintain dramatic momentum until the big finish. Look at *Raising Cain* or *Scarface*, *Blow Out*, *Carlito's Way* or even *Mission: Impossible*. I'm not interested in stories where the action is told mainly through dialogue. Or it has to be brilliant dialogue, like David Mamet's.

Like Obsession, Carrie *is centred around a mother figure. In the first film, the mother was absent, but in* Carrie *her influence is everywhere. How did you come across Stephen King's novel* Carrie?

At the time I was using a gym on 13th Street, next to my place on Fifth Avenue, in an apartment that William Finley's parents had handed down to me. I met a friend of a friend there, David Freeman, a writer and occasional novelist. "You should read *Carrie* by Stephen King," he told me. "It's very good." I asked who Stephen King was. "It's his first book," he said. "A horror novel." I went to the local bookstore on 8th Street, which is now a clothing store but was a really great bookstore back then. I'll never forget that day; it's engraved in my mind. I walked in and saw this hardcover book called *Carrie*, bought it, went home, and immediately started reading it. I thought it was great. *Obsession* hadn't been released yet and I'm not sure if *Sisters* had been distributed, but I was looking to make another film for a major studio. I needed to expunge the disastrous experience of *Get to Know Your Rabbit*, so I called my agent and asked if anyone owned the rights to King's book. I think Fox had them initially, but then the project ended up at United Artists, with Paul Monash as producer. Do you know who he is?

He produced Butch Cassidy and the Sundance Kid.

Among others. You know he also wrote the first draft of Orson Welles' *Touch of Evil*? He's been in the business a long time and knows everyone in Hollywood. He's had his fingers in so many projects over the years. *Carrie* was at United Artists with Monash as producer and Lawrence D. Cohen as scriptwriter. I put my agent George Litto on the case, begging him to get me the job. Luckily Mike Medavoy, who at the time was running United Artists, had heard about me from one of his clients, my old girlfriend Margot Kidder, and on the basis of *Sisters* decided, "OK, this kid can do *Carrie*."

Carrie *is a kind of perverted fairy tale. Cinderella goes to the ball, where everything turns into a nightmare.*

That's all in the book, which I followed faithfully, once the flashback structure was eliminated. I added some Catholic imagery – the kind of thing that's always resonated for me. As for Cinderella, I suppose you could say that about the book, but I always saw it as more of an ugly duckling story, about someone bullied in high school who gets her revenge. It's the kind of story that has always captured my interest.

Why did you remove most of the supernatural elements from King's novel?

His book was mostly about a girl with telekinetic powers. In the film I emphasised the idea of vengeful, marginalised child, someone who is a victim of her classmates, because that seemed to me to be everyone's high school experience.

Manipulation is one of the great themes in your films. Carrie is manipulated by her mother, but there's another, more sexual kind of manipulation in the film, as seen in the characters of Billy Nolan and Chris.

Absolutely. Chris manipulates Billy through sex. She teases him into doing what she wants. Sue Snell manipulates Tommy in the same way.

Carrie seems caught between heaven – the ball where there is "Love Among the Stars" – and hell, the grave where "Carrie White burns in hell."

You're talking about symbolic elements that I put in a film twenty-five years ago. It's hard to remember… I had to ask someone to write the graffiti, probably Jack Fisk. Maybe it's in the book – I don't remember.

The structure of the book is very different from the film.

Yes, but that's because I had a solid understanding of the book. When I was given the script, I immediately said, "I know how to do this."

The novel is from the point of view of Sue Snell, played in the film by Amy Irving, whereas Carrie's perspective is at the centre of your film.

As with *Obsession*, I identify with the vengeful child. The first draft of the script was told from Carrie's point of view. It starts with the shower scene, when she has her period for the first time.

That scene is the foundation of the whole film, which is why it makes sense that it's at the start of the film. But there's actually another scene before it, with Carrie and her classmates playing volleyball.

I needed a way of introducing the main characters and Carrie's relationship with the people around her. A volleyball game was ideal.

It's one of the few times in your films where you show people playing sports.

That's possible. I filmed the game in one shot, with a crane, which is the only way to do it. When you film someone catching a ball and throwing it back, you have to do it in one shot.

Is the shower sequence a tribute to exploitation films?

No, it's just the visualisation of an especially masculine fantasy. Every boy dreams about what happens in the girls' locker room, so I took the camera in there. We shot *Carrie* in the first half of the Seventies, when there were naked girls in every movie.

Was nudity a problem for the actresses?

It did cause a few problems, yes. Some of the actresses panicked, others threw up just before the cameras rolled. Some wanted to sit and discuss it with me. I heard every possible reason why I shouldn't film the scene that way. Fortunately Sissy Spacek took the lead. We spent the first few days shooting her close-ups in the shower, where she's soaping herself and starts bleeding. Seeing Sissy perform naked loosened everyone else up.

Much more embarrassing was when we screened the rushes. The whole crew was there, and I also asked the actresses to show up. I don't know if you've ever seen rushes, but the clapperboard is still in the picture and you can see the actors waiting for the director's cue. It's all a bit thankless. But with *Carrie* it was even more ridiculous because the first thing that appeared on the screen was a close-up of Sissy Spacek naked. Until I called "action" and Sissy lifted her thigh to start soaping up, the entire screen was filled with this red pubis. Plus, because I shot it in slow motion, at 48 frames per second, it seemed to take forever. Everyone was very embarrassed. You can imagine the ordeal it must have been for Sissy, being so exposed in front of everyone. But she was very calm, and at the end of the screening came up to me and said, with eyes blazing, "What a great shot Brian!"

Why did you ask the actresses to come to watch the rushes?

Because I wasn't happy with what we shot when Carrie comes out of the shower and stumbles into her classmates. I had originally planned to edit it differently, but there were two problems on the day. First, Sissy played the scene as if she was in a trance, and second the other girls were so hysterical that they jumped all over her. In everyone's defense, by that point we had been in that dressing room for days. It was very hot, the actresses were naked, and most of them had zero experience of filmmaking. The scene really didn't work because I wasn't able to follow anyone with the camera; they were all running around like mad, missing their marks. It was a disaster, which is why I wanted to show them the rushes. "Ladies," I said just before the screening, "what you're about to see is unusable. You were moving too fast and I can't see anything. We're all going to have to do better next time." They were disappointed, but at least they knew what they had to do to make it work during the re-shoot the following day. Sissy also realised that the scene would be better if she got out of the shower in a real panic and grabbed Amy Irving. In the end it turned into such a powerful moment when Sissy exits the shower and grabs Amy's arm that I decided not to cut and filmed it in a single shot, over Sissy's shoulder, cinéma vérité-style. I cut in other shots throughout the rest of the scene to give it more depth.

You don't reveal the origin of Carrie's powers, and instead leave audiences with the sense that it's menstrual blood...

...that unleashes her power.

You also shot a scene in which we see Sissy Spacek's character as a child.

That's right. We shot that but I cut it. Carrie causes it to rain stones. It was pretty wild.

You wanted to suggest that already as a child she already has these powers?

Absolutely, yes.

Why did you cut the scene?

Just as there are "false endings," there are "false beginnings," and we realised during editing that it had to go. The shower scene was the best opening. It really wasn't possible to begin anywhere else.

In the novel Carrie destroys the entire town, but in the film she destroys only the high school ballroom.

That change was made for budgetary reasons, but at the same time I didn't need to show the whole town. For high school students the highlight of the school year is the prom. That's Carrie's world.

And the prom is the highlight of the film. Why did you shoot Carrie and Tommy's dance in a counterclockwise direction?

I wanted an unsettling feeling of disequilibrium. The shot is at a slight low-angle; we see fake stars shining down on them. Everything moves faster and faster, like in a romantic daydream. The actors were on a rotating stage, which gave us control over their movements.

Carrie and Tommy vote for themselves in the King and Queen couple contest, which suggests that what happens is some kind of religious retribution, and that Carrie is punished for being prideful.

Yes, but remember that the election is rigged. We see Chris and Billy dumping a load of ballots and switching them with others so that Carrie and Tommy will win. That was filmed with a crane in a single shot. We start with the ballots and end with the bucket of blood. It's a complex camera move that took a whole day to shoot.

The most intense moments during the prom are just before the bucket of blood falls. When Carrie and Tommy go on stage to be crowned, the switching of points of view creates an almost unbearable dramatic tension.

That was inspired by *The Bridge on the River Kwai*, where a tragedy plays out in front of several people who all see something different.

Before the bucket falls on Tommy and Carrie, a piece of paper drops on the couple, which intensifies the suspense.

And shows exactly where the blood will fall. I meticulously storyboarded that scene, as I did for the rest of the film. There was a room in our production office entirely lined with my little drawings. Each visual idea was considered and assessed an incalculable number of times. I had never stayed so long in Los Angeles to work on storyboards. Month after month I shuffled my sketches, like a musical score where each note is carefully thought through.

Are you graphically attracted to blood? Red is such an essential colour in your films.

Yes, but the same could be said of Sam Peckinpah; just look at *The Wild Bunch*. There's more blood in that movie than anything I've ever done. And the blood in *Carrie* is pig's blood, poured over her head, like in the book. The producer didn't like it very much and asked if we could change it. I asked him what he wanted instead. "I don't know. We could drop something else on her head. Blue paint, for example." I said no, because precisely what makes it so horrible is the fact that it's sticky blood. And since 1976 I've seen that image of Sissy Spacek covered in blood everywhere! It's become symbolic of the film, and isn't going away any time soon. It's so viscerally effective. Blood plays a big part in *Carrie*, whether it's menstrual blood or pig's blood. Everything dramatic in the script is caused by its flow. That's why we couldn't use blue paint; nothing would have worked as well. It would probably be impossible to make *Carrie* today because the menstrual blood scene would be censored. That's why, when I hear about violence in American movies today, it makes me laugh. I mean, just take a look at movies from the Seventies... Do you really think today's movies are more violent? Of course not. Apart from that, I don't have any special interest in blood. I've never done a vampire movie, though I was offered *Interview with the Vampire*, based on Anne Rice's bestseller.

You use split screen in the scene where Carrie destroys the ballroom.

Yes, and today I see that as a mistake. The older I get, the less I'm into those kinds of gimmicks. We tend to go back to basics. When you're young you want to do everything with the camera, but the fact is that split screen doesn't work very well for action scenes because it's too contemplative. It's perfect for counterpoint, but not when it comes to cutting between shots really quickly. I did my best to make it work, but in this case it creates too much distance between action and audience.

Stephen King uses collage and counterpoint techniques in his novel, of which split screen would be the visual equivalent.

Yes, but that's a book. I was making a movie. And this is a big action scene. I shouldn't have used such a contemplative form. It's a good example of how a stylistic device can be used inappropriately.

How long did it take to shoot the prom sequence?

Maybe two weeks.

How did you shoot the amazing scene where Piper Laurie is crucified by kitchen knives?

In the novel Carrie induces a fatal heart attack in her mother. That's not very visual, so referencing the martyrdom of Saint Sebastian, which her mother has a reproduction of in her closet, I came up with the idea of crucifying her with kitchen knives.

They were all mounted on wires, and all we had to do was throw them and they would fly into the artificial limbs Piper Laurie was wearing. We used a series of quick pans. It wasn't difficult to do.

Did you use a model for the scene where the White's house collapses?

Yes. Jack Fisk built a small-scale one and we shot it in a field in Los Angeles.

The last scene of the film, with the hand coming out of the grave, one of the most famous in horror cinema, doesn't appear in King's novel.

No, but in the book Sue Snell does go to Carrie's grave. The idea of the hand coming out of the ground came to me during production, because we couldn't think of anything else. I shot the nightmare just as I imagined it, and really like the end result. Credit to Sissy, who showed unusual courage and determination. She didn't want a stand-in; that's her actual hand you see coming out of the grave. I did everything to dissuade her. "It'll be uncomfortable, you'll be buried alive, you'll have to wait for hours in the dark." But she wouldn't listen. I let her husband bury her because I didn't want anything to do with it. Jack Fisk dug the grave himself, put Sissy in a box, and covered her with dirt. She lay there for hours, disciplined and unafraid.

In final scene, when she goes to Carrie's grave, Amy Irving is walking strangely.

Yes, and if you look closely in the background you'll see a car driving backwards. I wanted to add an unreal touch to the scene, so I asked Amy to walk backwards and we reversed the footage.

What do you think of the film today?

I really like it. It's exactly what I had in mind when I made it.

Sissy Spacek and John Travolta were unknown before shooting Carrie. Were they your first choices?

Casting for *Carrie* was open to everyone. At the same time George Lucas was casting *Star Wars*, and since we were both looking for young actors, I suggested we do casting sessions together. Together we looked at everyone, though our choices didn't overlap much, except for Amy Irving. George thought for a minute about casting her as Princess Leia and I thought she would be good for Sue Snell. So we looked at the same actors and did some screen tests. Sissy Spacek wasn't my first choice. I had seen someone else I liked, but Jack Fisk, Sissy's husband, insisted she wanted to try out for the part. I said, "Jack, I love Sissy but I don't think this is for her." Mike Medavoy wasn't crazy about Sissy either. She had done two films for him that weren't very successful. When he heard I had cast her, Medavoy wasn't happy.

One day – I remember it vividly – Sissy called me to say that she had been offered a commercial in New York the same day as her screen test for *Carrie*. "Go to New York," I told her, "and do the commercial. I'm thinking of getting someone else." In the end, Sissy chose to do the screen test. Compared to her, every other actress looked ridiculous. When I told the studio I had cast Sissy, they vetoed it. "At least look at the screen test," I said, which they did, and gave her the green light. No one could have played the other roles better than John Travolta, Nancy Allen and Amy Irving.

Piper Laurie as Carrie's mother is one of your best pieces of casting.

Hiring Piper wasn't my idea; a studio executive at United Artists thought it was a good plan. He knew Piper, who was retired at the time and living in the same town as him. She wasn't always very objective about her work; she hated her lauded performance in Robert Rossen's *The Hustler*. She's fantastic in it, but go figure – she didn't like herself at all. As for *Carrie*, she played the part as if the film was a black comedy, which allowed her to bring a larger-than-life feel to her performance. Actors aren't always aware of what their character represents because they're so locked into their own conception. Piper was easy to direct. They recently did a *Carrie* reunion with Nancy Allen, P.J. Soles and Piper, who reminisced about the film. Piper has never been fully aware of the extent of her talent, something she has in common with Sissy Spacek. They're both quite inscrutable. She's very mysterious; you never know what she's thinking – a perfect trait for the character.

Was it your idea to play songs during the prom with lyrics that foreshadow the tragic fate of the characters?

That came from the producers. I thought it was a dumb idea and was resistant. Originally they wanted the song to accompany the opening credits. Can you imagine the shower scene with syrupy music?

Who wrote the songs?

Pino Donaggio wrote the music and Merrit Malloy did the lyrics. The producer wanted a pop singer, which annoyed me. "That would be a big mistake," I said. The studio head asked why. "Because it will spoil the whole beginning of the film," I said. "I'm not going to put a song like that on the titles when I have this great piece of music composed by Pino Donaggio." Eventually they moved the song to the prom.

You said you were disappointed by the way United Artists distributed the film. Would it have been an even bigger success if it had been released any differently?

Yes, because they handled it like a B-movie, the kind you release at Halloween. Their big prestigious production that year was Hal Ashby's *Bound for Glory*. 1976 was also *Rocky*'s year. Nobody was much interested in *Carrie*.

Horror films were very popular at the box office in the Seventies. The Exorcist and The Omen broke box-office records.

Those films all had big stars, and *The Exorcist* was adapted from a bestseller. The *Carrie* novel reached the top of the sales charts only when it was published in paperback, which coincided with the release of the film. It was the movie that made the book popular.

Carrie was also adapted into a Broadway musical.

Which became one of the biggest failures in Broadway history. Betty Buckley played the mother. I've seen footage of the show, but was out of the country when it was playing. In the late

Eighties, Paul Williams and I thought about adapting *Phantom of the Paradise* for Broadway. I wrote a script, which I must still have in my archives. Recently the French band Daft Punk asked to meet because they wanted to do a stage version of *Phantom of the Paradise*, but nothing came of it.

How do you explain the decline of the fantasy genre? In the Seventies, filmmakers like George Lucas, David Cronenberg, Steven Spielberg, David Lynch, John Carpenter, Joe Dante and you were all making fantasies.

It's the fault of the critics. They never take horror films seriously and have never tried to understand the genre. They focus only on the violence, which they dislike intensely. If a woman is killed in one of these films, it's even worse. According to critics, horror films are harmful, a bit like tobacco. Children have to be prevented at all costs from seeing them, and as a result good filmmakers have stopped making them for fear of not being taken seriously.

What do you think of the postmodern trend in horror films, like Scream?

It's the culmination of inanity. They did that kind of film much better in the Seventies. Look at *The Exorcist* – a more terrifying film doesn't exist. The same with *Psycho* and *Carrie*. The problem today is that the world is infatuated with American mass culture, which is becoming more and more regimented. Pretty soon everywhere will look like an American shopping mall, with the same stores and cafés. And on top of that there's TV, the great leveler. Americans think they live in the most fascinating country in the world, when in fact it's boring as hell. No one in our country is interested in what's going on culturally in Europe anymore. We can't read subtitles, so what's the point of watching foreign films? Hollywood films have never made as much money as they do today, but can you name one film that will go down in history? *Titanic*? No way! There's nothing artistic about these big machines. They might be hits when they're released, but in thirty years nobody will be talking about them. They'll suffer the same fate as Cecil B. DeMille's films.

Stephen King said he liked your adaptation of Carrie. *Have you ever wanted to make another one of his novels?*

Not really. *Carrie* is his best book. At least, the one I was best suited for.

Are there any other books you would like to adapt?

The White Hotel by D.M. Thomas. It's a great novel which would make a great movie. Quite a few directors feel the same way.

You wanted to adapt Alfred Bester's science fiction novel The Demolished Man, *which you read in your youth. What's it about?*

It takes place in the twenty-fourth century, in a society where crime no longer exists. Thanks to telepaths, the police are able to neutralise criminals before they act. Despite this, the richest man in the universe decides to kill someone. I should have made the film right after *Carrie* and had a lot of ideas about how to film telepathy, but the studio was worried about bankrolling such an expensive production. I figured that one way to reassure them would be to first produce a smaller film on a similar subject and make it a success. That's one of the reasons I agreed to do *The Fury*, though unfortunately it didn't make enough money and my Bester adaptation remains on the shelf. *The Fury*, though, I really like.

Are you interested in telepathy and telekinesis?

Not really, but it's an ideal subject for a powerful visual story.

The Fury *is a mix of horror, thriller, espionage...*

I've always liked complicated plots, with multiple levels of interpretation, and this one had a unique and rather surreal tone. It's adapted from a novel by John Farris that I never read because it was handed to me as a screenplay that Farris wrote himself. *The Fury* was also the best offer I'd had, an opportunity to shoot my first big studio film. Frank Yablans gave it to me because the subject matter was similar to *Carrie*. It's set in a world of science, which I always felt in tune with. But for me it was a genre film, and as much as possible I treated it as a fantasy. It was an exercise in style; there wasn't any particular message I wanted to convey.

The film seems to be one of your most personal. All your themes are in there – it's practically an all-in-one of your cinema.

There are things in it that resemble who I am and what I've experienced, but I wasn't aware of them while filming.

You're like Gillian and Robin, the two psychics in The Fury. *You once said that as a filmmaker you're constantly bombarded by mental images.*

That's an accurate analogy. Fortunately or unfortunately, I'm easily able to visualise everything I read and hear. Someone tells me a story and I can't help but see it in my mind. I'm powerless when confronted by such things. During a shoot it's hell because the images I'm filming linger constantly in my mind. It's impossible for me to escape them, even at night. But then, once the shooting is over, it's as if I've slain the dragon, because the images – fortunately – disappear. The worst of it is before shooting starts because anything can happen and everything is resting on my shoulders. Once something has been filmed, that's it forever. Nothing can be changed or improved. I have to live with it for the rest of my life.

So Gillian and Robin's gift is like an artist's imagination for you?

More like voyeurism. I see *The Fury* as primarily a film about the struggle of good science versus bad. The bad science takes over and exploits the children's gift for its own benefit.

Robin is a true mythological creature, a demigod, as represented by the physicality of Andrew Stevens, the actor you cast. He's one of your most distinctive characters.

The characters in all of my films have a similar complex; they literally think they're gods. There's Swan in *Phantom of the Paradise* and Tony Montana in *Scarface*, not to mention Sherman McCoy in *The Bonfire of the Vanities*, who considers himself a Master of the Universe. Robin and Gillian don't fit into any mold; they're disrupters, suppressed and co-opted by society.

Like many of your heroes, Robin witnesses a massacre and is unable to intervene. During the shootout on the beach at the beginning he's unable to help his father.

This theme appears in several of my films; it must be directly related to my childhood and family life. At home, when I saw my parents fighting or attacking my brother Bart, I could never get involved. I felt powerless. Those were traumatic times. Characters placed in dramatic situations where they're unable to intercede are clearly meaningful to me. I'm thinking especially of characters in *Blow Out*, *Body Double* and *Casualties of War*, where a woman is assaulted and no one does anything to help her. Even today I'm sensitive to this kind of situation because there's a lot of violence out there that we're powerless to do anything about. This is true even in the film world; I remember what Martin Scorsese went through on *Taxi Driver*. The studio executives wanted him to cut the final massacre, and when I saw him going through that ordeal I felt bad about not being able to help him. In the end I was able to do something about it by organising a screening for several influential critics, who liked the film. It convinced the studio to keep the original ending. Marty was being humiliated; the censorship board was threatening him with an "X" rating. It was awful to see him struggling like that, but there was nothing I could do about it.

When The Fury *was released, many critics regarded the film as a kind of sequel to* Carrie. *Few of them remarked on the true relationship between the two films, which goes far beyond telekinesis. Like* Carrie, *which was based on* Cinderella, The Fury *is a modern fairy tale. It's a* Peter Pan *adaptation, with Childress as Captain Hook, who kidnaps the children. And he's even one-armed!*

I never thought about it, to be honest, but now that you point it out I'm inclined to agree. The scariest thing about fairy tales is how they lash out at the most vulnerable among us: children.

Because of the kidnapping, The Fury *connects with three of your most personal films:* Obsession, Casualties of War *and* Raising Cain.

That's an exaggeration. *The Fury* shows overtly evil people kidnapping a teenager endowed with special powers, with the aim of using him as a weapon. *Raising Cain* tells the story of a shrink who tests his theories on children. It's very different.

The abduction of traumatised children – which The Fury *in particular depicts – seems to be a recurring theme in your films.*

Yes, in all those films the children are driven crazy. In *The Fury*, Childress shows Robin the film of the beach massacre, where Peter is supposed to have died. But I was never interested in the story specifically because it's about a kidnapping. In my films kidnappings are generally occasional threats, but I couldn't see myself making a film entirely centred around one. I was once asked to do an adaptation of Mary Higgins Clark's novel *A Stranger is Watching*, which is a really horrible story.

Maybe the fact that you're a father now is why you don't want to tell those kinds of stories.

The abduction of his children is a father's greatest fear. It's as if someone is attacking *you*, because for the first time you really have something to lose. Thanks to fatherhood, my own childhood has somehow returned. When I look at my daughters, I see myself at the same age. I relive everything through them.

Can a parallel be drawn between kidnapping and art theft, also one of your favourite themes? Childress gets rid of Peter so that he can kidnap his son, which is similar to Phantom of the Paradise, *where Swan gets rid of Winslow to steal his cantata. Are children comparable to works of art?*

A child is a work of art, insofar as every parent's dream is to give the best of oneself to a child, to raise them so they're prepared for anything in life. But a parent strives to be constructive, not manipulative, with their child. Some parents cause damage by using their children as buffers during arguments, which is what I experienced in my family. That's the dark side of parenting. But I agree with you about comparing Swan with Childress. We could also throw in Dr. Breton from *Sisters*.

Gillian is a lonely character because of her abilities. The only two people she feels close to are Robin, because he has the same abilities, and Peter, because, like her, he sees people dying around him.

Yes. But above all, what brings Gillian and Peter together is their need to find Robin.

There's a real irony in the film, in that Robin can levitate but dies by falling off a roof.

That's true. I don't remember why it was necessary for him to die like that. I hadn't realised until now. But yes, it is rather ironic.

With the exception of Gary Sinise's death in Snake Eyes, The Fury *is one of the few films where you show a suicide – that of Peter, who lets himself fall off the roof after seeing Robin die.*

That's right. Peter says to himself, "It's all gone wrong, so what's the point of going on living?" Kirk Douglas has played quite a few self-destructive characters, in *The Big Sky*, *The Arrangement* and *Ace in the Hole*.

When Gillian leans over Robin as he dies, why do her eyes turn blue?

To visualise the transmission of power from Robin to Gillian. There's a similar scene in *Dressed to Kill*, when Nancy Allen discovers Angie Dickinson dying in the elevator. Angie holds out her hand towards hers and their fingers touch. The person dying entrusts the one who lives on to avenge them. It's the same thing in *The Untouchables*, when Sean Connery dies.

Like all filmmakers who make films about psychics, you place much importance on the eyes of the characters, but in The Fury *hands and mouths are equally vital. Gillian has a vision after touching Charles Durning's hand and she blinds Childress by kissing him on the eye.*

Because hands and mouths, like eyes, are parts of the body that give identity to an individual.

In Carrie, *the heroine's powers are tied to her sexuality. There's nothing like that here.*

No, though at the very least the final scene evokes something sexual. We hear gasps, and the explosion of Childress' body obviously gives Gillian a kind of orgasm. But what's most important in the scene, for me, is that Childress, like Frankenstein, is destroyed by the monster he created.

How did you shoot the scene of Childress' body exploding?

We made a cast of Cassavetes' body, then built a dummy. The shot of the explosion is an optical effect. Remember the lamp that falls just before the body explodes? It was connected to a cable and always fell in exactly the same way, first with John standing behind it, then with the exploding dummy. We cut the two shots together as the lamp falls. Because your eyes follow the lamp and the camera doesn't move, you don't notice the jump in the image where John is replaced with the dummy. It's a nice bit of sleight of hand. When we blew it up there were ten cameras running at different speeds. The first time the pieces of the dummy didn't go in the right direction and the entire set was covered in blood. It took us ten days to get it back together and explode it again properly. Rick Baker built the dummy and A.D. Flowers, the special effects guy, blew it up. A.D. also worked on the carousel scene.

Many of your films end with a violent explosion.

Because it's dramatic and visual. Above all, I'm a stylist. I love to see action scenes, which is why I often end my films with a violent climax. It's like in music, with a crescendo and rising tension. I'm good at that kind of thing.

As with Sisters *and* Carrie, *the horror in* The Fury *is counterbalanced by scenes of comedy. This is especially true at the beginning of the film in the sequences in Chicago, when Peter escapes his pursuers by hiding with a family or when he kidnaps the two cops.*

When you make a science-fiction film you have to include moments where the audience can relax and laugh, otherwise people will laugh anyway, but at your expense, because they think you're taking yourself too seriously. One of those cops is played by Dennis Franz, who today everyone knows from his TV cop roles. I discovered Dennis Franz! *The Fury* was his first role; he was later in *Dressed to Kill*, *Blow Out* and *Body Double*, where he continued to develop the character he eventually played on TV.

It feels as if you weren't entirely comfortable filming the kidnapping of the two cops, which turns into a car chase.

That's true, I really don't like that kind of thing. They're so tedious. We've seen hundreds of chase scenes over the years. The best one ever is in William Friedkin's *The French Connection*. If you can't do better than that, it's not worth the bother. I'm not like James Cameron; I don't enjoy filming endless chases with trucks on bridges. It's not my style. *The Fury* was the first time I filmed a car chase. I took it as a challenge but was quickly annoyed by the whole thing, so to stylise it as much as possible I set it in fog. There's nothing more boring than filming in a car. What are you going to show? A guy moving the wheel and reflections on the windshield? There aren't too many ways of making it interesting.

Regarding windshields, quite a few scenes in The Fury *are shot through windows or glass, for example the image of the woman whose blood spills onto the glass table.*

Glass is like a mirror, a double. It's part of the visual ideas I get when I read a script. Then I talk about it with my set designer and it all ends up giving the film its style.

It's also the first film where you integrate elements of modern urban scenery – escalators, carousels or elevators – into the action, something we also see in Body Double, The Untouchables *and* Carlito's Way.

Playing with a space and then inserting characters into it is what I'm most interested in when I choose a location. I generally look for settings structured on several levels, which allows characters to observe without being seen. American shopping malls are good for this, train stations too. Unfortunately, in the United States there aren't many grand settings with impressive architecture, which is why I like Europe. I've filmed in every interesting spot in America.

Which sequences of The Fury *were shot in a studio?*

The interiors of the Paragon Institute, the room where Fiona Lewis is levitated, and the pursuit in the fog we talked about.

Cinematographically speaking, it's a very rich film. You make use of several techniques that have become your signature effects. The jump cuts on Amy Irving's face, in the last scene, just before Cassavetes explodes, evoke the ones you use in Carrie, *when Sissy Spacek blows up Travolta's and Nancy Allen's car.*

Hitchcock invented the technique in *The Birds*. Remember when Jessica Tandy walks into the house and discovers the corpse of the guy with his eyes torn out? Hitchcock, who was a pioneer of film grammar, uses jump cuts to bring us closer in on her face. That kind of editing technique is extremely effective in shocking the audience. Each jump cut is a jolt. It's much more effective than a zoom.

Slow motion is also one of your favourite effects, but you may have never used it quite as effectively as in the scene where Amy Irving escapes from the Paragon Institute.

Mention my name or my films and several images immediately come to mind: Sissy Spacek covered in blood in *Carrie* is one, Gillian running away from the Paragon is another. No one could have shot that scene the way I did. It's completely wild. With so much fast-paced action going on at once, it can be useful to slow down the pace so we can really look at what's happening. That's why I use slow motion. Sam Peckinpah didn't do much more than that. Most of the time I shoot with a single camera. It's when I'm using special effects – an explosion, for example – that I use more than one.

You and Martin Scorsese are two filmmakers whose use of slow motion is, at times, unexpected.

Scorsese's use of slow motion goes back to *Mean Streets* and *Taxi Driver*. I'll always remember the shot of an Alka-Seltzer dissolving in the glass of water. It gave a solemn, almost religious atmosphere to the scene. Marty also used slow motion in *Raging Bull* to convey Jake LaMotta's paranoia, which is made most obvious in the scene where he watches his wife with the gangsters. To him, every gesture is suspicious, and his jealousy is reinforced. I did the same thing in *Scarface* when Tony watches his sister dance with the guy from the Babylon Club. If a technique is effective, I use it in my own way.

At the end of the escape scene, you also use fades to show Carrie Snodgress dying.

The slow motion adds stylisation. The film becomes even more unreal.

The Fury has several special effects scenes. Cassavetes exploding is the most striking, but we also really like the carousel scene with the Arabs and the scene where Gillian has a vision of Robin on the Paragon stairs. Is that a blue screen shot?

Yes. I filmed Amy Irving against a blue background, then inserted the scene with Andrew Stevens. I do that a lot, like in *Body Double* when Craig Wasson and Deborah Shelton are kissing on the beach. In *Blow Out*, when Travolta holds Nancy Allen in his arms with the fireworks all around him, it's two shots blending together. Its way of freezing a moment in time.

The carousel scene is reminiscent of Hitchcock's Strangers on a Train.

I'm always irritated when people compare my films to Hitchcock's. I don't think they really know what they're talking about. Someone once told me that the scene in *Carrie*, of Sissy Spacek in the bath washing off blood, reminded them of the scene in *Psycho* when Anthony Perkins cleans the shower. But they have absolutely nothing to do with each other. It really isn't a useful comparison. Critics always need to build frameworks around everything. Objectively, the scene with the carousel in *The Fury* has nothing to do with the carousel scene in *Strangers* on a Train. What interested me was showing that Robin generates energy and how he accelerates the carousel just by concentrating on it, whereas in *Strangers on a Train* the carousel flies out of control because someone sabotages it.

Was the carousel in the script?

Maybe I added it. I don't know if there were Arabs either. I often have ideas just before shooting.

You worked with Kirk Douglas twice, in The Fury *and* Home Movies. *Each time he plays a father figure.*

A coincidence. Kirk was a friend of Frank Yablans, who sent him the script of *The Fury*.

How did you find the other actors?

I knew Amy Irving from *Carrie* but it took a while to find Andrew Stevens. I had seen Carrie Snodgress in a play in Pittsburgh. When I'm casting a film it's always helpful to work with a casting director, people like Lynn Stalmaster, Alixe Gordin and Marion Dougherty. I go to the theatre and watch TV movies; it's all about finding the best person for the role.

We heard that Gary Sinise, who you later cast in Snake Eyes *and* Mission to Mars, *was an extra on* The Fury.

That's what he told me, but I don't think you can spot him in the film. On the other hand, James Belushi can be clearly seen at the beginning in Chicago, when Amy Irving is walking on the beach. Do you know the girl who's walking with Amy? It's Melody Thomas, who played Marnie as a child in Hitchcock's *Marnie*. Gentlemen, how could you miss this?

There are joggers in several of your films, and your feelings about them seem increasingly satirical. You kill one in The Fury *during Gillian's escape, the joggers in* Body Double *aren't able to prevent Gloria's murder, and at the start of* Raising Cain *you film two joggers in slow motion as a threat to Carter, who has just chloroformed a mother. What do you so dislike about them? The California body cult?*

It's just something very contemporary that's immediately noticeable when you walk down the street. It's part of the scenery today. When you're scouting and thinking about what would make the backgrounds of a scene come alive, you have to take them into consideration. They became part of American life in the Eighties and Nineties. *The Fury* was filmed in 1977, so we were ahead of our time. That jogger must be the first in film history.

CHAPTER FIVE

HOME MOVIES – DRESSED TO KILL – BLOW OUT

You seem to enjoy working with students. You took film courses at Sarah Lawrence and then taught at several universities. One of your most personal films, Home Movies, *was made entirely with students.*

Film school is frustrating for me. Because students have energy and some have talent, they just want to work, but they're rarely given the opportunity. It's unfortunate. My teaching experiences with them were mostly about channeling their energy. When you get to know students you definitely see the promise in some of them – the more aggressive ones, those who think only about film. Nothing can divert them from the quest they're on. These are people who are prepared to do *anything* to make a film.

How did Home Movies *come about?*

When I got home from filming *The Fury*, I had the idea to go back to Sarah Lawrence and teach a class on how to make a low-budget film. There was only one way I could think of doing this: shoot a real low-budget film with students. During classes, as we discussed all kinds of ideas for a film, there was one that I really wanted to make, one that was very autobiographical. It was inspired by my own misadventures as a teenager when I used to spy on my father, hoping to catch him in an adulterous act. I had been thinking about this story for years and finally decided to make it as a slightly rambling comedy. The students wrote the script based on my treatment and we put it together during classes, after which we had to find the money to produce it.

I remember we convinced some accountants in New York and dentists in Des Moines that they would get a tax break if they invested. I had to put together $200,000 and persuaded two off-Broadway producers I knew, Jack Temchin and Gil Adler, to come up with $100,000. Some of the agreements we signed ended up being invalid, but in the end those kinds of problems were integrated into the classroom experience, because when you make a film with a small budget, it's a given that your financiers might disappear at the last minute. I had to find $100,000, so I called Spielberg and Lucas, who came to the rescue. Steven gave me $25,000 and George and I put in the remaining money. I promised to cover any additional costs, which was another lesson. I hired a bunch of actors I had already worked with. Nancy Allen played the bride; Gerrit Graham played my older brother Bruce; Vincent Gardenia played my father; Mary Davenport, Jennifer Salt's mother, played my mother; and Keith Gordon played me.

Keith Gordon is now a director.

And a very good one. I'm the one who discovered him. He was an actor but very interested in technique. I let him attend the course I was teaching at Sarah Lawrence.

And Kirk Douglas?

In the script, Keith Gordon's character is taking a course on mythotherapy and is learning filmmaking so he can process and overcome the trauma he suffered as a child. The filming of the movie becomes part of his therapy and is a way of bringing him out of the catatonic state he's in. Kirk, who was a big star at the time, played the professor who teaches these "star therapy" classes. "You have to be the protagonist in your life, not an extra," he tells students. "You have to be the star! The camera has to be on you at all times." In the process of completing the mythotherapy course, Keith discovers that his father is cheating on his mother with a nurse and begins filming them. Kirk gave us two weeks of his time for free and even put money into the film. It was great for the students to work with a star of that calibre.

Did your family have anything to say about the film?

Not really. It's always a problem for a parent whose child is a director, writer or poet because what they experienced as a child eventually ends up a part of their artistic endeavours.

Did the crew know how autobiographical the film was?

I think so. I knew it wouldn't make money, but I was driven to tell the story anyway. It had been nagging at me for a long time. There's an irony in the fact that I made it as a comedy, since when I was a teenager living through those events it wasn't exactly a happy time.

How was the film received?

It got good reviews, but I couldn't get the distributor to promote it, so I ended up paying for the publicity myself. That $10,000 cheque grates to this day. The movie played for five or six weeks, but it took about ten years to break even. Steven and George teased me about it. "What happened to our investment?" In the end I was happy to be able to make them a small profit. They knew the film was a student exercise but decided to support it financially anyway. I don't need to tell you that it's not often that they invest money in someone else's film, something they've never stopped reminding me of.

In Billy Wilder's Fedora *a character alludes to your generation of filmmakers by calling them "the young bearded ones." You all had beards – you, Coppola, Spielberg, Lucas, Scorsese.*

Yes, and I've been mistaken for Martin Scorsese many times because of it. People come up to me all the time and tell me how much they love *Goodfellas*. I always politely thank them. I think I was the first one to have a beard. The hot water was turned off in the building I was living in at the time, during the shooting of *Sisters*, and I couldn't shave, so I grew a beard. George and Steven didn't grow theirs until much later. Actually I think Francis Coppola had a beard by the time of *You're a Big Boy Now*, one of his first films, so he must have started the trend. Like Marty, he's had moments with and without a beard.

You're always dressed the same way, with that safari jacket of yours.

George Lucas and I have been dressing this way for more than thirty years. Marty has adopted a more formal style over time; he's fascinated by Armani suits. Steven has gone through a lot of different styles. Francis too, though he now wears mostly suits. Safari jackets are very comfortable and allow me to hide the fact that I'm overweight. Don't get me wrong, I was raised in a very conservative environment. I had to wear a suit and tie all through high school. I changed it up completely when I got to Columbia.

Along with Scorsese, Lucas, Spielberg and Coppola, you're part of the last group of filmmakers that could be described as a "wave" of American cinema. Today's filmmakers are more individualistic and don't much communicate with each other.

We were the "film school generation." Marty went to NYU, Francis to UCLA, George to USC and Steven to Long Beach. I attended Columbia and Sarah Lawrence. People always talk about me, Coppola, Spielberg, Scorsese and Lucas as a group, but we only ever saw each other at George's birthday parties. That was the only time all five of us were ever in the same room. I also think we were the last ones to make films that had something to do with our lives. Quentin Tarantino is very talented but he only works in terms of tributes and references, and the Coen brothers are only good when they talk about what they really know, like in *Fargo*, otherwise I find their work too affected. Today's directors look for inspiration in other people's films. It's pretty decadent. You might compare our era to the decline of the Roman Empire.

You have been described as a derivative director who makes films inspired by great classics.

There are plenty of misconceptions about me. Everybody thinks I'm always ripping off old directors and that I have no original ideas of my own because I learned my craft by studying Hitchcock so closely. But actually, I'm much more inspired by my own experiences. Take *Snake Eyes*. I know Atlantic City and the people who live there very well. When I made *Wise Guys* I lived in a casino for a month.

Another misconception is that because I often put female characters in danger, I'm considered the ultimate misogynist filmmaker, and when women meet me for the first time they seem to be expecting Bluebeard. But I'm constantly surrounded by women, and for good reason – I spent four years in an all-girls college. People have a hard time understanding this because it doesn't fit the image they have of me. People always ask me, "Why do you treat the women in your films so terribly?" No matter how many times I tell them that I work in the Victorian Gothic tradition, of the young woman trapped in a haunted house, I can't clear up the misunderstanding. It's like the famous ending of John Ford's *The Man Who Shot Liberty Valance* – "Print the legend," because it's more interesting than reality. I shall forever be seen as the misogynist director who stole everything from Hitchcock.

The filmmakers of your generation have all been knocked by American critics at one time or another. Martin Scorsese was attacked for Bringing Out the Dead *and George Lucas'* Star Wars: The Phantom Menace *was reviled.*

Maybe, but generally speaking, in America, Martin Scorsese is considered the greatest director of his generation. He gets an award every week and is acclaimed year-round. Everything he does is beloved and every critic talks about the "genius of Martin Scorsese." A new term has even been coined to describe young filmmakers: "Scorsesean." Steven Spielberg is a unique genius and a humanist, imbued with so many qualities that make him almost a God. It goes without saying that they're both very talented and among my closest friends, but I'm not in the same category. A movie of mine comes out and everyone says, "Here we go... he's doing the same old thing," and I get four hundred bad reviews, like I did with *Mission: Impossible*, *Snake Eyes* and *Mission to Mars*. The release of a new movie in the United States is always arduous, which is why I prefer not to be there when it happens.

What did you think of Peter Biskind's 1998 book Easy Riders, Raging Bulls, *which paints a rather negative picture of the directors of your generation? You're described in the book as being extremely jealous.*

It's full of gossip spread by people with bad intentions. Biskind interviewed our ex-wives and failed writers who were angry at us for being successful. He really doesn't understand us. We've always been very supportive of each other; we weren't trying to get in each other's way, like he says. Would we still be friends if we had?

Steven, George, Marty, Francis and I stayed in touch because we were going through the same things and could talk about them together. Who understands a director's problems better than another director? I can say to Spielberg, "Do you really want to get back to work?" He looks at me and says, "Not really," and I understand him because I feel the same way. Steven works *very* hard; he just made three films in a row. The first one, *The Lost World: Jurassic Park*, was routine for him. The second, *Amistad*, was disappointing. The third one, *Saving Private Ryan*, was an extraordinary war movie. It's understandable that he doesn't want to do it all again right away.

For Biskind, every director of our generation is a self-destructive artist at the end of his rope. It's true that some of these guys seriously messed themselves up, but maybe they're not in the game anymore because they weren't that talented. A director is judged in the long term. Biskind also misrepresented some of the events in his book. He said that I insisted Marty cut the scene in *Mean Streets* where Harvey Keitel and Bobby De Niro are in the back room. He also said that it was Jay Cocks who then convinced Marty to put it back in. The truth was that Marty asked me to help him edit his film. I worked on it and Jay Cocks was there too. We were all very close at the time. We all lived in California, struggling to get by.

Are you close to Scorsese today?

I see him when he's in New York. I think he's a little too isolated. It would be better if he spent more time with people. Every time we meet it's always very pleasant, but I'd like to see more of him. He sent me an email this morning. *The New Yorker* is writing an article about him in which they wrote about some things I said about him. He wanted me to confirm them, which I did.

Do you still show the first edits of your films to your filmmaker friends?

We did post-production on *Mission: Impossible* at George's Skywalker Ranch in California. Originally the film didn't include the scene where Jim Phelps discusses the mission with his team, as he does in the TV series. When I showed George the first cut he immediately asked, "Where's the scene where they're all around the table and he's explaining the mission?" He was certain the film needed it. I agreed, so we went back to London to shoot it.

You're friends with Spielberg but have never worked with him.

We flirted with a couple of ideas. Steven is fascinated by my films and Scorsese's too because they're so different than his. We're very different, but that doesn't stop us from being great friends. We've had our ups and downs, but there's a lot of mutual respect for each other's work. I don't know if there's the same spirit of healthy competition in young directors today. I just don't know them well enough.

Whereas you differ from many of your colleagues in that you've never made a film for purely commercial reasons.

Spielberg once said that I would be done as a filmmaker the day I agreed to direct a film like *Home Alone*. Whenever I've been successful, I've never hesitated to put whatever profits I make directly back into other films. For me that's just part of the creative process; it's what being an artist is all about. You can't be afraid to fail or go down in flames, because sometimes something new emerges out of the ashes. I made my best films when I was at rock bottom, depressed and unable to set up a project. I really do believe it plays a part. I'm not looking to fail, but I'm not afraid to take risks; I always want to go further. I have a lot of experience and know how to do a lot of things. A director makes his greatest films after fifty. You're more mature, you've had time to study the work of your elders, hopefully you still have integrity – which isn't easy, considering how much money you can make. It turns out that the old Hollywood filmmakers didn't earn very much. We came onto the market at a time when a director could become a multi-billionaire. In retrospect that wasn't a particularly good thing. It explains why the cinema of the Seventies was so innovative and the Eighties so conformist. Prosperity is a curse for the artist; it pushes you to take fewer and fewer risks. You have a business to run... or you end up cutting yourself off from the world, like Howard Hughes. You live like a god, surrounded by people who reflect the image you want to have of yourself.

George Lucas has completely given up on making any films other than *Star Wars*, which he's turned into an industry, like Walt Disney did. You could compare Francis Coppola to Orson Welles. His problem was having had such great success – *The Godfather*, *The Conversation* – at such a young age. That never happened to me. Today we wonder what will happen to Tarantino. It's hard to survive such successes because inevitably everything you do afterwards is considered a disappointment. If you win the race at fifteen, what will you do at seventeen? If you have enough money saved up, you retire to your vineyard and think back on the good old days. You really have to be motivated to keep making films. It's such a wildly difficult job. One day you say to yourself, "Do I really want to go through this hell again?" In the eyes of the establishment you're only worth what your last movie made, which means that the biggest genius for them right now is Michael Bay. That's who I'm competing with. Michael Bay!

Where you differ again from the filmmakers of your generation is in your persistent refusal to create a production company.

I was never interested. My assistant only works for me one day a week. I'm not in the least bit interested in running a company, and as you get older you become more and more aware of time passing. As far as I'm concerned, a production company would be a waste of time.

What are your thoughts on DreamWorks SKG, the studio that Spielberg founded with David Geffen and Jeffrey Katzenberg, two other prominent industry executives?

Steven, Geffen and Katzbenberg are big winners in this industry, so it's only normal that they would want to go even further together. They're thoroughbreds. You put them on a racetrack and they start running; it's in their blood. These kinds of alliances will lead to the formation of empires, conglomerates entirely devoted to new media. For us artists, this potentially means more work, and that's fine. But if the profession is becoming more and more competitive it's kind of the fault of Coppola, Friedkin and Spielberg, who launched the first blockbusters. Before *The Godfather*, *The Exorcist* and *Jaws*, nobody would have imagined that a film could make so much money. Thank God there's still room for different kinds of cinema.

Not being distracted from your work is obviously important to you. When you're working on a film you're so focused that the outside world no longer exists.

Yes, but it's hard to live like that; it messes up your life. You've seen how I've been living alone in the same apartment for twenty-five years. That's not the case for the majority of my colleagues. Most of them are cut off from the world, though I don't think they even realise it. These days George Lucas is really isolated. Sometimes I can get him to come out of his hideaway, which he seems to enjoy. Steven is also easy to get hold of. Scorsese much less so. It's hard to get him to come anywhere. Do we even know where Francis Coppola is today? In his vineyards or on his island? They're directors, for God's sake. They should be out and about.

What do you do to avoid the isolation of the rich and famous artist?

I go to festivals, especially in Canada. That seems to surprise people. Every time I go to Montreal or Toronto people look at me and say, "What are you doing here? You're a famous director." "I'm like everyone else," I explain. "I like to watch films. Why is that so odd?" It's completely beyond them. I find it strange that I've never seen another director go to a festival for fun. I'm rarely there to show one of my own films. And I stay until the very end because I want to see absolutely everything I can. What I like about Canadian festivals is that they screen films from all over the world. These days people are used to seeing me there, so they pay me no attention.

In the United States you're seen as a provocateur.

When you work in suspense or horror, as I do, you can get away with that because people don't take you seriously. What you show audiences makes them uneasy, but they deal with it by telling themselves that it's only a movie and has nothing to do with reality. But actually, I'm confronting them with their most primal fears, with their unconscious, though I do it in a seductive way. On the other hand, when I make a film that's neither fantasy nor thriller, like *Casualties of War*, audiences don't respond so positively. The problem is that the critics are just so pathetic. Most of them don't even try to understand what my films are about anymore; they stick strictly to appearances. For them, all I'm doing is putting on a big show. I do wonder if there are any decent critics in the United States anymore.

When I started out we had Pauline Kael and Andrew Sarris. Today all they do is feed the studios publicity material by reducing films to adjectives: "Dazzling," "The best performance by so-and-so..." To read their reviews you might think that there are more than thirty masterpieces released every year in the United States. These people know nothing about cinema. Kael and Sarris were different. They wrote with passion; you learned something by reading them, they were stimulating. Nowadays, people say that films have become less interesting. That may be true, but there has also been a decline in the quality of critical writing. Today's critics gang up on filmmakers of my generation for having allowed ourselves to be corrupted by money, fame, power, ease, while they have sold their souls and write the stupidest things in television magazines, which have considerable influence in America. It would be interesting to compare the evolution of film criticism with that of the actual scope of the films in the same country. In the United States, scripts and reviews have to be summarised in twenty-five words or less.

Dressed to Kill *is one of your most controversial films.*

Yes, because it was so successful. The reaction from feminists was vicious. They picketed theatres and urged people to boycott the film. The whole thing became political. I had to fight the censorship board and its chairman, Richard Heffner, and agreed to make some cuts, but the version you saw in Europe is mine. I cut some nudity for the US, including at the beginning where Angie is masturbating in the shower, but we put it all back for the laserdisc release.

Dressed to Kill *is a return to the Hitchcockian thriller, but it's more like* Sisters *than* Obsession.

I can only think of one real Hitchcock trick in the film – the idea of suddenly killing off the star of the film twenty minutes in, which was inspired by *Psycho*. As far as everything else goes, using Hitchcockian grammar is innate in me; I don't think about it consciously. *Dressed to Kill* is a mix of inspirations. Years ago I did some work on *Cruising*, a book that William Friedkin eventually made into a film with Al Pacino in 1980, about a cop who goes undercover in the gay community as bait for a serial killer. To this I added the story of a mother flirting in a museum and being picked up by a man. The idea had always been in the back of my mind because as a student I used to go to museums and pick up girls. I would walk from one gallery to another and look at the same painting as a girl, then start talking to her. In my version of *Cruising* there was a third story, involving a character who always carries a camera. It was a bit like *Hi, Mom!* – three characters and three parallel stories that come together at the end. There was the whole homo-sadomasochistic theme from Gerald Walker's book, but with two additional stories. Friedkin's film doesn't really work, though I wouldn't be able to say precisely why. In any case, my adaptation of the book would have been very different, though the original idea was fascinating: a guy who represses his underlying homosexuality and becomes a murderer.

By the way, the first time I met Steven Spielberg was in New York when he was scouting for *Cruising*, which would have been his first feature film, long before *The Sugarland Express*. Margot Kidder took me to the Plaza Hotel or the San Regis – I don't remember which – where I met him for the first time. He had a producer with him and believe it or not was about to go to a gay sauna, so I accompanied them. Bette Midler was performing there; she was singing in a gay sauna. Can you imagine? Steven and I scouting for *Cruising* in a gay sauna! Unbelievable!

Dressed to Kill is the flip side of Sisters. *In the latter, Danielle becomes schizophrenic following a surgical operation, whereas in* Dressed to Kill, *Dr. Elliot will be cured of his schizophrenia once he has a sex change.*

I first heard about sex change operations on a television talk show in the late Seventies, when transsexuals were being invited to talk on TV. In *Dressed to Kill*, Michael Caine watches one that made a big impression on me – *The Donahue Show*, featuring a former Chicago journalist who had undergone surgery and became a woman. The transsexual immediately seemed like an intriguing character to me. Feeling like a woman in a man's body, after all, is very close to schizophrenia. I read every book I could find on transsexuals and came up with a story of a transvestite who wants a sex change, represses his male side, and murders all the women who have the misfortune of turning him on. Later I had the idea of turning this character into a psychiatrist, but the initial story came very quickly; I wrote it in one go, at home, on my kitchen table.

    I was frustrated at the time because I couldn't get *Prince of the City* off the ground, which David Rabe was writing. When I finished the script I gave it to my agent, who auctioned it off. Several production companies were interested and we sold it for $200,000, which was a lot of money. George Litto wanted to do the film, and so did Sherry Lansing and Ray Stark. I was represented by ICM, who brought Michael Caine onto the project. From there we were able to get started. It's a situation that happens once or twice in a career, where suddenly everyone wants to buy your project and in a flash, things fall into place. Then I went to the Montreal festival where I met Angie Dickinson, who I had long been a fan of, and asked her to play Kate Miller. It didn't take long to cast the film. I knew Dennis Franz because we had worked together on *The Fury*, and Keith Gordon had been in *Home Movies*. Michael Caine said yes after reading the script.

Along with Dog Day Afternoon, Dressed to Kill *is one of the first mainstream films to deal with the subject of transsexuals. Today transsexuals are everywhere, including on the cover of* Vanity Fair. *There's also the television series* Transparent. *But at the time it was a bold move.*

I was ahead of my time. I recently saw a film at the Montreal Film Festival about transsexuals. Four hours long, and you see them naked most of the time. It was pretty crazy.

When you were writing the role of Kate, you said you were inspired by the character of Marion in Psycho. *Was it important to have a star like Angie Dickinson play the role?*

That's the point. The public immediately identifies with an actress of Angie's stature, so when she dies, the shock is even greater. It's like killing off Sean Connery in *The Untouchables*. I played around with that a lot. It was a pleasure working with Angie, who has a great sense of humour. I'm a big fan. As for Michael Caine, he's the nicest actor in the world and was excited to play the part. He had just done a grueling action movie and *Dressed to Kill* was like R&R for him. The role basically involved him just sitting and talking the whole time. He didn't even have to play Bobbi's scenes because for those I hired an actress, Susanna Clemm, who plays the policewoman. She did all the scenes where we see Bobbi walking around in her black raincoat. Michael Caine only had to dress up once, for his sequence with Nancy in Dr. Elliot's office. Every other time it's a double with glasses and a false nose.

Psychiatrists appear in several of your films. Have you ever consulted one?

Yes, actually – around the time I was writing *Dressed to Kill*. I made notes while I was a patient. Every scene in the film with the psychiatrist was inspired by my own experiences. I always work that way.

Dr. Elliot looks into a mirror whenever he's sexually excited.

He does that to pull himself together. His erection foreshadows the arrival of Bobbi, his double.

The first version of the screenplay of Dressed to Kill *opens with the image of Dr. Elliot shaving off all his hair and cutting off his penis.*

I shot that sequence of the poor guy shaving off every hair on his body with a razor but never included it because it was too much like the scene of Angie in the shower.

You used a double in the scene where Kate masturbates in the shower.

Yes, that was a model.

In every film you made with Nancy Allen, your wife at the time, she plays a prostitute. Was that a problem for her?

We never talked about it openly. I wrote the role of Liz in *Dressed to Kill* especially for her. Before that we had done *Home Movies* together, in which she played a perfect girlfriend character who turns out to have a split personality. But Nancy never said to me, "You're making me play a hooker again?" It never occurred to us. That may seem strange to you, but it isn't really. Each of these films contains a version of the female-in-peril character.

I actually once met Janet Leigh and asked her, "Did you realise when you were shooting *Psycho* that it was the second time you shot a scene in a motel, with a weird guy, in your underwear?" I was drawing her attention to the striking similarities between *Touch of Evil* and *Psycho*. I asked if Hitchcock knew Welles' film, and Janet said he probably did. I mean, how could he *not* have seen it? Norman Bates is so much like Dennis Weaver's character in *Touch of Evil*. Add to that the motel, Janet Leigh, and the fact that both films were produced by Universal. Strange coincidences.

There's a detail in Dressed to Kill, *when Angie Dickinson is standing on the steps in front of the museum, which is noticeable only if you're able to freeze frame the image. In the panning shot that moves from her to the stranger in the cab we clearly see Bobbi.*

I was invited to a film class taught by Robin Wood just to talk about this scene. He played it in slow motion until it landed on the image of Bobbi on the steps.

If the audience can't see her without freeze framing the shot, why did you include Bobbi?

Because she's standing there. It's not some random thing I decided to do; there's a shot of her picking up the glove immediately after. We also see her when Angie Dickinson starts walking down the steps. I follow her in a tracking shot in which you see Bobbi in the background just before she picks up the glove. Bobbi appears and disappears…

One of the surprising things in the film is Angie Dickinson discovering that her one-time lover has a venereal disease. It's a flash of her imminent death to come, and in some ways a punishment for cheating on her husband.

The scene is partly autobiographical. One day I ran into an old girlfriend in Greenwich Village who I hadn't seen in years, and she asked me to come up to her place, where we talked about what we each of us had been doing. During our conversation someone knocked on the door and a guy came in and whispered something in her ear. It all seemed very serious. It turned out that my ex had contracted a venereal disease and had to write down the names of all the people she had slept with. A real nightmare. That's where the idea for the film came from.

The big scene of Dressed to Kill *is, of course, the murder of Kate Miller in the elevator. Just before Bobbi attacks her, Kate finds herself in front of a woman and a little girl, who stares at her insistently. This provokes a feeling of guilt in Kate and foreshadows the punishment that follows.*

That's exactly it. The look in the girl's eyes reminds her of a lost innocence. Several shots from the scene were cut for the US theatrical release, so you're better off watching the video version instead. This scene was meticulously storyboarded: the mirror, Liz and Kate looking at each other, then Liz and Bobbi.

In the close-up where she sees Bobbi in the mirror, Liz looks like a pietà, a Madonna. She resembles the crucified Margaret White in Carrie. *It's quite unusual for a murder scene.*

As I told you before, Catholic religious iconography had a strong impact on me. I've always associated it with violence.

The character of Peter Miller seems a lot like the teenager you were.

He's an extension of the Denis Byrd character that Keith Gordon played in *Home Movies*. He's obsessed with technology, like me, and has all this camera equipment that he uses to spy on people, which is what I did when I was tracking my father. His computer looks like the one I built when I was in high school and his room is a replica of the one I had as a teenager. All of this made me feel at home on the set.

In terms of visual composition, Dressed to Kill *is one of your most accomplished films. The images are intricately layered, most obviously in the scene where Peter watches Dr. Elliot's office through binoculars. There is always something – rain, windows, glass or curtains – between him and what he's looking at.*

Like *Carrie*, *Dressed to Kill* is meticulously planned. I worked a lot on the storyboards and used complicated split screen, fades, fade-ins and fade-outs inside the split screens. For the scenes where Bobbi stalks Liz, I used every trick I could think of so we wouldn't see Bobbi's face. The film is a carefully crafted visual tapestry.

Dr. Elliot's office also looks a lot like your own office.

And for good reason. The furniture comes from the film.

Do you often keep props from your films?

No, but they were going to resell all this beautiful Danish furniture, so I told them I would buy it all for my office.

Was Dressed to Kill *easy to shoot?*

Absolutely. We finished on time, I enjoyed working with the actors, and the film was successful. Everyone was happy.

Where did you shoot?

Manhattan, except for the sequence in the museum, which we shot in Philadelphia because the Metropolitan Museum wouldn't allow it.

You said that you expected bad reviews because of the Psycho *reference.*

Yes, and oddly enough I got a bunch of very good ones. I was expecting a tidal wave of bad reviews, but critics finally saw one of my films as something other than a sub-*Psycho* knock-off. It surprised me that a lot of them seemed to understand what I was trying to do.

If the teenager in Dressed to Kill *is an extension of the hero of* Home Movies, *Jack Terry, the protagonist of* Blow Out, *seems a lot like Peter as an adult. Jack is a brilliant tinkerer who uses his know-how to solve a complex case.*

Once again, he's very much like me. I'm an analytical person who's always looking for the logic behind things.

Was John Travolta your first choice for Blow Out?

I actually had someone else in mind; I don't remember who. *Blow Out* was originally going to be a low-budget film. I don't remember if John sent me a script or if I called him to talk about something else, but he asked me what I was doing and I told him I was working on a script. He asked me what it was about, and when I told him he asked me to send it over. He read it and immediately wanted to be in it. You can imagine how that changed everything. It was staggering! I had convinced John Travolta, this superstar, to be in my little movie! He turned *Blow Out* into a huge movie with an $18 million budget. In the end it was a commercial failure. My most personal and boldest films have all been box office disasters. They didn't get the best reviews either, whether it's *Dyonisus in 69*, which lasted two weeks and then disappeared for good, *Hi, Mom!*, which lasted four or five weeks, or *Casualties of War*. And how could I forget *Body Double*! You can't imagine how many hostile reviews that film got. The release of *Blow Out* was a painful moment for me. I still remember an evening with the man who later became my agent. "I have revealed myself with this film," I told him, "and it's a complete disaster."

At the time you said that Travolta was wrong for the role, but he's very believable in the film.

It's always the same problem when you make a movie with a big star cast against type. Over time, people come to see the film for what it is, and today everyone agrees that John was excellent in the part, but at the time people said he was miscast. With an actor like the Travolta of 1981, people imagined that there would be a love affair with Nancy's character. They weren't expecting what actually happens.

John Travolta's film Moment by Moment *had just flopped.*

Yes, and at the time *Blow Out* was considered such a disaster that neither he nor I would ever work again. It was a difficult time.

But Travolta's career would never have taken off again in the Nineties without Blow Out. *It's the role that gave Quentin Tarantino the idea to cast him in* Pulp Fiction.

Yes, but twenty years ago who could have predicted that?

Did it help that Tarantino named Blow Out *as one of his three favourite films, along with* Rio Bravo *and* Taxi Driver?

Probably. It's always nice to hear that your films are an influence on young, talented directors. I talk with Quentin fairly often. The minute I saw *Reservoir Dogs* I asked to meet him and immediately saw how talented he was. I'm not saying that because he can recite *Blow Out* by heart, but he does really understand the film. His enthusiasm did me a lot of good. He's seen *Blow Out* countless times – more than I have, which is saying something.

The theme of political assassination is threaded throughout your work.

I'm obsessed with President Kennedy's assassination. From that starting point I came up with the idea of someone who, because they have some piece of evidence, is able to solve a riddle. I was interested in showing how pieces of the puzzle fit together. More concretely, the idea came to me while I was working on the sound mix of *Dressed to Kill*. My sound effects guy was playing me different sounds, telling me where he had recorded each of them. I imagined that one of them was the missing piece of a case as complex as the JFK assassination. Imagine that you've figured out what actually happened and you want to tell everyone about it, but no one pays you any attention.

You never had the idea, like Oliver Stone, to make a film about Kennedy's assassination?

No, and in *Blow Out* I don't even refer to it directly. I was more inspired by Chappaquiddick, which nearly ended Ted Kennedy's political career, but I reversed the fate of the two passengers. In my version the girl gets away and the senator dies. There are references to the Kennedy assassination in several of my films, but my feeling is that nobody really wants to know the truth. It's like the Jack the Ripper story; nobody will ever know what happened, and if they ever found out who did it, if a guy stood up and said, "It was me! I did it!," chances are nobody would believe him. In the case of Kennedy, no one believes that Lee Harvey Oswald acted alone, even though that's the most obvious explanation. But that's just too simple, so the details of the tragedy have been dissected down to the most insignificant level and endless conspiracy theories have developed. They are appealing in theory but difficult to imagine in reality. It's no easy thing to construct any kind of conspiracy on that scale. Sooner or later someone talks. The United States isn't a totalitarian country, where it's possible to keep a secret, but it's very human to think that we're being kept in the dark and that if we start playing Sherlock Holmes we'll find out what's *really* going on. It's a way of denying the absurdity of life, of reassuring ourselves that there is inevitably a logic, a deus ex machina, behind every mystery. But life sometimes defies logic.

How did you go about writing Blow Out*?*

Once I had the idea, I organised a screenplay contest and got the Canadian magazine *Take One* to assist. I promised I would shoot the best of the three finalists. It's no surprise that most of the scripts were completely over the top; not one of them developed the original concept in the same way. But it was interesting for me to see how these premises spurred people's imaginations. In the end the contest didn't yield a usable script, so I wrote the first draft myself, which was called *Personal Effects*. It wasn't difficult to find the money because *Dressed to Kill* had been such a big hit.

Was the film always set in Philadelphia, where you grew up?

I don't remember if the first version was in Philadelphia, but the Liberty Day ceremonies, with that huge bell, were always on my mind. The unique architecture of the city was also an inspiration. Walking through the streets you quickly realise the visual potential of the place, and I immediately saw the possibilities. Think of that helicopter shot where you see Travolta's car crossing the city and all these buildings intertwined.

The characters in your films are always professionals who enjoy their work. Blow Out *is the best example of this. In the sequence where Travolta edits the film of the accident, we feel the physical pleasure you get from making a film and the handling of celluloid.*

I'm a professional with a scientific background, always up on the latest techniques. I've always been comfortable around new technology, and know a lot about what's going on these days. It's something I'm proud of.

There's another autobiographical reference in the film. Travolta, like you, has a background in cybernetics.

His technical training was mostly in the police force, when he was an expert wiretapper. At the time I was supposed to be making *Prince of the City* with John. A lot of the research I did for that film ended up in *Blow Out*, especially the flashback where we see Jack working for the cops. I knew Bob Leuci well, the real-life "Prince of the City." I spent a lot of time with him, walking around the city and listening to him talk. He considered himself a traitor who had snitched on his colleagues and caused many deaths, all while saving his own skin. He was consumed with overwhelming guilt, a sentiment which would have been the basis for the film and which I ended up channeling into *Blow Out*.

Prince of the City *was ultimately directed in 1981 by Sidney Lumet. How would you have done it differently?*

I was very happy with the script I wrote with David Rabe, which was a character study, like *Scarface* and *Carlito's Way*. Bob Leuci was an incredible, very appealing guy. I wanted Travolta for the part because he would have brought a certain seductiveness. It was essential that the character be so charming that audiences would accept the dreadful things he does. Lumet cast Treat Williams, who isn't wildly charismatic, and because of this the film doesn't have much substance. Bob Leuci was the kind of guy who could betray his friends and still make you feel sorry for him. You would hear that a cop had been put away for life because of Bob's testimony and you would feel sorry for *him*. That's what had to be conveyed in *Prince of the City*.

I was mad as hell when the Orion executives kicked me off the project. I should have seen it coming, because Orion was formed by executives who left United Artists and they had previously turned down *Dressed to Kill* when the studio was run by Mike Medavoy. But I ended up getting my revenge. It's a bit complicated to follow, but bear with me. *Dressed to Kill* was produced under American International, which was its last film before it was bought by Filmways, which produced *Blow Out*. After the film flopped Filmways went bankrupt and was sold to Orion, which Medavoy was running, so he acquired the rights to *Dressed to Kill*, which he had previously turned down and the director of which – me! – he had removed from *Prince of the City*. Then we took legal action against Orion because we were owed money. I ended up suing Mike Medavoy. Another irony is that after directing *Prince of the City*, Lumet was supposed to direct *Scarface*, but they ended up dumping Lumet and hiring me.

Your take on the political thriller in Blow Out *is quite different from* Three Days of the Condor *or* The Parallax View, *which are about the individual against an organisation.* Blow Out *doesn't deal with that kind of thing.*

Because the whole assassination story is missing the big picture, and as usual the critics didn't get it. *Blow Out* is the story of a cynical guy who goes so far as to put the life of a girl in danger to prove he's right. He causes the death of an innocent girl, and what does he get out of it? Nothing. Ironically, he uses her scream for the soundtrack of a lousy horror movie, which becomes a sort of metaphor for his entire experience.

Travolta causes Nancy Allen's death, even though he tries to save her.

He finds himself in the same situation as Cary Grant in Hitchcock's *Notorious*. After throwing the girl into the arms of a murderer, he says to himself, "My God, what have I done?" And he can't get her out. Travolta has manipulated Nancy in order to prove that he's right. It doesn't occur to him that his actions might put the life of the girl he loves in jeopardy. For him, the truth is what's most important – whatever the price. It's a rather pathetic way of doing things.

Look at what happened in Vietnam or the beginnings of communism. At the start there was genuine idealism, ideas developed by people with real knowledge, but once implemented, those theories led to the deaths of millions. That's the price to pay for an idea to be viable. I can understand this state of mind because I was brought up in a scientific environment where only ideas counted, where the human factor was negligible. How many people were sacrificed in Vietnam in the name of the domino theory? If you talk about the domino theory today nobody knows what it is because it was so absurd. To think that if Vietnam fell into the hands of communists, then Thailand would follow, then the United States... [*laughs*]

How did you come up with the climax of Blow Out? *Sally's last scream is used by Jack in the soundtrack of the film he's working on.*

"Now that's a scream!" says the director. The idea came to me when I discovered that editors use reels of film as leader. A sound effects reel is made up of pieces of sound and leader, which is celluloid without a soundtrack. If you take these pieces and hold them up to the light, you'll see that they're actually pieces of old films. When a print is taken out of circulation it's shipped back to the studios where it's shredded and used as leader. One day, while my editor was cutting some perforations between two footsteps on the effects tape, I looked at the piece of celluloid in the light and discovered it was a piece of *Lawrence of Arabia*. A masterpiece of film history was being used as filler between two footsteps! That's also the idea in *Phantom of the Paradise*: every great song will one day be turned into elevator music. It's decorative, like wallpaper, but ultimately worthless. That's what inspired the epilogue of *Blow Out*. From this terrible situation, this tragic story about political assassination, what's left? Nothing but a sound effect in a film. A scream. It's the most desperate vision I've ever had. It's also the most ghastly ending I've ever seen in a film. People still talk to me about it today. You couldn't make a movie like that nowadays. The distributor was upset when he saw it, but it was too late to change anything. The film was finished and I had final cut.

The awful thing about the ending is that Jack is so focused on his work that he loses sight of his humanity.

In the end he's just an empty shell. That's a very powerful idea for me. When I make a film there's nothing else that matters; the outside world no longer exists. I have one obsession: to finish the project. I basically ignore my wife and children, which of course can lead to any number of problems. From that point of view, filmmaking is a ridiculous profession. People might explain to you how perfect and wonderful your film is, but you know what the real cost of it all was. It's really quite shattering. That's what I was trying to say with *Blow Out*.

It's a similar idea to one of my favourite books, *Sirens of Titan* by Kurt Vonnegut, one of the most cynical stories I know. Vonnegut basically says that humanity exists only to allow an alien spaceship to get from one point in the galaxy to another. Imagine their ship has a problem and that it lands on Earth just so they can tighten a screw, and that the entire history of mankind – all those wars, everything – only take place so that the aliens can leave. The tragedy that John Travolta's character lives through in *Blow Out* is reduced to this scream that spruces up his trashy movie.

Your endings are generally pessimistic. You once said that audiences shouldn't go home reassured, because life isn't like that.

Entertainment in all its different forms tells us that the world is fabulous, that people are young, beautiful and kind. This is especially true on television, where you'll never see anything disturbing or unsettling. It's the same with advertising. "Buy this product and your life will never be the same again!" We're bombarded with slogans day and night. My films push back against these kinds of falsehoods that we all take for granted. I always try to see what's hidden behind the facade. At the same time, the films I've made with happy endings – *The Untouchables* and *Mission: Impossible* – have been my biggest hits.

Blow Out *clearly seems to be influenced by two very different films: Antonioni's* Blow-Up *and Coppola's* The Conversation.

Two of my favourites. Actually, Antonioni's film hasn't aged well. I can't watch it these days; it's pretty boring, probably because stylistically it's so bound up in its era. But it was a strong source of inspiration. Surprisingly, many people today prefer *Blow Out* to *Blow-Up*, which wasn't the case when my film first came out. *The Conversation*, on the other hand, is still a great film. I watch it regularly; it's one of Francis' best. The idea behind it is fascinating, even if it's a bit of a cop-out when he changes the wording of the dialogue we've been listening to. *The Conversation* is a bit like *Vertigo*. There's a real problem with the script in the middle of the film, but the images are so fabulous, Gene Hackman is fantastic, and the direction of the actors is so breathtaking that you don't even notice it. When the film came out I interviewed Francis for *Filmmakers Newsletter*. I went to see him on the set of *The Godfather Part II* and even wrote an article about the film.

Like *The Conversation*, *Blow Out* is a story that could only be told in film. That's why I found *Blow-Up* so interesting. I was recently on an English TV show and they showed me the scene where David Hemmings studies the photo of Vanessa Redgrave in the park, looking over to the fence. It's pure cinema, brilliantly effective filmmaking. *Blow Out* has the same quality. We see how sound is synchronised with image. That's what cinema is all about and what solves the mystery. It's what makes *Blow Out* so original.

After Obsession, Blow Out *marked your second collaboration with Vilmos Zsigmond. How do you choose your directors of photography?*

I like Vilmos and Stephen Burum; they really understand what I'm after. That said, it's really all about who's available at the time. Vilmos is a great artist, demanding and with strong opinions. He would rather do nothing than have to work under poor conditions, which is why he disappeared for several years.

Something wonderful happened on the set of *Blow Out*. We were filming the car crash scene; there were cranes everywhere. The spotlights were placed in pods forty feet up, with an electrician in each of them. They had to stay up there all night; they couldn't even go back down to go to the toilet because it would have taken too long, so they pissed in cans. We spent a whole night up there. Vilmos had never lit such a huge set. "I've never done anything like this," he said. "It's so big!" By the time the lights were finally in place, the sun was coming up. And that was it – we lost a night. It was too much to do. But I liked working with Vilmos. We experimented a lot together. He likes to desaturate colours, something he did on Altman's films. He does what's called flashing, which involves exposing the film to light before shooting. It gives a milky quality to the image.

Is it true you shot the parade in Blow Out *twice because the negative was stolen?*

Yes. After the re-shoots we had so much of John that I was able to keep all but the most spectacular shots. The most expensive shots had to be redone entirely, over three days. I filmed it in almost the same way as the first time.

Pino Donaggio's score is particularly good.

It's my favourite. The main theme is very moving, especially during the end credits with the fade to black, as John covers his ears. It's very emotional, very sad. It's a shame there's no CD of the soundtrack because everything that Pino composed for the film is exceptionally beautiful.

Blow Out *was your final film with your wife Nancy Allen. How would you describe that collaboration?*

Complicated. I think we did too many movies together, which had a negative effect on our relationship. I didn't necessarily want her to be in *Blow Out*, but Travolta insisted on it because he liked working with her. In the end he was right, Nancy was never so good, but it was a difficult time for both of us. Relationship issues aside, the shoot of *Blow Out*, just after the success of *Dressed to Kill*, was a good one. I was making an exciting film that I was very invested in, and took great pleasure in returning to Philadelphia to do location scouting with my camera. It was the happiest time I've had as a filmmaker.

CHAPTER SIX

SCARFACE – BODY DOUBLE

Scarface *was your first collaboration with Al Pacino.*

I've known Al since the Sixties. I saw him perform on stage in his early days and we had a mutual friend, Jill Clayburgh. I always wanted to work with him. Long before *Scarface*, around 1970, we were planning a project for Warner Bros. called *Cop-Out*, based on a play by John Guare, but could never get it going. Al is an actor who comes to every film with a lot of ideas. He's extremely sensitive and already knows everything about the character he's going to play. On *Scarface* he worked with Oliver Stone, the scriptwriter, while it was being written and during rehearsals. Al's approach to acting is a realistic one, but his references come from theatre. For *Scarface* he was thinking about *Richard III* and was always talking about it, especially when we were shooting the part of the story where the character becomes increasingly insane and paranoid because of his intense cocaine use. Pacino's greatest talent is knowing how to turn the most stylised and abstract ideas into something realistic.

How did you get involved in Scarface?

Pacino loved the character after seeing Howard Hawks' version for the first time and originally thought of doing a literal remake set in Chicago during Prohibition. He went to Martin Bregman, his former agent, now a producer, and tried to set it up. They got in touch with me and David Rabe, but I wasn't interested in simply remaking the original, and said so. Bregman turned to Sidney Lumet who suggested that they modernise the story and set it in the Cuban community in Miami during the cocaine boom of the early Eighties. Everyone liked that idea and Oliver Stone, who Bregman had hired to write the screenplay, went to explore Miami and the Colombian network. In the end Lumet didn't like Oliver's script; he didn't think it was serious enough and felt it was too much like a comic book. Bregman and Pacino, who liked what Oliver had done, got in touch with me. I thought the script was very powerful and immediately signed on. Since I had been looking to work with Pacino for a long time, *Scarface* seemed like the ideal project.

Hawks' film was unknown for a long time in the United States. Its first major re-release was in 1979.

I discovered it long before that, when Martin Scorsese showed me a 16mm print he had. This was years before I was asked to direct a new version.

Did the fact that it was a remake bother you?

No, because my version is quite different. I'm not actually a big fan of the first *Scarface*. Hawks did a superb job – I think it's very well directed – but I'm not keen on Paul Muni's performance. Oliver Stone found a great way to tell the story.

How long was the script?

Long – about a hundred and forty pages. I cut some things, at the beginning in particular, including scenes in the Cuban refugee camp and with Tony's mother. Oliver wasn't happy about that and was critical when the film came out. He was disappointed and thought my direction slowed everything down. I think he really wanted to direct the film himself. He put his heart and soul into researching and writing the story, sometimes even risking his life. At one point the cocaine dealers he was dealing with in the Bahamas thought he was a cop because he was asking so many questions. He really could have been killed. But the authenticity of the film stems from his research. The dialogue in particular is extraordinary. To this day people on the street throw out lines from the film at Al Pacino.

Scarface *isn't the only remake project you worked on.*

Around 1990 I wanted to remake John Sturges' *The Magnificent Seven* and set it in the Medellin cartel. I worked with Daniel Pyne, who wrote John Schlesinger's *Pacific Heights*, on a really good script about mercenaries coming to the aid of peasants enslaved by cocaine traffickers, but over time I lost interest in the project. I also wanted to remake Billy Wilder's *Ace in the Hole*, which is a great indictment of the media. David Mamet wrote the script. In the end I made *The Bonfire of the Vanities*, which deals with the same kind of thing.

The cast of Scarface *is extraordinary. F. Murray Abraham, Mary Elizabeth Mastrantonio, Michelle Pfeiffer, Steven Bauer were all relatively unknown.*

The art of casting is to spot actors in other people's films who have untapped potential. I was lucky enough to work with casting director Alixe Gordin, who made some very good suggestions, including Mary Elizabeth Mastrantonio, who plays Gina, Tony's sister, and Steven Bauer, who plays Manny. At the time Steven was married to Melanie Griffith, but I didn't know him. Sidney Lumet originally wanted John Travolta to play Manny. I had actually thought of Travolta myself, but since Pacino was concerned about the Cuban accent he needed for the role, I thought that playing with a half-Cuban actor – which Steven is – would help him.

Tony's attraction to his sister Gina is more obvious than in Hawks' version.

Hawks and Ben Hecht were constrained by censorship. Our film is set in the Eighties, so obviously Tony and Gina's relationship is much more sexual. Before *Scarface*, Mary Elizabeth Mastrantonio had a small role in Martin Scorsese's *The King of Comedy* but didn't make the final cut. She was the only actress capable of playing every facet of Gina Montana – both the sweet little Latin sister and the wildly sexual, murderous woman who shoots at her brother before herself being shot. What Mary does in the film is extraordinary. She's a great actress.

Did you always see the film as having an exaggerated tone?

That's what the Miami atmosphere called for. Flowery shirts, a certain kind of personality, the drug dealing – it had to be larger than life. But those elements were in the script.

Would Scarface *have been such a grandiose film if your previous work hadn't been so fantastical?*

The fantasy genre taught me how to be a stylist. In other words, how to find visual ways to tell the story. *Scarface*, however, had to be realistic. It was the only way to make audiences accept certain excesses. I added newsreel footage to the credits showing the arrival of the *Marielitos* in Miami because I wanted to make it clear that this was real life.

Did Oliver Stone's script describe how the famous chainsaw torture scene should be filmed, the slow crane move from the bathroom to Steven Bauer on the street and back again to the shower? The use of sound and light in this sequence is very subtle. It inspired the torture scene in Quentin Tarantino's Reservoir Dogs.

In the script it was written that the Colombians would start cutting up Angel with a chainsaw. The scene took place entirely in the shower. I reconceived it and took the camera outside. In Oliver's script we hear the TV playing. I had the idea that the television should be showing Mark Robson's *Earthquake*. I thought it would be fun to have the rumble of an earthquake covering the sounds of a chainsaw.

Scarface, *like most of your films, including Swan in* Phantom of the Paradise, *is about the moral destruction of a man and his slow metamorphosis into a monster. Your characters become completely isolated, cut off from all emotion. You have the reputation of being rather detached yourself.*

The film business can be cold-blooded; you have to be pretty hardened to survive it. As for me being detached, I'm aware people feel that way, but it's my way of not letting myself be affected by anything that might distract me from the work. It's vital that I isolate myself. It's true that I don't talk much when I'm filming, either with the crew or the actors. That would be a waste of energy. I'm so busy on set that it's impossible to give everyone the attention they need. Besides, too many people who want to ask me something don't really have anything important to say; they just want me to pay attention to them. It can become exhausting very quickly. Film sets can bring out the worst in people if you don't take the necessary precautions, so when I'm working I have to live a bit like a monk, detached from earthly pleasures and temptations that might distract me from my goal. And God knows they're there. These days I'm much calmer than I was at the beginning of my career, so you can imagine how things used to be.

Every time a character speaks or acts from the heart in one of your films, we know something awful will happen to them. This is perhaps most obvious in Scarface, *when Tony refuses to kill the two children in the car.*

The film is a metaphor of the madness that can take hold in a capitalist world where greed is such a driving force. The more dehumanised the world we live in, the more we have to deny our feelings, otherwise we're crushed.

Scarface *could be seen as a political film. Links between American banks and traffickers are more than suggested.*

We had issues with the censors, who wanted all that stuff removed. We needed someone from the drug squad to certify to members of the censorship board that everything in the film was true. This guy was anxious that people see the film because he wanted everyone to know just what kinds of things he was dealing with. In Miami there was a television news report every evening about cocaine trafficking. The film simply pointed out what the news never mentioned, which is why people found it so shocking and saw it as excessive and gimmicky. But it's all based on fact, and the situation hasn't much changed since then. Looking back, it's clear that *Scarface* was ahead of its time. We now know a lot more about cocaine trafficking down there. The TV series *Miami Vice* made it all widely known, and showed that *Scarface* wasn't the product of my "wild and crazy imagination."

Did you shoot the whole film in Miami?

Initially we were going to shoot in Miami, but the Cuban community was hostile and blocked us, so most of it was filmed in Los Angeles. We shot in Miami for only two weeks at the end of the production. We worked in a studio a lot of the time because that was the only way of getting on film what I wanted – huge and imposing sets, like an opera. You had to feel the power and the excess of these people. *Scarface* would have been a different film if we had shot on location.

How long did it take to film the final shootout?

I don't really remember. Quite a while, because Al burned his hand while picking up a machine gun by the breech which hadn't yet cooled down, so he wasn't around for at least a week. We spent the time getting shots in which he doesn't appear. Seven days filming guys shooting at each other, waiting for my main actor's hand to heal. It got pretty boring.

This final sequence reminds us of Sam Peckinpah, a filmmaker who, like you, has been criticised for the violence and slow motion in his films.

I like Peckinpah a lot; *The Wild Bunch* is a great movie. But the final shootout of *Scarface* wasn't inspired by him. Peckinpah edited together shots that were filmed at different speeds. When I edit a slow-motion shot, I never cut it and never change the speed. Peckinpah combined shots filmed at 24 frames per second with others filmed at 48, or even 96 or 120. That was his signature. But he started out at a time when they were developing new techniques to make artificial blood gush out of bullet holes, and they wanted to slow it down to emphasise the eye-catching aspects.

You don't speak French, but have you seen the French version of Scarface?

No. Is it bad?

On the contrary, it's extraordinary. The French actor who dubs Pacino, Sylvain Joubert, does a fantastic job. Do you supervise the dubbed versions of your films?

Unfortunately not. It's not something I'm especially aware of because I don't speak the language. And frankly, I'm not that interested. Some directors go so far as to supervise the dubbed versions of their films themselves, but even if I like to exercise control, it doesn't go that far. This is definitely an important issue, though. In France in particular, I've been told that at least 85 percent of the revenue for an American film comes from the dubbed version.

Gérard Depardieu dubbed John Travolta into French for Blow Out. *Who knows if Depardieu's voice is recognisable to a French audience. The idea of asking him to dub Travolta might seem absurd, but it works brilliantly.*

I had nothing to do with that; it was John who asked Depardieu to do the job. They've been friends for a long time and admire each other. I don't know Depardieu well. I had dinner once or twice with him and Travolta.

How long did it take to shoot Scarface?

At least a hundred and ten days. Along with *Mission: Impossible* I think it's the longest shoot of my career. Almost all my "big" movies are long and difficult to make. The longer the shoot, the more problems and mishaps. It's exhausting.

The music of Scarface, *composed by disco king Giorgio Moroder, really contributes to the atmosphere.*

I immediately thought of Moroder, who was very fashionable in the Seventies. He literally invented Donna Summer and had a big hit with the *Midnight Express* soundtrack. Disco, loud and vulgar, with its repetitive rhythm, seemed to suit the character of Tony Montana perfectly. It's the music he would have listened to. Tony vibrates to the sound of disco, which becomes more and more repetitive, more and more intense as the film progresses and he sinks steadily into madness. Moroder composed two themes for the film: one for Gina and Elvira, which evokes Tony's ideal woman, and one for Tony, which has the rhythm of a funeral march, with repetitive accents. It's very different from the kind of music in my other films. No violin, no romanticism.

Scarface *has been influential in the hip-hop community. Many American and French rap singers refer to Tony Montana in their songs.*

I hear about that all the time. Every time I go to Florida I see the film's influence. When we shot it there were little old men on the streets of Miami, but today it's full of Hispanics in floral shirts and there are drugs everywhere, just like in *Scarface*. I went back to Miami once and was taken to a nightclub which looked like the Babylon Club, with bowls of cocaine and gangsters in every corner. I'm a hero to those guys; they know the movie by heart. But it's because of Al's performance and Oliver Stone's dialogue that *Scarface* became such a cult. People know the lines by heart, just like they did with *The Wild One*, where Marlon Brando gave an equally outrageous performance that inspired so many actors. Sometimes a character goes down in history for a single line of dialogue. In *Sunset Boulevard* it's "Mr. DeMille, I'm ready for my close-up." In *On the Waterfront* it's "I coulda been a contender." *Scarface* must have a dozen lines like that. Every actor I meet, no matter what age, can recite lines from the movie to me – Alec Baldwin, Bruce Willis, even Tom Cruise... It's crazy. In the end, I'm convinced my *Scarface* will surpass Hawks' film. His is pretty good, but you'll see... When people talk about *Scarface*, it's my film that will be remembered.

Oddly enough, both films are marked with an X. Hawks tried to integrate an X in every scene where a character was going to be killed. In your case, the X is the one that the censorship board almost gave the film.

Yes, but Hawks' *Scarface* had even more censorship problems than I did.

What specific problems did you have?

I've read so much nonsense about this that maybe it's time to set the record straight. Here's the whole story. When I submitted *Scarface* to the MPAA [Motion Picture Association of America], they said it was getting an X rating. I made a few cuts and sent it back to them, but they wouldn't budge. An X rating. I cut more footage and submitted the film a third time. Same thing. What bothered them was the scene where the clown gets killed at the Babylon Club. I cut that shot, but it was still too violent for them, so I appealed. I should point out that the studio did absolutely nothing to support me. All they wanted was to release the film, regardless of the cut. Martin Bregman and I created a huge media campaign to protest this censorship. I called a bunch of influential critics to explain what was being done to my film and went back to the MPAA with the first version of the film. I figured that if *Scarface* was going to be classified "X," it may as well be the cut I wanted, not a truncated version. The studio wanted me to go back to the MPAA with the third version. Finally they gave us an "R." What you saw was my cut of the film. Contrary to what I read in the press, I never filmed a woman with a chainsaw cutting off a guy's arm in the shower. No shots are missing. Everything's in there.

Critics didn't like the film when it was released in the United States, but today many consider it a major work. We think it's one of the most important American films of the decade, one that established a new aesthetic of film violence. Looking back, what do you think of it?

Everyone came down hard on me when *Scarface* was released. I was criticised for being excessively violent and sadistic, and overly dependent on foul language. My feelings about *Scarface* are unchanged. The problem is that nobody understood the film at the time. Nobody understood what I was trying to do. "It's a very old-fashioned script," people said to me. "It looks like an old Warner Bros. film noir." Well, that's exactly what I like about it. There hadn't been a film noir made in Hollywood for a long while, not since *Chinatown*. And for good reason – it's a genre that doesn't much appeal to audiences. Who wants to see a downbeat film that ends with the death of the hero?

With the exception of one single critic, nobody really knew what to say about *Scarface*. My direction wasn't to blame; I got some good notices. But critics said I had gone to a lot of trouble for a two-bit story that wasn't worth the bother, in which Al was doing his usual gangster act. But it was obvious to me that this was his best performance in years. The film didn't get a single Oscar nomination; it was rejected outright. In Europe, on the other hand, *Scarface* was a success. As you know, I'm pretty used to that kind of situation. *Body Double* was released to widespread indifference in the United States but was a big hit in Europe, especially France.

Body Double *did have one fan in America: Patrick Bateman, the hero of Bret Easton Ellis' novel* American Psycho, *who rents the film at his video store so he can masturbate to the scene with the drill.*

That's right! I forgot about that.

Body Double, *your next film, includes references to* Vertigo, Rear Window *and* Strangers on a Train, *but for the first time you reference them in a satirical way, as if you wanted to mix it all together before moving on to something new. Is* Body Double *a farewell to Hitchcock?*

I tried to learn as much as I could from Hitchcock's films, then develop my own style – one quite different from his, at least in terms of my visual approach. After having made several films inspired by him, I had the impression that I'd reached the end of a cycle and that it would be pointless to continue. In the case of *Body Double* I wrote a rough draft of the story but wasn't thinking of directing it myself. I liked the first film by Ken Wiederhorn, *Eyes of a Stranger*, about a young woman being stalked by a killer in Florida, and wanted to produce his next film.

Ken came to me with a scriptwriter he had worked with, Robert J. Avrech, and the three of us got to work. I gave them my rough draft and they went off and wrote the script, but in the end we never got it up and running. The people at Columbia told me that they would only make the film if I directed it.

How did you come up with the idea?

It's pretty much the same as *Vertigo*. You watch someone and take what they do at face value without suspecting that they're actually playing a role and involved in some kind of scheme. When he looks out his window and sees a girl masturbating, Craig Wasson's character believes what he sees. He's the peeping tom who says to himself, "I don't believe it! She's really doing it!," when in fact she's playing a role and trying to fool him. By taking the bait, Craig's character becomes the alibi for Gregg Henry's character, who can easily kill his wife.

Did you make any significant changes to Avrech's script?

His version was set in New York, but I moved it to California, and the Holly Body character was largely rewritten. Because of the nudity and sex in some scenes it was difficult to find an actress willing to play the part, so at one point I said to myself, "Why don't we just get a real porn star?" That's how I ended up with Annette Haven, who's quite incredible. It was only after spending countless hours with her, talking to her, filming her on video, having her work on the scenes that Melanie Griffith eventually played, especially the seduction dance, that I understood the character. I ended up completely rewriting the part for Melanie based on my time spent with Annette. Structurally speaking the film isn't much different from my first draft. The idea of the guy who moves into the house across the street, the husband in disguise – all that was already there. The rewrite fleshed out the character of Holly Body.

Why Annette Haven over another porn star?

I watched a lot of porn and of all the girls I met, Annette was the best actress. By that I mean that she was quite a character. Those films are usually shot without a script; the actors have to improvise, and Annette was very good at it. She intrigued me, so I contacted her and after meeting her I knew I'd found the right person.

Why did you finally give up on hiring her?

She couldn't act. She couldn't be seductive or provocative, and strangely enough wasn't at all sexy.

Body Double *may be a farewell to Hitchcock, but for the role of Holly Body you cast Melanie Griffith, Tippi Hedren's daughter.*

She's the only actress who agreed to play the role. The link with Hitchcock wasn't voluntary.

Why did you choose Craig Wasson to play Jake?

I had seen him in Arthur Penn's *Four Friends*, John Irvin's *Ghost Story*, and an episode of a TV series directed by Frank Perry, set in a mining town, where he played Karl Malden's son. The series lasted only one season. I've always liked him as an actor. I auditioned him and he exceeded my expectations.

Craig Wasson's mishaps in Body Double *make for an interesting commentary on Hollywood actors.*

That was a lot of fun. You see that kind of thing every day in our business. There's a lot in the film that comes directly from my own experiences. Early on I worked on lots of low-budget films and met a bunch of film producers who specialised in erotica. Annette Haven opened the doors to the world of porn to me, which fueled research for the *Body Double* script. The porn professionals I met were all very funny people. To my surprise, they had real perspective on what they were doing.

Your vision of California in Body Double *is a satirical one. Every possible cliché is there – the joggers, the outdoor life. You said the film was originally set in New York, but the film seems inextricably linked to Los Angeles.*

I set the story in New York because at the time I lived in an apartment overlooking Washington Square. From my window I could see into other buildings, like in *Rear Window*, which is what gave me the idea for the film. I said to myself, "What if I wanted to play a trick on someone?" It's something I've always thought about; you can find traces of it in *Home Movies* and Robert De Niro's character in *Greetings*. A pretty girl puts on a show by undressing in front of her window, which catches the attention of a man in another apartment, which means he'll be back every night to watch her get naked. Then something happens – like someone being killed. The peeping tom becomes a witness and tells the cops, "It wasn't the husband who killed the girl, it was someone else."

The murder is like a horror movie. The killer is in disguise and knows he's being watched.

The murderer is an actor, don't forget. That's why every character in the film is an actor. It's a great idea – for a murder as well as for a movie. An actor in disguise kills his wife and there's a witness across the street. It's the perfect crime.

Is Dressed to Kill *a reference point for* Body Double? *The two films are strikingly similar.* Dressed to Kill *is a female fantasy, while* Body Double *is more of a male fantasy. And in both films the murderer is disguised.*

Body Double is more of a cinematic meditation on the human body. What I mean is that the bodies you see on screen usually aren't those of actors. Audiences never notice, but doubles are often used in nude scenes. To fool Jake, Sam Bouchard uses the same kind of artifice that a film director does to fool his audience.

The most famous body double in the history of film is in Psycho. *It isn't Anthony Perkins who stabs Janet Leigh in the shower.*

That's true. Hitchcock asked another actor to play the scene.

Is this your way of telling the viewer from the start of the film that it's all an illusion?

Yes, because the film is about the fine line between illusion and reality. During the opening credits we see a desert shot and suddenly realise that it's a painted canvas being carried by two stagehands. In Hollywood, you never know what's real.

In some ways Body Double *has a structure similar to* Blow Out. *In each of them, the hero is a film professional unable to give his director what he needs. His involvement in a crime enables him to solve some technical issue and do his job. It's as if real life is only about solving problems in the life of a filmmaker, which is the only life that counts.*

That's true. Someone once said that I tend to live my life as fiction and that my films are my only true reality. This is all unconscious, of course, and it took me years to realise why certain elements always appear in my films. The other day a friend said to me, "Whenever you do something in real life, it's a kind of fiction for you. The only thing real for you is your films." I've come to the conclusion that whenever I'm not making movies, I'm constructing a kind of fiction for myself… and I'm pretty good at it. I'm a good actor, a good director, and I can get everybody involved and believing in the little melodrama I'm making. But for me it's fiction, because once I start working on a film, I drop everything. It doesn't matter if I'm married, in love, it doesn't matter what sort of fiction I've created. When I start a film, it becomes the only reality and the fiction, that is to say my personal life, suddenly stops. Believe me, it's very destabilising for my family who believe, with all their might, that it's reality. My life is similar to that of the hero of *Body Double*. He plays a vampire in a movie, and strangely enough his life begins to resemble that fictional character.

In the scene where Jake is tortured by the drama teacher, you seem to be making fun of the Stanislavski method, as taught at the Actors Studio.

Again, this scene was inspired by an actual event. I attended a similar class where I saw a teacher crush a student.

But you helped discover actors like Robert De Niro, who have taken this kind of acting to its limits.

Stanislavski's teaching, properly applied, can be useful to actors, but there are too many teachers who take Stanislavski's method to an absurd level and mistreat students. By exercising power over people, they manipulate and unsettle them.

During the audition, Craig Wasson explains that as a child he used to play sardines, a variation of hide and seek. Is that something you used to play?

Yes, especially with my girlfriend when I was in college. I recall hiding behind a stove. There was already an allusion to this game in my script for *The Demolished Man*; that's how much it's part of my life. For the record, the girl I was playing the sardine game with had a twin sister, who was the spitting image of her, except that she was mentally retarded. The two sisters were always together, and when I went out with my girlfriend I also had to deal with her sister, who was with us at every moment.

What did you think of Paul Schrader's Hardcore, *which is set in the world of pornography?*

It's a realistic and dramatic approach to the world of porn, which my film represents in a more humorous way. The premise of *Hardcore* – a father discovers that his daughter is doing porn – is a powerful one.

The difference between traditional film and pornography is that the sex act is authentic.

Yes, and in this respect amateur porn, which these days generates huge profits, goes even further because it's no longer actors in these kinds of films, but real couples who have been sleeping together for years. They don't necessarily look the part, but you know they're having real sex. This is different from traditional pornography where things are staged and directed. The actors might moan and groan, they might have real intercourse, but for them it's not much different from imitating a kiss in front of a camera. They just go a bit further. But it's still a performance, as opposed to something spontaneous that happens for real. Most porn movies are completely predictable; that's what makes them so fake.

What do you think about the way Hollywood movies do sex these days?

Hollywood doesn't do sex any more. The feminists and the virtue leagues have killed it. It's a shame.

Paul Verhoeven's Basic Instinct *led to a wave of erotic films that featured more and more sex.*

If you have full frontal nudity or penetration in a film, it won't get released in American theatres. The censors won't allow it; it's as simple as that. All this talk about so-called erotic films being made in Hollywood is mostly a way to promote them and start a media buzz. If the public hears that a film has had problems with the censors, they're more likely to want to go see it. It's the same thing when a dirty book comes out; everyone wants to buy it. "We can't tell you what it's about," the media says, "but trust us – it's shocking!"

Have you seen David Cronenberg's Videodrome?

Yes. I liked it, though the sadomasochistic folklore doesn't do anything for me. It's too crazy and weird. Plus, I find it visually repulsive. My films work because of the beautiful imagery. That's what makes people hate me the most, that my films are beautiful to look at. It's also why they can't dismiss them as crap.

What is your definition of pornography?

It's kind of a meaningless word to me. Artists should have the right to create whatever they want. They have always had to work within societal limits, though this hasn't prevented them from doing remarkable things. Painting endless crucifixions probably wasn't ever wildly exciting, but at one time it was the only thing people were interested in, so that's how painters made a living. "You can paint my ceiling but only if it's a crucifixion." The term "pornography" was entirely fabricated by society. It's completely relative and has nothing to do with artistic expression. I'm repeating myself here, but an artist should have the right to draw from *everything* that exists – violence, nudity, beauty… anything. Society then decides what is pornographic and what isn't.

Are there any so-called pornographic films that you feel have artistic value?

The ones I've made! I'm only half joking, because at one time or another every one of my films has been described as pornographic. *Taxi Driver* was considered a pornographic film in its time. As for pornographic cinema, I remember a Japanese film where naked girls were tortured in public places, in a shopping mall or a highway, something like that. In one scene a girl was force-fed laxatives and then followed by a camera until she defecated. That kind of thing goes beyond pornography, but there was still something fascinating about it. What was happening on the screen was outrageous, yet everyone was watching, drawn in. I'm not sure what to say about it. A film like that would probably be considered pornographic by any society that's even remotely evolved. Even so, I'll bet you wouldn't be able to avert your eyes if you were watching it.

Did you immediately think of claustrophobia for the condition that Jake has in Body Double? *You probably needed something that echoed James Stewart's vertigo in* Vertigo.

Yes.

Are you claustrophobic yourself?

No, but my ex-wife Nancy Allen is. When we filmed the scene at the beginning of *Blow Out*, when the car goes into the river, I didn't want Nancy to be inside because I knew how difficult it would be for her, but she insisted on doing it. I'll never forget the moment when we had to get her into the car. She turned deathly pale and started to cry. I immediately told her we could get a stuntman to do it. Picture the situation: Nancy had to get into a transparent cube that was submerged in a car filled with water – a total nightmare for anyone claustrophobic.

You shot a similar scene with Lolita Davidovich in Raising Cain.

Yes, but it was less painful for Lolita because she could get out of the car very quickly if she wanted to, and the vehicle wasn't so deep in the water. Nancy was trapped in the cube. Even though there were divers at hand, she had a panic attack and didn't want to go in. I got angry, she got angry, so much so that I said, "Let's stop this. I'll find another way to shoot it." I hadn't finished my sentence when Nancy turned around and walked back into the cube. I've never seen anyone so hysterical. So I know the effects of claustrophobia because I've seen them up close.

The problem is that it's difficult to transmit feelings of anxiety visually. It's much easier to communicate a feeling of vertigo to an audience. You shoot a subjective shot on a high floor and anyone even slightly prone to vertigo can say, "Holy cow, that's high!" If you get into a roller coaster car with a Cinerama camera, what you shoot will probably come close to what a roller coaster feels like. But there's no equivalence for claustrophobia.

In *Body Double* I used every possible trick in the book, but it's not easy to recreate on screen because watching a film – the very fact of sitting in a cinema – is already claustrophobic. Filmmakers need to focus on what cinema is able to do more effectively than any other art form. The close-up, for example, is the only way to capture real emotion on a human face. Ingmar Bergman understood that better than anyone. The actors' faces fill the entire screen in his films; it's as if you're going inside someone's head. Action films, similarly, create sensations of speed and movement that theatre and ballet could never convey with the same intensity.

You make good use of typically Californian settings – shopping malls and underpasses, the hotel on the beach, egg-shaped elevators, the farmers market, not to mention Sam Bouchard's incredible house.

That spaceship-shaped house really exists; it's not a set. It's called the Chemosphere and was designed by John Lautner, a former student of Frank Lloyd Wright. My direction relies heavily on camera movement, so it's always important that I find visually interesting places to shoot.

You're good at using natural settings in dramatic ways.

Absolutely. I do meticulous preparation before shooting, carefully surveying the sets and photographing every angle. Today I can move even faster thanks to a computer programme that's designed for architects, which I use to create environments. That's how I've done the action scenes in my recent films.

This passion you have for computers is shared by Spielberg.

I'm always telling him about new software. Spielberg is unbeatable at video games, especially flight simulators, which are the most difficult to master because they're designed for professionals. Steven was the first person I knew who used a cell phone. One time we played a joke with it. We parked in front of a girl's house, called her to say we were coming over, and a second later were knocking on her door. You should have seen her face.

The cities in your films are often characters in themselves: Miami in Scarface, Philadelphia *in Blow Out, Hollywood in* Body Double, *New York in* Greetings, Hi, Mom!, Carlito's Way, The Bonfire of the Vanities, *Florence and New Orleans in* Obsession, *Chicago in* The Fury *and* The Untouchables.

The architecture of a city has always been an important source of inspiration for me. The problem today is that people only want to see American actors in American settings, but the most interesting spaces are in Europe. I'm good at filming them – take a look at *Mission: Impossible*. That said, I'm not a creator of spaces like Stanley Kubrick, who paid attention to the smallest visual aspects of an environment, to the point of being able to recreate them from scratch. Kubrick's stories would never have had the same impact without this kind of work, which he did on every film. Hitchcock did the same thing; he created everything in the studio. And I could do the same thing too, but my feeling is that it's always better to rely on a pre-existing reality. Because they're great filmmakers, Spielberg and Kubrick can conceive of the most fantastical places and give them a touch of reality. I like to start with a natural setting, if it exists. That's why I'm not a director who creates imaginary worlds. In fact, that would really throw me off, because I wouldn't have any reference points.

One of the gutsiest parts of Body Double *is the murder scene with the drill. Did you set out to parody the chainsaw scene from* Scarface?

No, the chainsaw was Oliver Stone's idea. But the idea of a power tool becoming the weapon of a crime is a fantasy I've had since *Sisters*. I would have liked one of the characters in that film to use an electric knife to kill someone and for the plug to get pulled. I ended up using the idea in *Body Double*, with a drill. I don't set out to include scenes like this in my films because it always creates problems. I know I'll struggle with the censors and the critics will call me crazy, whereas all I'm doing is trying to make the most effective horror film possible. In this case, the idea of someone being chased by a killer with a drill seemed frightening, and the only question I asked myself was: "Should I drop this idea because the censors won't go for it?" The answer was no.

Just as Sam is about to deliver the final blow to Gloria Revelle, you frame the drill between his legs, as if it were a penis.

It's an indication that it's actually the husband who is doing the killing. I didn't want audiences to see the drill go into Gloria's body, but I did want it to go through the ceiling, which is even more shocking, so I chose the longest drill bit possible. People said to me, "You have to be pretty screwed up to imagine such a long drill," but my choices are always pragmatic. If I had used a smaller one it wouldn't have gone through the ceiling and it wouldn't have been as effective. The image in my mind was Craig looking up and seeing the bloody drill go through the ceiling so the viewer could imagine what the guy was doing to Gloria.

Do you think the Steadicam, which you use in Body Double *and in most of your later films, has had an effect on the way you work?*

It's a useful tool for filming long takes with complicated movements, and contributes to the overall sense of reality. A shot filmed with a Steadicam feels like it's happening for real; it's like the spontaneity of cinéma vérité. It also forces a certain truthfulness on the image, because you work without a net when you shoot with it.

The scene where Craig Wasson follows Deborah Shelton is reminiscent of the museum scene in Dressed to Kill. *It's intense even though nothing much happens. The tension is created by your use of the subjective camera.*

The subjective camera shot is one of the most important elements of film grammar there is. It allows the viewer to discover information at the same time as the character in the film, which is only possible in film. I'm often called a voyeur because I use this technique so often, but voyeurism has always been an essential component of cinema.

The entirety of Body Double *might be the invention of Jake Scully in his vampire coffin. He fantasises the story in order to find the strength to overcome his claustrophobia – which he finally does.*

I don't see it that way. *Casualities of War*, *The Bonfire of the Vanities* and *Carlito's Way* are films where the action is seen through the eyes of a narrator. By this I mean that there's a prologue, which introduces us to the narrator, then his story unfolds in flashbacks, and finally there's the epilogue, which shows him giving us the moral of what we saw.

But in Body Double *you film Jake being buried by Bouchard, then suddenly we're back on the vampire movie set that opens the film, and Jake finally gets out of the coffin.*

Maybe this is confusing, but for me it's a mental projection that Jake makes for himself when he's about to be killed by Bouchard. In order to get out of the grave and overcome his claustrophobia, he has to imagine that he's being pulled out of the vampire coffin, which is where he had his first attack. I admit it's a bit far-fetched.

When Jake plays an X-rated film on fast forward on his VCR, the images remind us of the horror film at the beginning of Blow Out.

That's what you always do with a porn tape. Voyeurs have their finger permanently on the fast-forward button, moving from one naughty scene to the next.

You filmed a scene from Body Double *like a music video.*

That's a real music video, for the song "Relax," by Frankie Goes to Hollywood. Jake and Holly Body meet while shooting it.

You later shot a music video for the Bruce Springsteen song "Dancing in the Dark."

I did it mostly as a favour to Springsteen; it was his first video. He started with a different director but they had a falling out, and Jon Landau, Springsteen's manager, who I know well, asked me to give them a hand. I listened to a few songs and an image of Springsteen in the middle of a concert, bringing a girl from the audience up onto the stage, came to mind. Springsteen liked the idea so much that he incorporated it into his show afterwards. Courtney Cox played the girl; it was her first on-screen appearance.

It was actually an idea I first came up with for *Fire*, a screenplay about a rock 'n' roll star that I had written for John Travolta. It was supposed to be a movie about The Doors but we never got the rights to their songs, so I rewrote it and turned it into a story about creativity, a kind of rock 'n' roll version of *The Red Shoes*. One character was a reporter investigating a Jim Morrison-like rock star who had apparently died in a plane crash. The reporter discovers that he's still alive and hiding in South America. There were three points of view, all telling the same story – a bit like *Citizen Kane*.

The video "Relax" in Body Double *isn't the one that the band Frankie Goes To Hollywood used to promote the song.*

No, they didn't like it and made another one. I don't remember where I got the idea for a porn video; I just know that it sounded intriguing at the time. MTV was just starting out and since I was the producer of *Body Double*, I thought this video would be a good way for us to promote the film on MTV. Everyone liked the idea and we convinced Frankie Goes to Hollywood to participate. We filmed the video a few months after the end of the shoot of *Body Double*; that way we could integrate it into the film. Apart from those two experiences, I'm not interested in music videos and I've never thought about shooting any others.

Body Double *is the film that inspired the title of Quentin Tarantino's* Reservoir Dogs.

Really? In what way?

In the final sequence, a dog jumps into a tank... a reservoir dog!

Good point! *[laughs]* By the way, did you know that the white dog was the one used by Samuel Fuller in *White Dog*?

What do you think of Body Double *today?*

The basic idea is good, but some parts are unconvincing and don't really work. In *Vertigo*, it's easy to believe that James Stewart falls in love with this woman supposedly possessed by the spirit of someone else because the film is a love story, a full-on romance. In *Body Double*, Craig Wasson falls in love with Deborah Shelton because he sees her masturbating. That's pretty weird, right? I'm not even talking about the scene on the beach when they kiss and the camera swirls 360 degrees around them, which is borderline ridiculous. The audience laughed at that moment because I filmed it as a romance, but there's nothing less romantic than a dissatisfied wife who sleeps around. Why does this guy fall in love with her? When I was writing it I was already asking myself, "Is this romantic or is it gritty?" Anyone can make a mistake.

But doesn't the kiss happen only in Craig Wasson's head?

It's not clear enough. Anyway, when the audience starts laughing at the expense of your main character, you're in trouble. Nobody laughs at Jimmy Stewart in *Vertigo*, but in *Body Double* they were definitely laughing at Craig Wasson. At the time I thought audiences would buy that they were watching a romance, because I was showing – as with *Vertigo* – an obsessive guy following a woman. What spoiled it was the scene where Jake sees Gloria at home masturbating, which isn't an especially romantic image.

CHAPTER SEVEN

WISE GUYS – THE UNTOUCHABLES – CASUALTIES OF WAR – THE BONFIRE OF THE VANITIES – RAISING CAIN

Wise Guys *and* The Untouchables *were clearly a change of direction for you.*

After the failure of *Body Double* and all those feminist attacks, I wanted to distance myself from Hitchcock thrillers. I had to reinvent myself. I've always thought that a filmmaker shouldn't be afraid of changing direction because things can get a little stale over time. If I'm doing something new it's so I can detach from old ways of thinking and demonstrate that I know how to make different kinds of films. I think about how things were done back in the golden age of Hollywood, when directors churned films out one after the other. They were continuously honing their craft while thinking about what to do next.

We don't really like Wise Guys. *It's so unlike you.*

I thought the script was pretty funny. I wanted to do a comedy, so I met with the producer Aaron Russo and with Danny DeVito, who I'd been friends with for a long time. It didn't seem like much work and I thought the film would be a hit. It ended up a disaster. I had a lot of problems with the producer, who kept telling me what to do, so I got rid of him and took over everything myself, which wasn't easy. MGM/UA, the studio behind the film, had changed management and none of the new people supported the project. We had to fight with them just to get it released. It was all a huge disappointment. I had a "pay or play" clause in my contract and could have pocketed the money and not done the film, but I made a commitment to Danny and stuck with it. I won't make that mistake again. If I had known it was going to be that hard I would have jumped ship at the start. It's a kind of weird and silly film. The oddest thing is that I got good reviews in America, where no one saw it.

Who was the scriptwriter?

I don't remember his name. He became a director. He must have made one or two films by now.

The Untouchables *isn't one of our favourites either.*

That's OK, guys. I forgive you.

How did you end up making it?

After the catastrophic failure of *Wise Guys*, I was in desperate need of a hit. I was good friends with Dawn Steel, who had been Martin Scorsese's girlfriend and at the time held an important position at Paramount. Art Linson was working on the script of *The Untouchables* with David Mamet and Dawn thought I would be a good choice to direct. She introduced me to Art Linson and the two of us went to see Ned Tanen, Paramount's production head, who gave us feedback on the script. Then we went back to Mamet and began reworking the relationship between Ness and Malone, which originally wasn't an important part of the story. I felt it should be the heart of the film, so Linson and I talked things through with Mamet. The studio was open to casting suggestions so long as they didn't have to spend too much money, and I thought of Sean Connery for Malone. I had met him at the film festival at Avoriaz, where John Boorman had introduced us. Kevin Costner was a young actor who came highly recommended by Steven Spielberg and Lawrence Kasdan, who had worked with him on an episode of *Amazing Stories* and *Silverado*. Art also thought it was a great idea. I brought Robert De Niro onto the project, though initially there were contractual issues and we signed Bob Hoskins instead to play Al Capone. In the end we paid off Hoskins with a pile of cash and De Niro did it. I wanted to make a kind of classic Western – good guys against bad guys, with a strong throughline: the Ness/Malone friendship. When the older guy gets shot, the younger guy avenges him by throwing his killer off a roof.

The most famous scene of The Untouchables *is the* Battleship Potemkin *homage, with the baby carriage at the train station.*

People always think that my films are planned down to the last detail, and that's true, but sometimes things happen and very quickly you have to find solutions. I improvised that train station scene at the last minute because we didn't have money to shoot the car/train chase that was in the script. David Mamet refused to change a line, so I said to myself: the important thing about this scene is that Ness and Stone corner Capone's accountant in a train station. I told my assistant to find a big train station with stairs. The staircase reminded me of *Battleship Potemkin*, which is where I got the idea for the baby carriage. From there it was a piece of cake. It took six nights to shoot. Mamet hated it when he saw it.

Did you get along with Mamet?

Not really. He's an arrogant guy, convinced that everything he writes is great. I really didn't like him. It didn't take him long to sense that I wasn't wildly impressed by the cult following he has. It wasn't until Art Linson began mediating between us that we got a good script out of him.

Does he like your films?

I don't think so. He said a bunch of nasty things about me behind my back. He was about to direct his first film and figured he knew everything.

Even if you were a director-for-hire on the film, you seem to like some scenes more than others.

There's Malone's death, with the transfer of power from him to Ness. I also like the baby carriage sequence and the scene at the opera. What we're talking about, actually, are elements that weren't in the original script and that I added myself.

What about the scene where Capone smashes the head of one of his associates with a baseball bat?

That was in the script, but I found an effective way to film it.

It's reminiscent of a scene from Nicholas Ray's Party Girl.

I don't know that film very well. Mamet was inspired by a real episode in Capone's life.

Even so, The Untouchables *isn't entirely historical.*

That's for sure. We're somewhere between fiction and myth, as with most Westerns. Wyatt Earp, the gunfights at the O.K. Corral – it's all legend.

Was Budd Boetticher's The Rise and Fall of Legs Diamond *an influence? There are traces of it in* The Untouchables *and* Scarface.

I know that film, and even thought of remaking it at one point.

The Chicago of The Untouchables *is reminiscent of Boetticher's film, yet Boetticher never set foot in Chicago and filmed entirely in Los Angeles. The scene in* Scarface *where Pacino kills Robert Loggia is taken from Boetticher's film.*

I don't remember much about Boetticher's film. All I can say is that it had an impact on me the first time I saw it, and I thought it would be good to remake that kind of movie. Art Linson and I watched it together with that in mind when we were at Paramount.

Your take on Eliot Ness is interesting. He's quite passive, an observer throughout most of the film, until at the end he erupts.

That kind of dynamic always works. Sometimes you have to trust the old ways of doing things. Look at John Wayne in *The Quiet Man* and Alan Ladd in *Shane*. The character waits and waits, then finally flies off the handle. It's the same thing in *Unforgiven*.

And Taxi Driver.

It's especially true of Paul Schrader's scripts. The character is passive at first, observing without saying anything. Then, finally, he freaks out.

What did Sean Connery think about playing a character who gets killed off?

He hated it. I think it was the first time he was killed like that in the movies, with so many bullets. While we were shooting the scene, when he was using the machine gun, he got powder in his eyes and had to be taken to the hospital. He was furious with me and I had to beg him to come back to the set and do a second take. I said, "You're James Bond and no one's ever shot you?" Connery wasn't easy to work with. He always thought we were messing with him, and kid gloves were needed at all times. In the end he turned in a magnificent performance that won him an Oscar, but there was a lot of friction. One day I asked him to come to the set and he ended up sitting around all day, waiting to shoot something. I thought he was going to kill me. I apologised to him. "Sorry, Sean, but the sun has gone down. There's no more light. What do you want me to do?"

The Nesses must be the only happy family you've ever filmed.

Yes, and that's probably the biggest problem with the film.

The first time we see Ness in his home, it looks like a Norman Rockwell painting.

I don't think David Mamet had much faith in that scene when he wrote it. It's like something out of a bad Hollywood movie, the cliché of the ideal family. Eliot Ness with his perfect family life.

The Untouchables marks your first collaboration with Ennio Morricone.

That was a great experience. He's a phenomenon. Every time I went to see him, he would play me eight or nine versions of the same theme, and together we chose the one that ended up in the film. That's how we picked the main theme.

Were you surprised by the film's success?

No. Studios love these kinds of films. Test screenings go well, critics love them, and Oscars are waiting for you at the end of the year. You're Genius of the Week.

Dawn Steel, who has been important to your career, worked at Paramount for a long time.

A very stubborn lady. I owe it to her that I was able to get back on track. When she came to Columbia, the first project she greenlit was *Casualties of War* – the most depressing, miserable story you can imagine. And she let me make it precisely as I wanted. It's a rare thing to be backed by a studio executive in that way. Believe me, when a film isn't a success everyone gets the blame. I've always been very comfortable with women in senior positions, whether Dawn or Sherry Lansing at Paramount. Remember, I spent four years at Sarah Lawrence, an all-girls college. I have no issues with brilliant, powerful women. I very much appreciate them. And yet I'm considered a huge misogynist.

These "executive women" work in a world dominated by men and often produce very masculine films. Sherry Lansing made Fatal Attraction *and* Indecent Proposal, *for example.*

And Gale Anne Hurd, my second wife, produced *The Terminator*, which isn't a bad contribution to the genre! [*laughs*] I've worked with women all my life. I've always gotten along with them, the actresses too. The feeling was mutual. I respect their opinions and unlike some men, I'm not in the least bothered by working with powerful women. And yet I'm seen as a man who hates women because I show them as victims in my films. That would mean that I just want to chop them into pieces, which is just cheap, stupid criticism. I wouldn't be interested in putting Mel Gibson in danger in a film; that's not my thing. I like to photograph women. I always say that if I painted nudes, I would paint women, not men. [*laughs*]

Casualties of War is based on a true story that first appeared in 1969 in The New Yorker *and later in Daniel Lang's book* Casualties of War. *During the Vietnam War, Sergeant Meserve forces his men to rape and kill a young Vietnamese woman. Only one soldier, Ericksson, risks his life by refusing to join in. Back at base camp, he does everything he can to bring his fellow soldiers to justice. What interested you about the story?*

Ericksson's helplessness. He's afraid to desert, and because he's also afraid to be at odds with everyone, he has no choice but to watch this poor girl suffer. He is unable to prevent these crimes from taking place, even though he knows they will haunt him for the rest of his life. When he returns to camp and tells people what happened, everyone says, "What's wrong with you? We're at war! This guy saved your life, and now you want to turn him in?" They can't believe it.

Have you met the real Ericksson?

No. And nobody else has either. He's out somewhere in the Midwest. Daniel Lang and his wife met him, but he hasn't been heard from since, not even when the book or the movie came out either. I sometimes wonder if he's seen the movie and what he thinks of it.

You weren't the only director interested in telling the story.

It inspired two films: *o.k.* by Michael Verhoeven, which was screened at the Berlin Film Festival in 1970, and *The Visitors* by Elia Kazan, not to mention the many scripts that were never made. In any case, a director can take on a project like this only after a big commercial success. It was the triumph of *The Untouchables* that allowed me to make *Casualties of War*. Nobody will give you money to make a film about a Vietnamese girl being raped and killed by American soldiers.

The script was written by David Rabe, with whom you had already collaborated on Prince of the City.

David is a Vietnam veteran. I had seen one of his plays about the war, *Streamers*, when it premiered on Broadway. I still remember it as one of the most shocking plays I ever saw in the theatre. It's terrifying, really chilling. I also knew David well because he's married to Jill Clayburgh. He's a rather mysterious man, quite withdrawn, with an inner rage burning under the surface. He always ends up falling out with collaborators, including Joe Papp, who produced his plays, Mike Nichols, who directed some of them on Broadway, and finally me. We don't talk anymore. He always blamed me for the ending of *Casualties of War*, which he said spoiled the whole film. He has a very troubled personality. He needs a father figure to fight against, and we've all played the role of his father at one time or another.

How did you work with him on the adaptation?

Our first discussions took place when we were working on *Prince of the City* in 1980. Around 1987, I started to describe to him more precisely what I had in mind. Several Vietnam movies, including *Platoon* and *Full Metal Jacket*, had been successful that year, so I asked to meet with Ned Tanen at Paramount and we signed a deal and bought the rights to the story. Our first decision was to follow Daniel Lang's book fairly closely. In the first chapter, Ericksson, living in the Midwest, sees a Vietnamese woman on a bus. That's what brings the whole incident to the surface. We kept this structure in flashbacks. David wrote his remarkable script very quickly, but we had trouble agreeing on the ending. At one point I thought of including a rather surreal climax. In *The Visitors*, Elia Kazan, imagining what the rapists would do once they're released from prison, has them go to Ericksson's house. We played around with that – Ericksson haunted by the idea that these guys will be back for revenge. In one version of the script there was even a sequence where Ericksson dreams they come back and the rape begins again, this time with his wife as the victim. A real nightmare of an ending.

Did you shoot it?

No, I stuck with the flashback structure. The idea came to me on the set in Thailand while talking on the phone with David Rabe. When Ned Tanen read the script he said, "You can't make a movie about a bunch of soldiers raping and killing an innocent girl. No one will go see it." Fortunately, I had a clause in my contract that allowed me to offer the project to another studio if Paramount turned it down, so I took it to Dawn Steel, who had just been made head of production at Columbia.

The film begins on a San Francisco subway train the day of Nixon's resignation, which is revealed on the front page of a newspaper that a passenger is reading. Why start the story on that date?

I was looking for a headline that could immediately situate the action. Nixon's resignation in 1974 was ideal.

Why did you want to start the film in the United States?

I was making a film for an audience that had never been to Vietnam, so it was better to start the film in America rather than Vietnam because for most people Vietnam only exists through what they've seen in documentaries and movies. When I lived in Northern California, my wife and I lived near a military hospital. I would see Vietnam vets hanging out, and it was clear from their faces that they had come back from hell. They were wandering around, haggard. I remember one guy who thought he was a traffic cop. He would show up at an intersection, then head back across the street and go inside. You're dealing with people whose experience is incommunicable and most of whom have come home crazy. I had to find a way to relate this experience and could only do it by connecting it to a reality we all know, which is why I chose the flashback structure.

It's the same actress who plays the girl at the beginning and end of the film, as well as in the flashback.

She's wearing a fake nose in the San Francisco sequence, but it's her – it's Thuy Thu Le. It wasn't an easy role to cast because apparently there are no actresses in Vietnam. But I was determined. It's important that she was Vietnamese, because Thai and Filipino girls look different. We searched for an actress all over the world and finally found her in Paris, where she was a student. She had no acting experience. I think her father worked in the diplomatic corps. I auditioned her using the scene after the rape, when Ericksson talks to her and tries to persuade her to run. We rehearsed and she spoke only Vietnamese. I was very moved by her performance.

Every one of the performances is remarkable.

To find the American soldiers I organised casting sessions in New York, Chicago and Los Angeles. I insisted on having young actors because it really was kids who were sent to Vietnam. I was still in college when I was exempted from the draft. I also wanted to train them to be more believable as soldiers, so I hired Dale Dye, a Vietnam veteran, who had worked with Oliver Stone's actors for *Platoon*. He and another veteran, a former LA cop, spent weeks training the actors, and in the end they moved like a real patrol. Sean Penn was the most committed; there was no better soldier than him. Once he entered the jungle, he never left. He didn't talk to anyone; he really became Sergeant Meserve and took charge.

It turned out that one of the trainers was a real psychopath and the actors were coming to rehearsals kind of beat up. "You're being too hard on them," I told the guy. "They just need to *look* like soldiers." He was doing mock assaults in the middle of the night in the river and my guys were dropping like flies. The area was really dangerous, full of snakes. Another time the guy phoned Sean Penn in the middle of the night. "Gather your men in the perimetre at zero two hundred." That's two in the morning. "You're crazy!" said Sean. "This is a movie we're making here. We aren't fighting a real war." I ended up replacing that weirdo with Dale Dye.

Were Michael J. Fox and Sean Penn your first choices for Eriksson and Meserve?

Sean Penn was brought on by his friend, producer Art Linson. Michael wasn't our first choice. He had heard about the film through our mutual agent, and after he read the script he immediately wanted to do it. At the time he was best known for his roles in comedies and the TV series *Family Ties*, but he very much wanted to take on more serious roles. He was a huge star and the film was made at Columbia on his name alone; it wouldn't have been possible with only Sean Penn. At one point Dawn Steel worked for Michael's production company. He brought a lot of innocence and integrity to his role. He reminds me of the kinds of characters that James Stewart played. Audiences have no trouble identifying with them because of their moral strength and integrity.

One of the most surprising aspects of Casualties of War *is that by first presenting Meserve as a hero who saves Ericksson, the audience identifies with the sergeant who then orders the girl to be raped.*

It was important to justify his behaviour. Meserve is the guy who was in Vietnam too long. His best friend died there, and he wants revenge.

Is Ericksson a hero, or a snitch who betrays his patrol?

In this respect there are comparisons to be made between the film and Elia Kazan's *On the Waterfront*. When someone in America denounces his comrades, the blacklist inevitably follows. Are Ericksson's actions justified? With his strong moral foundation, can he stand up to the officer, played by Dale Dye, who tells him that bringing charges is absolutely the wrong thing to do? No matter how much everyone around him says otherwise, Ericksson knows he's right and won't budge. That's what makes him stand out from the crowd and confide to the chaplain. It gives him the strength to denounce his commanding officer and his patrol, and send them all to jail. "It's war, it happens," everyone says. "But you can't kill people like that," says Ericksson. A voice inside him tells him he can't step back from this.

How did Fox and Penn get along on the set?

It was a strange relationship. Sean hardly spoke to Michael at all. He got very seriously into character and when he wasn't shooting, he hung around with the actors playing his solders. He was determined to be the best sergeant possible. Michael, who's a really nice guy, was repulsed by Sean's behaviour. They were staying in the same hotel but never spoke to each other. There's an incredible moment when we were shooting the scene where Michael runs into the tent, after Sean's men have tried to kill him with the hand grenade. Just before a take Sean went up to Michael, looked at him like a piece of shit, and punched him in the face. If you could have seen Michael's eyes… It's in the movie, by the way. When he says his line you get the sense that Michael *really* wants to kill Sean. His crazy eyes are up there on screen. There was palpable tension between the two of them.

They have different backgrounds. Fox has worked primarily in TV, Penn in cinema. That must have contributed to the antagonism.

Sean spent a lot of time teasing Michael about that. Remember at the end of the trial when Sean whispers something in Michael's ear? In one take I think he called Michael "nothing but a TV star," and in the others something like, "I've screwed your wife a few times. Now it's your turn." On every take Michael had the same look of terror on his face, like, "Holy mackerel, what's this guy going to say now?" Sean played the dangerous guy all the way through. Michael never knew how Sean was going to act, what he was going to do, which fit with the characters they play in the film.

Did other actors have to deal with Penn's behaviour?

Yes, the Puerto Rican actor John Leguizamo, who plays Diaz; it was his first big film role. I'll never forget that scene when Sean shakes him and asks him to kill the girl. He was slapping him so hard that it was unbearable to watch. "Kill her! Kill her!" he kept repeating like a madman, take after take. *Casualties of War* was a really difficult film to make. Even today just thinking about it gives me the chills.

You filmed in Thailand.

I called Eric Schwab, my assistant on *Body Double* and *The Untouchables*, and sent him to Southeast Asia to search for locations. He concluded that Thailand would be the best place to shoot; we couldn't imagine going to Vietnam at the time. Eric went all over the country and found a beautiful location, with a backdrop of mountains that was perfect for the village in the film, which we built from scratch. I think Oliver Stone used the same place for *Heaven and Earth*. We started shooting in the south in Phu Ket, where all the jungle scenes were filmed. Then we went to Bangkok and from there up the River Kwai to shoot the bridge scene. It was literally the bridge on the River Kwai!

The military camp was a set designed by Wolf Kroeger. For the jungle scenes we built an open-air studio in the middle of the rainforest. We set up water ramps because of the rain, which was essential, because it's so confusing at night. You walk thirty feet and you're lost, so imagine what a movie crew had to deal with. What we built really looked like a studio, except that we were in the middle of the jungle at night. To give the illusion that we were shifting locations, we simply moved the trees, which were fixed on railings, like in a theatre. For the scene where Ericksson gets stuck in a hole above the underground tunnels, we fixed up the side of a cliff to make it look like a trench.

Why did you choose Wolf Kroeger for the sets?

I liked his work, and for this kind of film it was essential to have a British crew because the English really know Southeast Asia. My assistants, Brian W. Cook and Michael Stevenson, were used to working in that kind of climate. We really had it rough. The weather was terrible; it rained all the time and shooting took forever. Weather like that is normal in the tropics, but you really have to experience the downpours that last all day to believe them. The heat was intolerable; the temperature was close to 120 degrees. We all had to drink a lot of water just to keep ourselves upright. All that plus perspiration – everybody was sweating all the time – insects and snakes.

To really understand that kind of country you have to spend time there. Thailand and the Philippines are very different to back home; the people there live and think differently. And their conception of women… It's probably nauseating to us, but prostitution is almost normal for them. People there don't see any problem with it. When you absorb this notion it's much easier to understand how those soldiers could have kidnapped that girl and done what they did. Many women in those countries end up selling themselves. We saw that ourselves in Bangkok, so you can imagine how bad it must have been during the war in Vietnam. Bangkok today is a lot like Saigon probably was during the war – an open city where anything can be bought. To understand how this atrocity happened, you have to understand the world these soldiers were living in. From that vantage point, it doesn't seem so strange.

Consider the fact that these guys were wandering through a foreign country that they couldn't begin to fathom, a country where notions of morality seemed upside down, where you couldn't tell good guys from bad, the Vietcong from other Vietnamese. Everyone looked the same. These eighteen-year-olds, who visited brothels every night, didn't see the harm in kidnapping a village girl. "She looks like the whore I fucked last night," they would say. This was an absurd setting for a war. The soldiers couldn't even see who they were shooting at. And the concept of borders, and the Western idea of conquered territory, didn't exist. You're in the middle of a nightmare that's impossible to escape from. Physically, the soldier is in constant discomfort, and he's usually out of it because of the drugs that everyone smokes to kill time. There are sudden explosions of violence, which come from who knows where. Don't forget, this was a sniper war. I tried to recreate that atmosphere, which would have been impossible if my guys hadn't gone through training.

How long did it take you to shoot the battle scene that opens the film?

We shot that first. It was endless. Every night for a month.

How did you create such a feeling of collective fear in the film?

On set, everyone was scared. We were in the middle of a jungle, there were insects and poisonous snakes everywhere. My assistant director, Michael Stevenson, was a madman. A colleague of his had been bitten by a snake during a previous shoot in the same area. Despite the training they went through, the actors were always on edge. All it took was for someone to yell "cobra!" and the set was evacuated immediately. We had specialists with us, guys who knew how to handle snakes and whose job it was to find and get rid of the critters so we could get back to work.

The most intense moments of the first battle in the film are in the tunnels, which give the impression of an entire underground city.

I was inspired by a book called *The Tunnels of Cu Chi*, which describes these underground cities. The idea of falling in there and not being able to get out… It's actually a bit like *Jaws*. Ericksson is in danger of losing his legs.

And when Ericksson is saved by Meserve it makes their relationship…

…even more ironic, yes.

How did you film the murder on the bridge? The focus is on both Ericksson and the background, where you can clearly see Clarke stabbing Oahn.

I shot it by attaching a prism to half of the lens to vary the diopter so I could focus on foreground and background at the same time. I used this kind of effect a few times in *Casualties of War*, including the tracking shot of Sean shaving. I wanted to show that everything is happening behind Ericksson without him being aware of it. What interested me here once again was the powerlessness of the character and the irony of the situation, because Ericksson has a clear view of who he's shooting at, but doesn't notice that the girl is being murdered behind his back. As usual, I prepared very carefully, for the first time on new storyboarding software. Until then I had been drawing everything by hand.

The sequence where Michael J. Fox wakes up in the military hospital, surrounded by injured soldiers, is particularly impressive. It's like something out of Jacob's Ladder, *the horror movie written by your friend Bruce Joel Rubin.*

That all comes from my father, who was a surgeon in the Navy during World War II in the Pacific. He would arrive by boat on the beaches after the assaults and pick up any wounded who could be operated on. He once told me about a guy who had no legs, beating the ground with his stumps. That's what inspired the scene where Michael wakes up in the military hospital. Being a surgeon in a war really is the most horrendous job. My father didn't talk about it much. He did it for three years, so you can imagine what he must have been witness to.

When they kidnap Oahn, Meserve's soldiers insist that she's Vietcong.

It's obviously absurd what they're saying. They do that to justify what they're doing to her. The team does question what Meserve is doing, but he's so persuasive that they end up taking his side. All Vietnamese are alike to them. It isn't as if the Vietcong have "Vietcong" written on their foreheads. A communist, a Republican – how can anyone tell the difference? The moment someone tells them "She's Vietcong," everyone believes it, except Ericksson. It's like Al Pacino in *Serpico*, when he says he doesn't take money. He sticks to his guns even after being told that all cops take money, and as a result, like Ericksson, alienates himself.

An individual in the right, up against the majority. A very American theme.

Absolutely.

The kidnapping takes place because the soldiers are forbidden from visiting a brothel when a curfew is declared and they can't enter a nearby town. What pushes Meserve over the edge is sexual frustration.

Yes, but don't forget that Brown, Meserve's best friend, has just been killed. That's what really turns him around. That plus he isn't allowed to get laid. So, yes – he's frustrated and, importantly, in charge of everyone else. In the book I remember he can't get into the brothel because the Vietcong are already there, so he says to himself, "Fuck it, I'm going to get a girl, right guys?" The others ask if that's allowed, and then, later, they figure that if Meserve says it's OK, then it's OK. Meserve is the father figure. He's the sergeant, the soldier who knows what he's doing.

Everyone expected that the rape sequence would be graphic, especially coming from you. But you film it from a distance.

I did that because Ericksson is watching from a distance. I also wanted to withhold Oahn's bloody and swollen face from audiences until the moment when Ericksson goes into the hut. She turns around and faces him; it's the moment when he sees what Meserve and the others have actually done to her. I still have trouble talking about it. It was a terrible scene to shoot, really awful.

What's your understanding of the exchange between the soldiers after the rape? They talk about the last time they had "a real woman." Meserve replies: "She was real. I think she was real." Does that mean they enjoyed raping her?

They feel so guilty that they do all they can to think of something else. They talk about cars, about God knows what. Meserve forced them to rape her, and none of them really enjoyed it. They try to act like they got off on it, but they didn't – not by a long shot.

Every one of the characters in that scene, except Diaz, is in near darkness.

We shot from Michael's point of view, with a long lens. The rape was filmed on the same axis with the same focal length, punctuated by a series of crossfades. The distance between Michael and what he's looking at makes for a powerful image, especially because immediately after this there's a cut to his face in an extreme close-up, which is the tightest shot in the entire film. Ericksson sat there, watching the girl being raped, for hours, without being able to do anything. The viewer sees the scene from his point of view and feels the same sense of helplessness. It's as if you're in a room and on the floor above a girl is being raped for three hours, and all you can hear are her screams. If a camera was pointed at you, imagine what you would look like. That's what I tried to capture with that extreme close-up.

For us, the key scene of the film immediately follows the rape, when Meserve goes to see Ericksson.

"I hate the Army," Meserve tells him, to which Ericksson replies, "This ain't the army, Sarge." "Though I walk through the valley of evil, I shall fear no death, 'coz I'm the meanest motherfucker in the valley," says Meserve.

This exchange of lines encapsulates the entire film. It's clear that Meserve isn't really himself anymore. In that shot, when he speaks those lines, in the rain, under the moonlight, he looks like a werewolf.

I'm interested in characters who have sold their souls to the Devil. After all, we've all dirtied our hands a little. Given the world we live in, how could it be otherwise? We filmmakers handle millions of dollars when we go to work, so our hands are bound to get a little soiled. But unlike Meserve, there's a line we won't cross.

Casualties of War *is one of the few films about the Vietnam War that tackles a real moral issue.*

Keep in mind that it's based on a true story that had already been the subject of a book in which the issues were clearly defined. Perhaps I'm repeating myself, but I only really understood the story once I went to Vietnam. If you don't go there you can't fully understand it, which is why the Vietnam War remains so impenetrable to this day. It's like trying to describe an LSD trip in words. People can say, "I saw a flash, I felt myself regressing to a molecule," but it's not possible to fully share in that experience unless you've actually lived it.

After The Untouchables, Casualties of War *is the second film in which Sergio Leone's influence is clearly visible. We're thinking of that close-up on Fox during his exchange with Penn, in the rain.*

That's a stretch... There's only one close-up like that in the whole movie. I'm a great admirer of Sergio Leone; *Once Upon a Time in the West* and *Once Upon a Time in America* are brilliant films. But you have to understand that at this point in my career I'm really not aware of these things anymore. Since *Dressed to Kill*, actually probably since *Blow Out*, I don't think about Hitchcock or Leone or anyone else.

Casualties of War is one of the few films about Vietnam with a soundtrack that isn't saturated with rock'n'roll.

I did everything I could to steer clear of clichés. There's only one rock song, "Time Has Come Today," by the Chamber Brothers, when Michael J. Fox talks to the chaplain.

Even Kubrick used rock songs in Full Metal Jacket.

Yes, but his film isn't based on fact, and doesn't really have much to do with the Vietnam War. The idea of putting kids through that kind of training is more of a World War II concept. The kids sent to Vietnam were very inexperienced. They were handed rifles and told, "Now shoot in that direction." The beginning of *Full Metal Jacket* is brilliant, but it's a boot camp movie. Turning those guys into killing machines is the reality of Parris Island, South Carolina. The fact that Kubrick didn't film in Asia is problematic. As you know, he recreated everything in England, which was a bad idea. Vietnam is an experience that can't be recreated on a set, even by such a brilliant director. His film is an intellectualised view of Vietnam. It isn't based on any reality, just like the New York of *Eyes Wide Shut*. It's one of the film's weaknesses. That and the script, which wasn't good enough.

What do you think of The Deer Hunter, Apocalypse Now *and* Platoon, *the other great American films about the Vietnam War?*

I thought Oliver's film was pretty accurate; he did a good job of capturing how contradictory everything was over there. *Platoon* was so successful and *Casualties of War* so unsuccessful because Stone's film ends like a Western, with the good guys winning. But it didn't go down that way. In fact, everyone lost in Vietnam. *Platoon* might be accurate in many ways, but it doesn't do justice to what Americans went through in Vietnam. Despite his own experiences as a soldier, Oliver clearly wanted to give his film some kind of cathartic climax.

But Vietnam is a gaping wound that will never heal, which is why at the end of *Casualties of War*, when Michael J. Fox is clearly still so haunted by his experiences, it could only be a Vietnamese woman – not an American – who tells him his bad dream is over. I can accept the idea of redemption to a certain extent, but not for

Erickson. That guy will be marked his entire life by that story. It's a bit like John Boorman's *Deliverance*, where the characters are in the same dilemma. If you want to go on living, it's vital that you try and forget certain things. Erickson wasn't responsible for this tragedy; he was overwhelmed by the events and he can't go on blaming himself for the rest of his life. That's how I view childhood, which can sometimes have an adverse effect on adult behaviour. Parents hand down neuroses to their children, which can lead to destructive behaviour, but at some point we have to wipe the slate clean and say, "OK, I understand. I wasn't well treated, but am I going to spend the rest of my life punishing and destroying myself, or am I just going to move on?"

Do you like Michael Cimino's The Deer Hunter?

It doesn't do a great job of capturing what the war was really like. We Americans, who usually think in such plainly black and white terms, who need to separate good guys from bad, weren't able to function in a country like Vietnam, where the line between good and evil was so blurred. That really was the image of the war, which we watched from afar on television, something made very clear in *Greetings*. We listened to our politicians explain how we were winning without suspecting for a moment that what they were telling us was bullshit. In the first draft of *Casualties of War* there was a scene where, on the plane back to the United States, Erickson asks his seatmate, "Why were we sent here?" The response he gets: "They have this arsenal, and they want to see if it works." We have a huge military-industrial complex; armaments are one of our key exports. Without a conflict every now and then, who would we sell things to? How can we justify such a large arms industry if we don't fight a little war every now and again? This, in my opinion, is the most sensible explanation. Of course, the French were in Vietnam before us, and since they helped us at the end of the Second World War, we told them we would help them out in Indochina, so we took their place and the Vietnamese ended up hating us as much as them. [*laughs*] After reading a lot of books on the subject and visiting the area, I see only the waste.

What did you think of Apocalypse Now?

The idea of transposing Joseph Conrad's *Heart of Darkness* to Vietnam is still an exciting one. I remember George Lucas working on an early version of the script in the early Seventies. The problem with *Apocalypse Now* is that Francis Coppola never came up with a convincing ending. Colonel Kurtz, played by Brando, is basically Attila the Hun. He's a monster, a brutal, fascist leader, but he doesn't really have anything to do with Vietnam. And politics aren't Francis' strong point; he's just not interested. The beginning of *Apocalypse Now* is brilliant, everything else is brilliant, but it's not about Vietnam. The character of Kurtz should have been some kind of summation of what that war was all about. When you get to his lair at the end, it's important that we have some understanding of who this guy is, how he became what he is, and what all that has to do with the Vietnam War. But the film doesn't show any of that. Add to this the fact that the ending lacks any dramatic progression. It might be wonderfully shot and directed, but the story just stops dead.

I still remember the four-hour version Francis showed me. Two years later, after several re-shoots, he still hadn't got the ending right. By the way, a film that is rarely discussed is the Hughes brothers' *Dead Presidents*, which shows, very accurately, what the Vietnam War was like from the point of view of black people in America. At one point there's a soldier who had been carrying around a severed head in his pack, and everyone tells him to get rid of it because it stinks so much. That's a spot-on image. Black men were on the front lines in Vietnam, which was essentially a race war. They had it rough, with no way of escaping the draft. They were basically sacrificed.

We especially like the scene where Eriksson talks with the chaplain. They aren't of the same faith, but they understand each other because they're the only ones who still care about the value of human life.

That's all in Lang's book. As the film shows, Erickson tells everyone what happened, and they all tell him to just forget about it. Then they try to silence him, even kill him, because he's talking too much. All this puts Erickson on edge. Finally he unloads on this Lutheran pastor, who has to decide whether or not to do the right thing.

We like the way you filmed the trial scene. It's very stylised, very quick. You never show the judge, just the soldiers answering questions. It looks like the Last Judgment, which makes it the opposite of the usual way of doing things in Hollywood, where every speech is included and trials last for hours. We can imagine how much you would hate having to shoot that kind of material.

You're right about that. And I had to deal with a lengthy trial scene in *The Untouchables*, too. The courtroom scene in *Casualties of War* was longer in the script and included Ericksson on the stand. It was a bit like the inquest in *Vertigo*, where the official in charge hammers James Stewart by saying, "He was incapable of saving the girl. How unfortunate!" Ericksson is under attack from the court because at one point Meserve saved his life. But as I edited the film, I saw how excessive the scene was. This poor guy had been tortured enough already, so I tightened everything up. Originally the camera held on each defendant for much longer.

Casualties of War is a tragedy, but in the final scene, as Ericksson talks to the Vietnamese girl, there's a glimmer of hope.

She sets him free by telling him that his nightmare is over, which makes the film different from *Obsession* and *Blow Out*, which have tragic endings. In any case, David Rabe didn't like the ending of *Casualties of War*, but as far as I can see it expresses truths about what Vietnam was for us. It's ironic that today the Vietnamese, who suffered by far the most casualties, want to put the war behind them and move on.

Ennio Morricone's music is magnificent.

He wrote it in record time. I made him a tape with different pieces of music, the kinds of things I wanted. For the final scene it was John Williams' wonderful theme from Spielberg's *Empire of the Sun*. A voice starts singing a cappella, then a choir; it fit perfectly with the images. There was a piece that accompanied the scene where Ericksson sees Oahn's face after the rape, but in the end Morricone didn't listen to any of it. I just described the music I had chosen, one piece after the other, and that was enough for him. For *The Untouchables* we groped around for a long time to find the two main themes, but for *Casualties of War* he hit the nail right on the head. We recorded the music in Rome around Christmas 1988. It was magical.

Choirs and elegies appear in several of your films, including Obsession *and* Carlito's Way. *The choir at the end of* Casualties of War *suggests Ericksson's redemption.*

Yes.

The critics hated Casualties of War.

I remember reading the reviews and watching the lines in front of theatres. Ironically, it was right here in New York that I was attacked the most fiercely, by *The Village Voice*, which even put my picture on the cover. I didn't dare leave my house because Frances FitzGerald, author of *Fire in the Lake*, a famous book about Vietnam that had won the National Book Award, dragged me through the mud. I have never received such an overtly negative review in a magazine with my picture on the cover! The first review of the film I read was Pauline Kael's positive notice in *The New Yorker*, and then I end up with this horrible *Voice* review. Kael called *Casualties of War* a feminist film. Reading her review made me so happy; she really understood the film. So it started there and ended with a vicious attack in *The Village Voice*. As usual I was the token misogynist. It really knocked me sideways. I thought I'd never be able to walk the streets again. [*laughs*] My picture on the cover of *The Village Voice*!

Casualties of War *failed at the box office. Ned Tanen of Paramount was initially worried, saying the story was too depressing and that no one would go to see a film about a girl killed by American soldiers. What convinced you otherwise?*

Platoon was a big success, but it had a much happier ending than my film. Downbeat films sometimes make a splash, and you always hope your film will be one of them. But my darkest films – *Blow Out* and *Casualties of War* – weren't successful and could have killed my career on the spot, like *Sweet Smell of Success* did for Alexander Mackendrick. It's a miracle if you escape that kind of failure.

What's your opinion of Casualties of War *today?*

I'm especially fond of it, for all sorts of personal reasons. I find the story – which I wanted to tell for many years – very moving, and was overjoyed when I finally managed to convince a studio to finance it. I think the acting is great, even though it's a film I still have a hard time watching because it's so disturbing. It's one of the most horrific stories you can imagine. Not to mention its commercial failure.

It's interesting to compare you to Steven Spielberg. Even when he's dealing with the Holocaust in Schindler's List *or D-Day in* Saving Private Ryan, *he gives it a positive spin – like a thousand Jews saved from the death camps or a family reunited. You do the opposite. You see only a desperate solution to a dramatic situation.*

Yes, and that's the genius of *Schindler's List* and *Saving Private Ryan*, with all those Jews travelling to Schindler's grave and that guy breaking down at his sergeant's grave at the end of *Ryan*. It's sentimental, but it works. No one wants to hear that, but it's true, and even though I might think, "My God, isn't this all too easy?" Spielberg manages to pull it off. His endings are genuine and honest. You can't leave audiences with a bitter taste in their mouths, like I do, though I know people who in their own way really like *Casualties of War* and who have seen it quite a few times. Personally, I find it hard to watch.

Like you, Spielberg comes from a broken home.

Yes, but he managed to build a new one for himself. It's pretty amazing. Steven has seven children and a very happy family life. I see them quite often. It's a joyous atmosphere over there.

Spielberg deals with reunited families, but you're interested only in broken families. Ericksson is completely alone at the end of Casualties of War.

As is so often the case in my films, it reflects my own life.

When did you discover Tom Wolfe's novel The Bonfire of the Vanities?

While shooting *Casualties of War*. I immediately thought it was a great book, but didn't think about adapting it at the time. It was the producer Peter Guber who later suggested it to me, after other directors had declined the offer. I expressed an interest and a meeting was organised with Warner Bros. executives, during which I explained my vision of the film to them. They liked it and we immediately got to work.

Your initial idea was to make it a dark comedy, like Dr. Strangelove.

That, for me, was the tone of the book, and I wanted any film adaptation to reflect it.

Were you offered the job because you live in New York?

Possibly, but initially Peter Guber was looking for someone unflappable, because he knew it wouldn't be an easy project to take on. It's a bit like adapting Nabokov's *Lolita*. The critics are out there waiting to pounce, which is why lots of directors refused the job. I knew the film would be controversial, but I didn't think it would be *that* controversial.

Have you met Tom Wolfe?

Just once.

How did you feel when you started work on the film?

Making *The Bonfire of the Vanities* was a way to forget the terrible disappointment of *Casualties of War*, which had thrown me into a depression. It was good for me to get out of my own head. It's not easy for me to recall the shoot because on set I'm so focused that I don't pay attention to anything else.

Julie Salamon's book The Devil's Candy, *about the making of* The Bonfire of the Vanities, *has become as famous as the film itself. No one is spared. Details of your childhood are revealed, and the fickleness of the Warner Bros. executives is exposed. It was the first time since* Picture, *Lillian Ross' report on John Huston's* The Red Badge of Courage, *that a director allowed a journalist to chart every stage of a film's production. Why did you allow such a thing to happen?*

Most reporters who interview me don't really know anything about Hollywood filmmaking. They think we're still living in the 1930s. I'm always being asked questions like, "Did the studio boss force you to use this actor? Was your cut re-edited behind your back?" I always want to say, "Are you kidding? The whole system has changed. The studio bosses don't just barge onto the set and fire the director and have a new staff of writers rewrite the script." I decided to bring a reporter onto the set and show her how things *really* work. Julie Salamon is a friend; she's an excellent reporter and a film critic. She wanted to become a novelist and I encouraged her, but after she published a really good novel that didn't sell, I told her, "You're a great journalist. How would you like to write a report on *The Bonfire of the Vanities* and turn it into a book?" Once I made that decision, I never looked back. I got her access to every meeting and let her listen in on every phone conversation. There was a lot of animosity from people around me who didn't want all that out in the open, and her book made the whole *Bonfire of the Vanities* catastrophe even harder to live with. Warner Bros. executives felt betrayed. The problems with the film were made a whole lot worse by the existence of the book. But anyway – it's a valuable document, exactly what I hoped it would be, and will remain a key reference work for a long time, because there will never be another director stupid enough to let a journalist follow him from A to Z throughout the production of a film.

Steven Bach wrote the same kind of book about Michael Cimino's Heaven's Gate *when he was at United Artists.*

And look what happened to him! These days he lives in Germany and has nothing to do with the film business. The same goes for producer Julia Phillips, who settled accounts in her book *You'll Never Eat Lunch in This Town Again*. Telling the truth about Hollywood is unforgiving; they'll never let you make a film there after that. But if you want to be a serious journalist, you have to know what's really going on. I've always liked what John Boorman wrote about Hollywood in his *Projections* diary "Bright Dreams, Hard Knocks: A Journal for 1991." That was an act of courage, especially since diaries of that kind are usually pure self-promotion, where the filmmaker puts himself in the spotlight. But that's not at all what John did.

Playwright Michael Cristofer wrote the adaptation of The Bonfire of the Vanities. *Did you choose him?*

No, Warner Bros. hired him long before I arrived. He had already written a draft of the script which I didn't like. But I did like Michael. We had similar ideas and got to work together on a new draft.

How did you work with him? Did you take turns writing?

No. When I work with a writer on material that we're adapting, I never write a line. I hadn't seen Michael's plays but I liked him as a person and thought his script was very good. We got along well. Once we decided on the tone and the flashback structure, the writing went pretty quickly. We didn't do more than two versions.

Like Casualties of War *and later* Carlito's Way, *the film is built around a flashback, as told by Peter Fallow, the narrator.*

The studio really wanted a narrator. They liked the style of the book, and for them a voiceover was a way of getting more Tom Wolfe into the film. I felt we had to have Fallow in the prologue and epilogue, and frame the entire story from his point of view.

The Bonfire of the Vanities, *like many of your films, deals with issues of morality. Every one of Sherman McCoy's problems is because of the hit-and-run he was involved in. If he had acknowledged at the time that he had hit the boy with his car, the media wouldn't have torn him apart.*

That's for sure. A good comparison is what happened to Hugh Grant a few years ago, when he was caught with a prostitute on Hollywood Boulevard. Grant was very smart and immediately jumped into the eye of the storm – on TV, Larry King – to apologise. That's the opposite of seclusion, which is the last thing any famous person should do when something like that happens.

He immediately exposed himself, answering any questions people had. It was exactly the right thing to do. In America if you say, "I'm sorry, I won't do it again," people forgive you.

The casting of Tom Hanks as golden boy Sherman McCoy was controversial.

The Bonfire of the Vanities is an interesting example of a film that was misunderstood when it was released. Tom Hanks gives a great performance, which in a few years I'm sure will be re-evaluated. People accused the film of being racist, of disrespecting the black community, but I never felt that. Everyone seems to have forgotten that one of the most sensitive characters in the film, one of the most human, is Judge White, played by Morgan Freeman. He's the only character who really knows how to assess the people standing on front of him. Unlike everyone else in the film, he doesn't let himself be blinded.

Did you expect protests from the black community during filming?

That kind of thing always happens when there's a minority involved, like the Cubans when it came to *Scarface*.

In Tom Wolfe's novel the judge is Jewish. Why did you make him black?

The judge in the novel was very unsympathetic. There were already a lot of unsympathetic Jewish characters in the film, and it didn't make much sense to add another. That's why we rewrote the role. The characters in the book are all stereotypes – horrible and corrupt – like in Mackendrick's *Sweet Smell of Success*. The judge in the book is a colourful but tough character. I actually met the person who inspired him. My concern was that we were dealing with a Jewish judge who was attacking a black man. It was an anti-Semitic caricature, and given the size of the Jewish community in Hollywood I knew it wouldn't fly, so I suggested we get a black actor, but that made the studio nervous. They wanted a Latino, like Edward James Olmos. I felt it was important to have a respectable black character in the film.

A judge named White.

Exactly. And he gives that final monologue, the speech of justice, which isn't easy to interpret. Morgan Freeman lends dignity to every other black character in the film. Today I probably wouldn't do that. My biggest mistake was watering down the nastiness of Tom Wolfe's novel. I should have been more faithful to the book and less worried about the direction I wanted to take things. I should have played the *Sweet Smell of Success* card, making everyone even more cynical and harder. But I couldn't make Warner Bros. see it that way. There was too much money at stake. Before we had even shot a roll of film, $20 million had been spent. The failure of *Casualties of War* really shook me up. If that film had been a success I might not have made those compromises. *The Bonfire of the Vanities* might not have been a success either, but it would have cost less.

We like a lot of the film, especially the whole first half, but it falls apart once the trial starts, and we don't much like Freeman's final monologue. What he says is so unlike you.

I don't agree. I believed in that speech. My only regret, as I say, is that I wasn't harsher.

You cut a scene at the end of the trial.

There was a riot. People attack the judge while Sherman defends him with the sword of justice. It was burlesque.

It sounds like the custard pie fight excised from the end of Dr Strangelove.

Kubrick cut that sequence because he thought it changed the tone of the film. In my case, I liked the sword fight scene, but somewhere along the way, once the trial was over, you wanted to get out of that courthouse. There's another scene I cut that would have and should have been the real ending. The young black man, Henry Lamb, wakes up, finally out of his coma, and leaves the hospital as if nothing has happened, unaware of anything that has transpired while he's been in a coma.

The opening shot, under the credits, is a wonder. The Bonfire of the Vanities *marks the beginning of a series of long takes in your films, culminating in* Snake Eyes.

Doing a shot like that in *The Bonfire of the Vanities* is a bit like traversing a tightrope. It's a challenge, and provokes the same kind of excitement. I wanted to walk the audience through all those spaces before reaching the reception, like walking backstage in a theatre. It's physical environments that inspire me, though it's only once I'm in a space that I work out a way of filming it.

Where did you shoot the opening shot?

In the *Wall Street Journal* building in Manhattan.

Was it difficult?

Yes. We rehearsed for one night and shot it the next. It's almost five minutes long, and we kept running out of film. We did it thirty-four times – not complete takes, of course. We had a lot of problems, especially between the basement and the elevator. The idea for the scene came from a memory of Truman Capote, who I once saw arrive completely drunk at a literary ceremony. It immediately sets the tone for the film, and is the ideal way of introducing the character of Peter Fallow. The crowd applauds a guy who can barely stand.

You appear in the shot.

And for good reason: it was impossible for me to direct it without at some point finding myself in the camera's field of vision, so I decided to play an extra, a guard who accompanies Bruce Willis and Rita Wilson through the basement. I shaved my beard so I wouldn't be recognised. When I'm walking ahead of them and talking on the walkie-talkie, I'm actually giving them instructions. I'm also in the scene in *Greetings* where De Niro goes for his army physical.

The cinematography throughout has shallow depth of field.

Sherman McCoy is supposed to be a Master of the Universe, so he has to inhabit a world that looks enormous. The images reflect this scale. That's why I used a wide-angle to film his apartment and the Stock Exchange, where he works. There has to be an element of surprise when audiences see those places.

Are some directors more likely than others to use a wide-angle lens?

Wide-angles make everything bigger. The directors who have an eye, like Kubrick and Welles, use wide-angle lenses, which reflects their relationship to space. That's what directing is all about – setting characters in space. But you can't teach someone to have an eye; either they have one or they don't. I also like directors like John Ford or Howard Hawks, who weren't so focused on technique and who worked very differently from my way of doing things. I'm like anyone else; I go to the movies to relax and look at worlds different from mine. I'm not necessarily interested in seeing films by directors who have the same sensibility as me. Kubrick creates a world without God, with people who are barely human. He's the master of cynicism, something I can relate to, though I'm an optimist in comparison. At least I believe in something: redemption, love. *Full Metal Jacket*, which seems to have been made by an entomologist, is darker than *Casualties of War*. You can't do that kind of thing too often, which is why Stanley made so few films.

Would you ever take on a film to test a new technique, as Kubrick did?

If it can lead to a new kind of imagery, absolutely.

Your assistant Eric Schwab created two memorable shots for The Bonfire of the Vanities: *the Chrysler Building, during the opening credits, and the Concorde landing at Kennedy Airport.*

I had a hundred dollar bet with Eric that you would never see a shot of a plane landing in one of my films. He promised me he could shoot one so spectacularly that I would *have* to include it in the final cut. He won the bet.

Was it important that all the exteriors were shot on location in New York?

Absolutely. We could never have recreated the Bronx, especially since we chose the worst street in the worst neighborhood. The scenes of Sherman McCoy's apartment, the restaurant where Maria's husband has his heart attack, the scene with the photocopier and the girl, and Bruce Willis' apartment were all filmed in a Los Angeles studio. I don't like filming in California. They have the best technicians and crews, but they don't understand space and how I like to make use of it.

Truffaut said that a director should convey either the absolute pleasure or the extreme agony of making a film. Perhaps more than any other American director today, your work reflects the pleasures of filmmaking. Yet you say that the experience of filming is difficult for you, which seems paradoxical, given the jubilation expressed in so much of your imagery.

Shooting is unpleasant because my lifestyle changes so radically. I'm constantly on the go, constantly anticipating what may or may not happen next, whereas I would rather just be at home, reflecting, working according to a schedule that I set for myself. I like to be in a state of total availability and have time to wander around. I'm constantly thinking about ideas for films; it's my way of life and it makes me happy, whereas when I'm shooting I feel like I'm in the army. I have to get up at a certain time and go to bed at another. There's a work schedule that absolutely has to be followed. I become extremely vigilant. In that way I'm the opposite of John Ford, who allowed himself a few drinks. I'm very careful because I know that whatever we shoot will be on film forever. It's an extremely disciplined regime, which is why as soon as shooting is over, I disappear. Living in such a regulated way is completely foreign to me. I can't think anymore; I just have to get things done. The shooting of *The Bonfire of the Vanities* was even more exhausting because I was both director and producer so I had to attend every meeting with Warner Bros. executives.

They weren't very understanding towards you. In her book, Julie Salamon writes that they were unhappy when you refused them access to the set during rehearsals, which proved their total ignorance of the creative process.

It was a mistake on their part, and I did all I could to defuse the situation. The production of *The Bonfire of the Vanities* was riddled with those kinds of mistakes, decisions that should never have been made and that seriously compromised the film. But I was one of the people making those decisions. Was there a lot of pressure? Absolutely. But there's pressure on any big-budget film. Sure, the studio wasn't always very astute, but I'm not trying to blame them for the film's failure. They did the best they could. I'm responsible for what you see on the screen.

What role did producers Jon Peters and Peter Guber play during the shoot?

None. They were appointed to run Columbia just before the film went into production, but weren't actively involved. They had nothing to do with filming or post-production, even though they get a credit. I had a couple of meetings with them, that's all.

George Miller couldn't believe that The Witches of Eastwick, *his little comedy about the war between the sexes, ended up costing $40 million. He blamed producers and the studio. Did you have the same problems?*

No. They have a way of working in Hollywood and there's nothing you can do about it. No one is going to adapt or change for you. I don't think that's the way to make good movies, but there's nothing you can do. You just have to live with it. The problem is that you're doomed to be a success. George Miller was, I wasn't.

Terry Semel and Bob Daly were the Warner Bros. bosses when you made The Bonfire of the Vanities. *How was it for you working with them?*

They were like any other bosses running any successful business. My conflicts with them were no different than those I had with other bosses at other studios. You have to understand that these guys aren't sadists out to sabotage your project at any cost; they just want everything to work. They want the machine to run smoothly. They don't like having to interfere, but they expect you to finish the film on time and within budget. Then they pray it makes money. They don't have time to deal with additional problems. Semel and Daly ran Warner Bros. successfully for over twenty years, and they were embarrassed when *The Bonfire of the Vanities* became a media target. The film was Warner Bros.' biggest financial failure since… Well, I can't think of a bigger flop.

Kevin Costner's The Postman *lost as much money, if not more, than* The Bonfire of the Vanities, *and Warner Bros. didn't have any problems with that.*

First of all, Kevin is a star, which makes a big difference. And most importantly, he didn't humiliate the studio executives. I made Terry Semel and Mark Canton look like idiots, which is unforgivable. The problem with our system is that you have to spend your time doing PR, which just wrecks you. "How was the movie?" *Great!* "What was it like working with the studio executives?" *Fantastic!* "What's Tom Hanks like?" *He's the greatest guy I've ever worked with!* "Melanie Griffith?" *Absolutely wonderful – I just love her!* "Bruce Willis?" *What a great guy! It's so exciting to be around him!* And so on. It's an utterly exhausting circus. The way TV reports on Hollywood is ludicrous. No one tells the truth because no one wants to be unemployed.

I remember a TV show about old Hollywood where they interviewed actors, producers and directors from years ago. They were very frank. One of them was asked if he had enjoyed working with Paul Muni. The old man replied that he hated him. "Was he a respectful actor?" "No, he was always trying to steal the spotlight, on every line. It was hell." The guy bad-mouthed Paul Muni the whole time. Muni was apparently a jerk to his co-workers, but no one would have known that if this old guy hadn't decided to say it out loud.

Every director of your generation has had a commercial and critical failure like The Bonfire of the Vanities. *Coppola had* One from the Heart, *Spielberg had* 1941, *Lucas had* Howard the Duck, *which he produced, Cimino had* Heaven's Gate, *Scorsese had* New York, New York *and Friedkin had* Sorcerer.

That's true. The most upsetting thing for me is that the film was completely misunderstood. I still think it's a very funny film, but it was released at the wrong time and the establishment crapped on it. Today people are always telling me things like, "Hey, I saw your movie on cable the other day. It's not that bad. I had a good laugh."

Home video gave the film a second chance.

Yes, but that doesn't really help get over what happened, all the vitriol that was thrown at me. In ten years I'm sure they'll take back what they wrote, like they did with *Scarface* or *Blow Out*. I turned fifty just before the first test screening of *The Bonfire of the Vanities*, and everyone was telling me I was a genius. I had shown the film to the people at the studio and they were ecstatic. Everyone was celebrating, convinced they had made a masterpiece. Mark Canton, head of production at Warner Bros., said it was the greatest film the studio had ever produced. Who could have predicted what actually happened? I don't think I ever recovered from the failure of *The Bonfire of the Vanities*, and I don't think I ever will. Every time a critic writes about Tom Wolfe they mention the "disaster" of *The Bonfire of the Vanities*, as if it were one of the worst films in the history of film. That was my ticket to the Nineties. [*laughs*] Tom Wolfe is an American icon, and in the eyes of the establishment I turned his masterpiece into the dumbest movie ever.

What do you think of it today?

I'm proud of it. It works in the exact ways I wanted it to. It's my vision of the book, and I think it's very funny. If people don't laugh, all it proves is that my sense of humour is marginal, to say the least. What allowed me to survive the film's failure was the actors. Tom Cruise loved *Scarface* and *Carlito's Way* and wanted to work with me. In that way, Martin Scorsese and I are in the same boat. However badly our films do at the box office, we've done work that sticks in the memory of people who grew up with them. Actors basically like me because I'm not afraid of anything. They like the way I do things.

Your French fans are divided when it comes to Raising Cain. *For some, it's one of your best, but for others it's the absolute worst.*

You know that Quentin Tarantino really likes it? My fooling around with the chronology of the story was an influence on *Pulp Fiction*. The films I write myself are usually more experimental, less bound by genre conventions, than the others. When I'm the sole author of a script I generally ignore traditional narrative forms; it keeps audiences on their toes. They never quite know what's about to happen next. I started making films in the Sixties, when conventions were being thrown out the window and everyone was looking for new ways of doing things. Film has become so conservative since then. The problem with movies today is that everything is conveyed through dialogue and stories are constructed in such a way that the climaxes are almost entirely verbal. The images do nothing but illustrate what the actors are saying, like on television. The new generation of directors has learned everything from watching TV and MTV, which explains their taste for linear stories and frantic editing. If fifty shots go by in thirty seconds, audiences have the impression that there's more going on. But nothing could be further from the truth. When you go to the movies today you usually know from the very first shot what kind of film you're watching. When you think about the many ways in which filmmakers could tell their stories, it's a drag that they all use the same techniques – like the old theatre-inspired, three-act dramatic structure.

Some of Kubrick's films, like *The Killing* or *2001*, play with traditional narrative structures. I like it when two parallel stories play out and collide near the end, which is why I admire Tarantino's work so much. The narrative structure of *Reservoir Dogs* is extraordinary, and *Pulp Fiction* goes even further. I love the way he throws his characters into one story, then abandons them to start another, then returns to the first, even if some of the characters have been killed in the meantime. He defies all rules and has fun with structure. It's not easy to do because more often than not experimental stories lose their dramatic progression and audiences find them disorienting. But Tarantino knows how to play with the rules and create something that people actually want to watch. With *Reservoir Dogs* and *Pulp Fiction* he had small budgets and wasn't beholden to a big studio, which helps.

How did you come up with the idea of Raising Cain?

By watching Michael Powell's *Peeping Tom*, especially the scene where the father studies the effects of fear on his son. A question came to mind: what if a child developed a second personality which assumes his traumas? It seemed a rather wild idea and quite powerful at the same time. I once had an affair with a married woman who fell asleep at my place. The next morning, when she woke up, she panicked, wondering what she was going to tell her husband. I'd always wanted to include that scene in a film. I had to create an antagonist, and that's when I added the whole schizophrenia thing, symbolised by the character of Dr. Nix, the shrink who becomes the villain of the story.

After Emile Breton of Sisters *and Dr. Elliot of* Dressed to Kill, *Nix is the third of your mad psychiatrists. Do you have a score to settle with them?*

For me, the psychiatrist is an abstraction in my films; I don't try to make them realistic. *Raising Cain* is playing with the same ideas as *The Strange Case of Doctor Jekyll and Mister Hyde*. Imagine a psychiatrist or a psychologist who listens to his patients recount their problems all day long. He has his own theories about split personalities – a bit like in *Doctor Jekyll* – and wonders how he can test them. Patients talk about how the source of their problems lies in childhood, so the shrink sets about applying his ideas to his own kid. Will that turn the boy into a schizophrenic? He traumatises him, then observes his behaviour. For sure he's going to split. Mission accomplished. It's the concept of the mad scientist who works for the good of humanity, but creates a monster along the way.

Elements of Raising Cain *remind us of* Dressed to Kill. *Was this a way of reassuring the studio after the failure of* The Bonfire of the Vanities?

I was so shaken by *Bonfire* that all I wanted to do was make a medium-budget film that I could shoot at home in California. At the time my wife, Gale Ann Hurd, was pregnant, so I didn't want to be too far from her. And frankly, I was exhausted. *Casualties of War* and *The Bonfire of the Vanities* really drained me. I scouted all the locations for the film myself and shot it within a five-minute radius of my house, practically in my backyard.

Did you immediately visualise that wonderful opening sequence, with the television screen showing Carter in the arms of his sleeping daughter? It's an image that sums up the whole film.

There are poignant images at the start of every one of the films I've written myself. But the truth is I was never wildly happy with *Raising Cain*. The original idea was to tell the story in a much more elongated way, starting with Jenny's story. We wouldn't have known that her husband was crazy until he smothered her with the pillow. We don't know anything about Carter; he's just a passing figure. But when we were editing we realised that this kind of structure required a detailed flashback. The husband smothered his wife with the pillow and from there we went to the scene that's now the first one in the film: Carter chloroforming the mother, followed by the appearance of Cain, followed again by the scene where Carter puts the woman in the trunk and takes the kid to his father, Dr. Nix. Then came the whole part with Jack, the scenes in the park where Carter sees his wife with her lover. At one point I remember telling the editor that we needed to add title cards throughout the film so audiences would know what the hell was going on. We ended up restructuring the film into three parts, following a linear chronology.

The other day my editor suggested that we go back to the original edit of *Raising Cain*, because the released version opens with Cain's scenes. Audiences are immediately thrown into the world of schizophrenia – a guy with twenty-seven personalities – which doesn't do much to prepare them for the romantic fantasy of Jenny and her story. Audiences laughed at test screenings. The story of a woman dreaming of her past loves felt outdated, especially after being confronted with the problems of some guy with multiple personalities. This change in tone spoiled the film and I had to cut the scenes with Jenny in order to make the story coherent. But by doing that, I lost the tone I was hoping for. It always bothered me that I couldn't solve this problem at the time. I worked out how to fix it only later.

Is schizophrenia a theme that interests you? Had you read much about it? Do you know Sybil *by Flora Rheta Schreiber?*

Of course. I read all these books when I was preparing *Dressed to Kill*. *Sybil* is one of the best known.

You never show Cain and Carter together in the same shot, as, for example, David Cronenberg does in Dead Ringers. *Would you have considered that cheating?*

It's such a cliché. We've seen it in a million movies, so I stayed away from it.

Raising Cain *is one of your most stylised films. We particularly like all the scenes in the forest with Jack and Jenny, which have a dreamlike atmosphere. The vegetation symbolises the imagination, or the Garden of Eden.*

If the film had been edited as it should have been, it would have worked, but when they appear in the second part, those romantic scenes never really cohere.

Did you ever see Jean-Luc Godard's sketch in Paris vu par…? *Anna Karina writes a letter to her husband and another to her lover, and when she puts the letters into envelopes she switches the two. It's the same thing when Jenny mixes up the gifts she's giving to Jack and Carter.*

I haven't seen it, but yes – it's the same idea, the kind of absent-mindedness that can turn a whole life upside down. It also happens in *The Bonfire of the Vanities*, when Sherman McCoy goes outside to call his mistress from a phone booth and accidentally dials his home number.

When we think about your films, it's generally not dialogue that comes to mind, but rather action and music. But the scene in Raising Cain, *where Dr. Waldheim tells the story of Carter and his father – the longest monologue you've ever filmed – is an exception. Like the opening shot of* The Bonfire of the Vanities, *it was done with a Steadicam.*

The Steadicam shot is just a storytelling technique, to be used sparingly. How was I going to make all that explanatory dialogue in *Raising Cain* interesting? I had to find a way of making a lengthy scene pay off in terms of action, and came up with the idea that the characters would go down to the morgue to look at a corpse, which, once it's been revealed, would surprise the viewer. Of course, before the scene starts the audience is convinced that the body fished out by the police is Jenny's, so you get used to the idea of her death throughout the scene, and then, once you arrive at the morgue – *bam!* We discover it's the body of the woman assaulted by Carter in the first scene. This surprise helps to make sense of a long, tedious exposition scene that the Steadicam makes so enjoyable to look at.

Several phrases uttered by Dr. Waldheim during this scene – "Money from other people's misfortunes" – could be you talking. There are ideas like that in all your films.

The exploitation of other people's misfortunes – it's like the O.J. Simpson trial, which, believe me, made a lot of money for a lot of people. One thing about society today, at least in America, is that everything can be turned into a money-making machine. That's what *The Bonfire of the Vanities* is about.

Why did you make Dr. Waldheim a woman with cancer?

The character needed to wear a wig. Carter needed one to escape, and cancer was the first idea that came to me.

When she hypnotises Carter to get in touch with his other personalities, it's like being in a séance. "Who are you?" she asks.

That's how it works. That kind of thing is described very precisely in the books I read before filming. You hypnotise the patient, then ask, "Who's there?" because you never know which personality is going to show up. "Who am I talking to?" "*Oscar.*" "Oscar who?" "*None of your business.*" It's a great starting point from which the imagination can run wild.

The scene is reminiscent of John Boorman's Exorcist II: The Heretic.

That movie was wild! I love it. Boorman and I have had the same problem with audiences. Our films are so baroque, so stylised, that people laugh in the wrong places.

There's a baby carriage at the end of Raising Cain *at the motel. A reference to* The Untouchables?

I wasn't too keen on using a baby carriage precisely because of *The Untouchables*, but I was looking for a way to make it clear that the baby was being taken somewhere else without actually having to show a baby, because filming with young children is always problematic. The solution was simple, especially because I used computer storyboards. Without this software that allowed me to visualise the sets, I wouldn't have been able to film it so precisely. The falling child, the oranges, the three different floors – the scene wasn't difficult to shoot once I had the storyboards in place, but it took me months to design it in such detail.

Hitchcock said that once a film was storyboarded, his work was done. Do you feel the same?

Not really. The visualisation might be complete, but you still have to bring the characters to life and get to work with the actors. If my visual designs get in the way of the actors and somehow impede them, and the end result isn't what I'm looking for, changes have to be made. Hitchcock didn't really care about actors, which shows in his later films. Sometimes a producer with a strong personality – like Selznick – would force him to develop a story and interesting characters and not resort only to audacious imagery and visual concepts, no matter how brilliant. That's what I learned from Hitchcock. I see his strengths, but also his weaknesses.

Did you write the role for John Lithgow?

He did an incredible job; I had him in mind from the start. He had to create all these different characters, each of which was more believable than the others. It's rare that I write with an actor in mind. What inspires me for my characters is more the people I know – my friends and family.

Lolita Davidovich was a newcomer.

I found her in an audition. I had seen her when I was casting *The Bonfire of the Vanities*. She auditioned for the role of Maria Ruskin, the role played by Melanie Griffith.

Did critics like the film?

American critics were confused because I was playing around with the narrative. It reminded me of how conservative we've become.

How did Raising Cain *do in the US?*

Not bad. It grossed about $22 million, which isn't that much, but it only cost $10 million to make. And because I was paid a percentage I still get money for it. I get cheques all the time. All said and done it's made a pretty good amount of money. So for me, *Raising Cain* was a hit.

CHAPTER EIGHT

CARLITO'S WAY – *MISSION IMPOSSIBLE*
SNAKE EYES – *MISSION TO MARS*

When Carlito's Way *was released in France, many critics saw it as a work of great maturity.*

When I started the film I was going through a personal crisis. Within two years I had gotten married, had a child, and then divorced. I found it difficult to balance my personal and professional life, something that most of my friends seemed to be able to do. I was very much questioning myself; it was the classic mid-life crisis. Somehow it was this aspect of *Carlito's Way* that intrigued me. What, essentially, is the film about? It's about a guy who's just been murdered and who says to himself, "My God, I'm dead… How did I get here?" And he looks back on his life to understand the sequence of events and to accept what has happened to him. That was my situation at the time. To make the film, which reflected how I was feeling, I laid myself bare. I couldn't have made *Carlito's Way* when I was thirty, or even forty. It deals with love, betrayal, fatality – but at a distance, and as a result the characters had more depth. It's less of a thriller and more of a character study. I think that's why people were so moved.

Was it Al Pacino who asked you to direct the film?

Al and his friend, producer Martin Bregman, had been looking to do *Carlito's Way* for years. They worked with Edwin Torres, the author of the two books on which the film is based, and kept telling me that it was very different from *Scarface*. When I read the script I could see that it was indeed very different. The tone was more fatalistic, the story took place in the Seventies, and there was this agonising voiceover that reminded me of Billy Wilder's *Sunset Boulevard* or *Double Indemnity*. I was immediately hooked.

David Koepp wrote the script. Did you know his work before reading Carlito's Way?

I had seen two films he wrote – Curtis Hanson's *Bad Influence* and Robert Zemeckis' *Death Becomes Her* – but it was his script for *Carlito's Way* that I really connected with. He worked hard on it with Bregman and Pacino for four years.

Carlito's Way *has a different tone to* Scarface. *The footage at the start of* Scarface *is grainy documentary footage showing the arrival of Cuban refugees in Miami, while the slow motion footage at the start of* Carlito's Way *is stylised, in black and white, with a voiceover.*

Different aesthetic choices are made for every film. For *Carlito's Way* it was important that the audience know very quickly that this is a story about a man on his way down, so over the credits there's a voiceover and slow motion imagery. I also had to disguise the fact that the entire film is a flashback told by a man dying in a train station, so that at the end, when he meets his girlfriend on the platform, we don't expect him to be shot. That's why I stylised the opening sequence as much as possible, to blur the lines and prevent audiences from having too many reference points. The opening is the one big change I made to David Koepp's script.

Scarface's *watchword is "The World is Yours," whereas Carlito's is more modest. It appears on a billboard he continually stares at in the street: "Welcome to Paradise."*

Scarface is a kind of mafia version of *Richard III*. "Who shall I kill? How will I kill? Who can I lie to? Who should I seduce?" In *Carlito's Way*, the recurring motif is a cliché of paradise, an advertisement for Florida with a palm tree on a sunset background. It's less ambitious than the watchword of *Scarface*, which is the American Dream. Carlito doesn't want the whole world, just his own heavenly little piece of it. In *Scarface*, Tony Montana moves blindly towards his and everyone else's death, but Carlito – full of regret and disenchantment – well knows what's happening to him, that he's going down. It makes his voiceover commentary on his life an ironic one.

Carlito's Way is a slower, more contemplative film than *Scarface*. Even so, there are similarities between Carlito and Tony Montana, and both have their weaknesses. The day he allows himself to feel human, instead of staying an unbridled killer, Tony Montana's fate is set in stone. When he refuses to blow up the car full of children, he crosses the line and signs his own death warrant. Likewise for Carlito, whose troubles begin when he follows his heart. His big mistake is thinking that the lawyer who saved his life is also his friend and that he has to return the favour. Tony Montana and Carlito are betrayed by their feelings, which is also what happens to Sean Penn in *Casualties of War*. He saves the life of someone who later puts him in prison. The cruel irony appeals to me.

Another irony of the film is that Carlito is a legend for many people in his community, but all he wants to do is get out of there and leave it all behind.

We always come back to that famous line from John Ford's *The Man Who Shot Liberty Valance*: "When the legend becomes fact, print the legend." This is what gives the history of America its novelistic dimension. Take Eliot Ness, who was a regular police officer, not much more than an office worker. Who wants to know about his day-to-day life, his family and all the paperwork and administrative problems? The mythology explored by *The Untouchables*, on the other hand, with its speakeasies, machine guns and violent shootouts, fascinates everyone.

What is it about criminals that you find so interesting?

Killing someone is a mythical act that can turn you into a star. You move from obscurity into the limelight in a flash, even more so if your victim is famous. Crime is like an equaliser; it raises you to your victim's level of fame. Look at Lee Harvey Oswald or John Hinckley, who shot Reagan. Those guys were nobodies before they committed their crimes, which made them legends.

When he becomes a nightclub manager, Carlito seems like a reference to Bogart in Casablanca, *a man on the verge of retirement.*

Carlito's Way is a contemplative film about life and death, the final opportunity we might have to change our life, and Carlito is somehow reminiscent of Bogart in *Casablanca*. Like all cynics he's a romantic, looking to step back from the action and spend his final years in peace. His ultimate obsession is to reach paradise and head to Florida with the girl he loves. Any allusion to *Casablanca* is a way of framing the film within a specific genre and conveying certain references to the audience.

The final twenty minutes of Carlito's Way *are a spectacular chase on a train and in a train station. You seem to have a liking for train stations, since many dramatic scenes in your films take place there.*

It's really just a coincidence. I spent months choreographing that final chase, which was originally supposed to take place on the escalators of the World Trade Center. It's a sensational location, but after the terrorist attack we were never going to get permission to shoot there. I didn't want to shoot the scene in an airport, as it was written in the script at one point, so on the advice of my set designer I looked at Grand Central Station, which also has escalators. I only had twenty-four hours to do rewrites, which wasn't easy. When you tell me I'm always shooting in train stations it sounds like criticism because I don't want to be accused of repeating myself, but circumstances sometimes force things on you. For *Carlito's Way* I'm convinced that it was my loss because the escalators in Grand Central are quite small, very different from the ones in the World Trade Center, which were massive. I had to reconfigure my entire plan and adapt it to the physical spaces of Grand Central, which is why the chase starts in a train, because it couldn't take place entirely on escalators as small as the ones in the station.

There were going to be lots of edits in the sequence I originally planned for the World Trade Center, but when I found myself in Grand Central and saw that my idea wasn't going to work, I thought of using a Steadicam. It took us thirty takes to get that one shot, which lasts more than two minutes. To this day, it's one of my fondest memories. Al was moving with the grace of a ballet dancer; it completely blew my mind. The funniest moment was during the shooting of the final chase, when Al moves from car to car. We were on one train and Al was on another, both running parallel. It was really tricky stuff.

We spent three months shooting that chase scene; we started in March and finished in July – in the middle of a heat wave. Al was in a winter outfit, that black leather jacket, and was dripping with sweat. We were in the subway at three o'clock in the morning and were having trouble getting a shot where he moves from car to car. We couldn't see him make the move because the pilars were obscuring him. We spent all night working on it. At one point the train Al was on disappeared. My assistant, Chris Soldo, came to me and told me that Al had gotten off the train. We went to his trailer and found him. He was melting, sweating gallons. He must have lost four or five pounds that night. He looked at me and said, "What the hell are you doing?" I explained, "Al, this is a very complicated shot. The Steadicam is in one car, you're in another, the two trains aren't going the same speed. We can't see where you are. We can't see the guys chasing you!" I begged him to come back.

Pacino has a tendency to overact, but he's really quite restrained in Carlito's Way. *Did you find it difficult to control him?*

You have to keep an eye on Al at all times. He's a very great actor, but as a director you have to be careful not to let him dominate. It's not unlike working with a magnificent musical instrument. You mustn't play it too loud or for too long – it has to be handled with tact and sensitivity, otherwise you end up playing wrong notes. In *Carlito's Way* there are silent shots where all you see is Al's face, which is all that's needed. His grace and elegance shines through if you look closely enough.

Did he like the film?

He was very moved. He really does like the two films we made together. *Scarface* might be the favourite of his films. He has always spoken positively of it, and says it's one of his best performances. Of course, I love hearing that.

He wasn't nominated for an Oscar for Carlito's Way, *but ended up winning for one of his worst films,* Scent of a Woman.

What can I say... He played a disabled person, which the Academy adores. Play a blind paralytic homosexual and you're sure to get an Oscar.

Sean Penn plays against type in the film as David Kleinfeld, the corrupt lawyer who accelerates Carlito's decline. Did you always think he was right for the part?

Sean is unpredictable; you can never guess in advance what he's going to do. He often plays the little badass, but he has a broad range. In Amy Heckerling's *Fast Times at Ridgemont High*, for example, he played a middle-class high school student. There's a moment in *Carlito's Way* where he literally loses his mind; he snorts cocaine and begs Carlito to get on his boat. When we shot that scene Sean went into a state that I'd never seen in him before. We must have done twenty takes. By the fifth he had it down perfectly, but he insisted on doing more. He was pissed off when I told him enough was enough. I wouldn't want to direct Sean in a movie where he plays a killer because I really don't know how far he might take it. [*laughs*] He has a choirboy quality, an innocent, charming smile that was perfect for this lawyer character. Don't be fooled by how the media portrays Sean. In private, he's a very pleasant guy, the opposite of his public image. For *Carlito's Way* I told him, "Sean, you have to be as friendly and charming as possible. No one can suspect that you're such a traitorous scumbag or it's never going to work." The difficulty of the part lies in its ambiguity. Sean had to be the most charming and vulnerable guy in the world because at a certain point in the story he removes his disguise and makes way for the biggest asshole on earth.

Whose idea was his hairstyle in the film?

His. I wanted him to look like a gangster lawyer who was a little too much into drugs. We've all met people like that.

It seems to us that Melanie Griffith is the ideal actress for you. Because she can play both innocent and depraved, she could have played all your female characters. It's too bad she isn't in Carlito's Way. *She would have been better than Penelope Ann Miller, who gives a very one-note performance.*

It's true. I've often thought about that. The problem with the character of Gail, who Penelope plays in *Carlito's Way*, is that she was originally going to be a schoolteacher. Then we decided to make her a stripper, but Penelope had already been cast. I agree that Melanie would have been a better choice. *Carlito's Way* is a love story, and the female character should have been as developed as Carlito, but that never happened. Penelope is no Melanie. But the role of Gail wasn't big and we didn't have the budget to bring in an actress as famous as Melanie, so we had to compromise and get someone who wasn't a star but who could stand up to Al and move the way I wanted her to for the dance and striptease scenes. It wasn't easy finding someone; we auditioned a lot of girls. Penelope was the best.

Patrick Doyle wrote the music for Carlito's Way.

My friend Régis Wargnier asked him to write the music for *Indochine*, which impressed me a lot, much more than the music for Kenneth Branagh's films – *Henry V* and *Dead Again* – which he also composed. Ennio Morricone was my first choice, before Régis told me about Patrick, who is a very good, very knowledgeable composer. I worked closely with him and in the end he did a superb job. For the opening credits he took a very Mahlerian approach, which is very beautiful, and what he did for the subway chase is mind-blowing. I think musicians are a little afraid of me. Nothing and nobody intimidates me, and I never compromise.

The film takes place in the Seventies, so there's lot of disco music in Carlito's Way. *Did you select the songs?*

Yes, though a specialist, Jellybean Benitez, did a pre-selection.

When Carlito goes to see Gail in her strip club, we hear the Bee Gees song "You Should Be Dancing." Were you asked to do Saturday Night Fever?

Kind of. I met the author of the original article. You may not know this, but *Saturday Night Fever* was inspired by an article by Nik Cohn in *New York* magazine. When I met him there wasn't even a script, let alone John Travolta. I was asked to meet this guy to see if I wanted to work with him on the script. I said no, and he moved on to another director.

Scarface *was two hours and forty-five minutes long and* Carlito's Way *is almost two and a half hours long. The average big American film is getting longer and longer. Why do you think that is?*

Two hours is plenty for me. I don't set out to make long films, although some stories need that kind of length, depending on their complexity and the number of characters. I've never been precious about the things I've shot. My inclination is to remove whatever I can. For *Scarface* and *Carlito's Way* I didn't make any cuts to the script. If I had, the films wouldn't have been as good. I haven't heard any complaints about the length of *Carlito's Way*. Anyone who objected to the 260-minute running time did so only as they left the theatre, not while they were actually watching the film.

    Every film has its own particular rhythm, but the studios are the first to pressure you not to go over two hours so they can pack as many screenings as possible into one day, and you have to commit to making a film that's no longer than two hours and ten minutes. Anything over that length and you lose one-fifth of projected revenue. Occasionally the studio recognises that a film is better when it's two hours and twenty minutes and backs off. It all depends on how powerful the director is. The chase sequence in *Terminator 2* was way too long, but James Cameron wanted it that way and insisted, regardless of what the producers said.

How did Carlito's Way *do in the United States?*

Badly, as usual, which in this case was depressing because I thought we deserved better. A lot of talented people worked very hard and the script was excellent, but American critics long ago made up their minds about my work and nothing I can do will make them think differently.

Did you know that Carlito's Way *was voted best film of the 1990s by* Cahiers du Cinéma?

Excellent choice! I'm going to move to Paris. Woody Allen should do the same. [*laughs*] What's the saying? "No one is a prophet in their own land." David Lean wasn't particularly admired in England either. But in the end, I'm free to do what I want. I go my own way no matter what, and I think that's why my work is getting more and more interesting, because I don't really care what people say – even though it's not always a particularly pleasant way to live.

After Carlito's Way *you were supposed to do a film written with Jay Cocks called* Ambrose Chapel. *What was it about?*

It was a variation on John Frankenheimer's *The Manchurian Candidate* and the theme of the programmed assassin, who in our version was a brainwashed woman. She was programmed to watch Hitchcock's *The Man Who Knew Too Much*, which then returns in her dreams. It was set in Mexico City, a place that has always fascinated me. Unfortunately I could never get the financing together.

Ambrose Chapel is the name of the church where James Stewart's son is isolated in The Man Who Knew Too Much.

Yes. I write a lot of scripts that I don't even try to sell; I just put them aside because often the stories aren't completely finished. Scott Spencer wrote *Act of Vengeance* for me, a great script about the murder of Joseph Yablonski that was eventually directed by John Mackenzie with Charles Bronson. Around 1984, I was planning on making a film called *Carpool*, which would have been *Rear Window* on wheels. Instead of seeing everything from a window, the hero watches from his car. Robert Zemeckis and Bob Gale wrote the first draft of the script, I think for Universal.

This was before the release of *Romancing the Stone*. I also wrote a remake of *The Treasure of the Sierra Madre* which switched out gold for cocaine, so it was more in keeping with the times. This was long before *Scarface*. And for a short time Spielberg and I considered working together on *Congo*, a Michael Crichton adaptation, which he would have produced and I was going to direct, but things dragged on and we moved on to other things.

Were you offered The Truman Show? *You would have been the perfect director.*

Yes, but they gave it to someone else when I said I didn't want Jim Carrey. Tom Hanks was my choice.

After Snake Eyes *you planned to make* Nazi Gold, *another script written with Jay Cocks. Why did that project fall through?*

We sold the script to MGM, but the studio went bankrupt not too long after that. I tried to put the project back together elsewhere, but no casting ideas, no package I could put together, made it viable. I even found foreign co-financing, but in the end there was nothing I could do with it. In hindsight, I think the subject matter – the Holocaust – bothered a lot of people in Hollywood, and they didn't want to spend the money. Since I'm not Jewish I have a hard time analysing clearly why, especially since I think it's a wonderful story. Many of my Jewish friends liked it.

You also wrote a script about Howard Hughes with David Koepp, which Nicolas Cage was going to star in.

Yes, *Mr. Hughes*. We sold the project to Disney Touchstone but they backed out at the last minute. When I did find someone to co-finance the film, Cage couldn't commit and it fell apart.

Why didn't he commit?

He had done four films in a row and a fifth was too much for him. I'm waiting until he's available.

There were several other planned Howard Hughes projects.

That's always been the case, but most will never see the light of day. I'm not concerned; I just need Nic to find some space in his schedule. David Koepp wrote a really good script based on ideas we came up with together. I found an original way to tell the story, through the eyes of his biographer Clifford Irving, author of *The Hoax*, who projects himself onto Hughes. He asks his assistant to interview him, and as he does we dig into the *real* story of Howard Hughes. It was reminiscent of *Fire*, my Doors-inspired script. Nic Cage was going to play both Irving and the Hughes he imagines himself to be. I'm convinced it's the best way to tell Hughes' story. I've managed to make most of the movies I've wanted to, but sometimes, after years of developing a script, the day comes when it's finally possible to shoot it and I don't want to do it anymore. That actually happens quite often.

An adaptation of the TV series Mission: Impossible *seems like the ideal project for you. Each episode of the show is a self-contained story, a perfect metaphor for the process of mise en scène.*

I never watched the show, but I did always want to make a spy film in Europe. Espionage is the perfect genre for me. I love showing people being followed and people spying. It's very cinematic – full of surveillance, voyeurism and double lives.

If The Untouchables *was faithful to the spirit of the television series that inspired it, the same can't be said of* Mission: Impossible, *which from the start is quite different from the original series.*

That was my intention. I wanted to do the unthinkable, something transgressive. In the series, the mission is always accomplished. With the film, the idea was that everyone dies and everything ends badly.

How did you get involved in the project?

After the commercial failure of *Carlito's Way* I was in urgent need of a hit, so I left my agent Marty Bauer and signed with Michael Ovitz and Creative Artists Agency. Ovitz immediately offered me *Mission: Impossible*. I had met Tom Cruise at Steven Spielberg's place. Sydney Pollack had been working on the project for over a year with the writers of *American Graffiti*, Gloria Katz and her husband Willard Huyck. I think Pollack wanted to get out of the job so he could focus on his *Sabrina* remake, and I jumped at the chance. I listened to Cruise's suggestions and got to work with Katz and Huyck, but because of their ironic approach I knew that Tom wasn't going to like their script.

Was Huyck and Katz's version set in the United States?

Yes. I suggested taking it to Europe, even though it's become as expensive to shoot there as it is at home. The Czechs, in particular, asked for a lot of money to shoot in the Prague locations I had selected. Back in the mid-Eighties, when Miloš Forman made *Amadeus*, filming in Eastern Europe was relatively cheap, but that's all in the past now. Nobody liked the Katz/Huyck script, so I told the producers, "Let me go to work with Steven Zaillian, the writer of *Schindler's List*, for a few days and see what we can come up with." We ended up inventing the entire story. Originally I wanted a *Dirty Dozen* structure with Cruise recruiting his crew from all over the world. Jean Reno was imprisoned in India, Ving Rhames was on an Irish island. It was all really good material, but I kept running into the same problem: "This is *Mission: Impossible*, so let's get straight to the mission!" Given that Tom Cruise was the star of the show, one problem was five characters working together as a team. Tom was the hero, so I suggested we kill off his four sidekicks right at the start. All of this was in our twelve-page treatment that David Koepp based his script on.

What did Robert Towne contribute to the script?

Tom Cruise insisted that he do the final version, which involved Towne beefing up the characters. I had to fight to keep the helicopter chase I had been working on for months because Towne preferred that dialogue scene with the three of them in the baggage compartment. I put my foot down. "We can't end with all that chit-chat," I insisted. "It's *Mission: Impossible* – there has to be some action!" Tom ended up proving me right and I'm happy with how it turned out. No regrets. I worked hard and created the story from scratch, and made all kinds of compromises to protect my vision and keep it all coherent.

How did you get along with Tom Cruise?

Once I had convinced him to do the film, it was easy going. He was skeptical at first, insisting that the script wasn't good enough and that he was wary of making the film. But once we starting shooting, we were on the same wavelength. Tom always wants to make the absolute best film he can. He's a smart guy, and once things get going he considers every option until the right one comes along. He wields enormous power and can get almost anything done. But working with him is tiring. The worst of it was just before shooting started, when the two writers were each in a different hotel. Robert Towne was rewriting David Koepp's work and vice versa. It was a nightmare. I was shuttling back and forth between the two.

Like Ed Pressman, Frank Yablans and Martin Bregman, Tom Cruise is a producer with a strong personality. You're one of the few American filmmakers to have recognised the creative contributions of producers.

The Hollywood system is an agglomeration of talent, the opposite of cinema *à la* Godard or Truffaut, where the director makes every decision. I think it's a good thing because it pushes us all together towards the end result. Look at *Citizen Kane*. Will there ever be another collection of so many extraordinary talents working at the same time on the same film? Probably not. You had scriptwriter Herman Mankiewicz, a producer able to handle Welles' ego, and Orson Welles at the top of his game, with the right of final cut in his contract – the first time in Hollywood history. That conjunction of talents is miraculous, which is why *Citizen Kane* is such a unique film.

No one paid attention to the fairy tale-like construction of Mission: Impossible. *Even the prologue, with Emmanuelle Béart brought back to life by Tom Cruise with the help of a syringe, is reminiscent of Sleeping Beauty awakened by Prince Charming. Danny Elfman's music reinforces the phantasmagorical aspect. The film is actually a version of* Tom Thumb. *There's the ogre, played by Jon Voight, who kills all his children. Tom Cruise is Thumbelina, who makes his way through the forest, which here is Prague, thanks to Internet messages that replace the pebbles of the fable.*

I fought hard to keep that perversity in the film.

This mythological subtext seems to come from Joseph Campbell's theories, which influenced George Lucas when he wrote Star Wars.

Campbell was my teacher at Sarah Lawrence College! I read his books, including *The Hero with a Thousand Faces*, and went to his class every Friday. We talked together from three to six in the afternoon, usually alone. That's the advantage of Sarah Lawrence; the student is really one-on-one with the teacher. It's obvious that his teaching has been an influence on me. *Mission: Impossible* is like a descent into darkness. The Internet works like the Pythia of Delphi. Tom Cruise embarks on an odyssey. He's a bit like the cosmonaut in *2001: A Space Odyssey*, and the CIA vault in the film, where the heist takes place, resembles the ship from *2001*. It was designed by Norman Reynolds, who did the sets for *Star Wars*. I had already drawn up plans on my computer using software for architects, but Norman gave it a science fiction touch.

Your films always feature powerless characters. But unlike your previous films, the hero – in this case Tom Cruise, unable to rescue his team – watches the drama play out on his wristwatch.

What he sees is actually a lie. The point was to show that film is a machine for manufacturing illusion. Cruise thinks, as does the audience, that Voight has been shot. Only later does he realise that it was all a set-up. Once again, cinema is a lie, twenty-four times a second.

Unlike its sequel, by John Woo, there are only one or two shots fired in your Mission: Impossible, *which is rather rare for a Hollywood action movie.*

I felt that the film should focus on betrayal, deception and conspiracy, not guns.

One of our favourite scenes is in the restaurant with the exploding aquarium. It's the kind of situation you like so much: a public place with only one person who understands exactly what's happening.

We shot at Pinewood Studios in England. The scene scared everyone because Tom had to do that big jump. We used a stuntman on the first take, but it just wasn't working, and I told Tom he had to do it himself. The great thing about Cruise is that he's not afraid of anything. The stunts he did on the train at the end of the film were really dangerous and could have injured him, but Tom was willing to try it all. He's the hardest working guy there is – on set all the time, and very supportive, too. We explained to him in detail what was going to happen and a stuntman walked him through the scene. Everything was meticulously prepared. "You know," he said just before shooting, "I'm just an actor." "Trust me, Tom," I said, "everything will be fine." He was a bit nervous about the thought of all that water coming up behind him.

The final shot of the sequence shows Ethan running, with the fish from the aquarium in his wake.

That was a stuntman. Considering the amount of water, we needed someone who could move *very* fast.

All those fish behind him evoke the Red Sea. It's a biblical image that announces Job, the traitor of the film.

Precisely. They were rubber fish, by the way.

How did you come up with the film's climax, the CIA heist?

As you can imagine, I've seen *Topkapi* by Jules Dassin. When I was working on *Mission: Impossible*, Jay Cocks showed me a lot of heist movies. *Topkapi*, with the scene of that guy hanging by a thread, really made an impression. I had the idea of shooting a scene in complete silence, in other words the opposite of most American action films. No music or sound effects, just silence. I wanted to use all those audio tracks to build a world of silence. The idea was to push it as far as possible.

Which character in the film do you identify with more – Cruise or Voight?

Cruise mostly. He finds himself in a position comparable to that of the hero of *Phantom of the Paradise*. He's both manipulator and manipulated.

That's clear in the scene at the train station where Cruise and Voight meet again and take turns lying.

It's an interesting idea because you're lying while you have in your mind what really happened, and even if you hear someone lying to you, you reconstruct in your mind what you think is the truth. It's quite a bold explanatory scene, and some critics and audiences were confused by it.

Was that scene in the script from the start?

Yes. It's certainly more interesting than showing what actually happened. Voight lies and Cruise basically reconstructs the truth. I wondered if audiences would understand it, and in the end figured it would work. Ideas often come to me as soon as I wake up. On a shoot, during lunch break, I'll take a nap and usually wake up with an idea. It's as if I've been solving problems in my sleep. That's why it's so important for me to find time to sleep when I'm making a film. Bernard Herrmann was the same. He said that the muses speak to us while we sleep.

How much flexibility is there on a production as huge as Mission: Impossible?

None. I know exactly what I want, and I usually edit pretty quickly. I hate that expression "give and take." The most important thing when I shoot a scene is to visualise exactly what it's about, and to ensure that the setting and camera movement make sense in terms of what the characters are thinking and doing. In *Mission: Impossible* we had a scene in an airport at the end where Tom Cruise meets Ving Rhames after the mission is over. Tom is going to catch his plane; they're saying goodbye. It was a classic epilogue, but I wasn't happy. Three days before the end of the shoot I had an idea while sleeping. I woke up and realised that after the long sequence with the train in the tunnel, we couldn't have another scene in such an artificial and confined world as an airport. The nightmare is over, and we had to show that there has been some kind of return to regular life. We needed to see reality – the streets, one of those English pubs. If we hadn't done it that way the film would have felt abstract and too cut off from reality. It wasn't an easy thing to change because we had planned everything in this airport, but I knew it was the wrong space for the scene, so we re-shot it outside a pub.

The only thing that doesn't work in the film is the relationship between Tom Cruise's character and Emmanuelle Béart's.

True. Originally they had more scenes together, but we cut a lot of them. It's not easy to say why it doesn't work as planned. I'm a great admirer of Béart. I met many French, English and Italian actresses when I was casting the role and she was certainly the best. I really liked the chemistry between her and Tom. In the test footage we shot in Paris they looked great together. I was surprised that it didn't work out as well in the final film.

Perhaps a romantic subplot was never going to fit in a film like this.

It's a different kind of problem. I can't say why, but American cinema is resistant to foreign actresses. Wonderful actresses like Emmanuelle Béart – who exude warmth and magic when filmed by filmmakers from their own country – don't work when they have to act in English with American actors. I can't really figure out why. There are exceptions of course, like Sophia Loren or Ingrid Bergman, who was Swedish and became a big American star. For French women it's more difficult. Catherine Deneuve and Isabelle Adjani are great stars in your country but they never found their place in America. I don't think a French woman has been fully accepted by the American public since Claudette Colbert, who managed to become a big Hollywood star. Maybe Juliette Binoche will succeed. It must be a cultural thing. I don't know.

Was it your idea to cast Jon Voight?

Yes. I've always liked his work. I've known Jon since the Sixties. He should have become as big a star as Pacino or De Niro, but he took a different path and voluntarily disappeared in the Eighties.

What are your thoughts on Max, the character played by Vanessa Redgrave?

It was Tom's idea to turn that character into a woman. He was friends with Vanessa and asked if she would play the part. I saw Max as a kind of Peter Ustinov character and was immediately intrigued when Tom told me to change him into a woman, especially since Vanessa is such a great actress.

Did you first see Jean Réno in Léon*?*

No, I had seen him in other Luc Besson films – that great one about free diving, *The Big Blue*, and also in *Le Dernier Combat*, which I like a lot. Réno is a great actor and a good guy to work with.

Mission: Impossible's *beautiful score is by Danny Elfman. Initially you hired Alan Silvestri, Robert Zemeckis' composer.*

Alan Silvestri wrote a score which we began recording, but after five days he had to start rewriting half of it because it just wasn't working. I didn't have time to supervise that new material. He came in with the new material and went straight to the studio to record it, without listening to my suggestions, but it wasn't what we were looking for. It was too melodic, and no matter what we did there was always something excessive in his music. We kept making changes, but after four sessions I told my editor, Paul Hirsch, "This is never going to work. Tom isn't going to like this music." Cruise was shooting *Jerry Maguire* at the time. It wasn't easy to find a good composer who was willing to work with Lalo Schifrin's themes. Alan Silvestri was replaced and I started working with Danny Elfman. I went to his house every day and we went over each piece on his computer.

You never thought of using Lalo Schifrin?

I didn't think Lalo was right for the job. We set out to hire the very best people, but most of them wanted to write their own *Mission: Impossible* theme.

Your original idea was to film on the Eurostar.

They wouldn't allow it, so we ended up on the TGV instead. Tom took an SNCF boss to dinner and persuaded him to give us permission. That's the advantage of working with a superstar.

What was the hardest thing to shoot on Mission: Impossible?

The very first scene, where Tom is disguised as a Russian and tries to get the other guy to talk. We filmed it three ways, each time with different lighting. It wasn't an easy shoot because everyone was arguing. The makeup guy was complaining about the light, which drove [my cinematographer] Stephen Burum crazy. I'd never seen him so infuriated.

Is the scene where Cruise takes off his Jon Voight mask a digital trick?

That was a real rubber mask made by Rob Bottin, our chief makeup artist. First we filmed Jon, then Tom removing the mask on the same axis and with the same shot size. The two shots were then morphed together.

What's your best memory of the film?

Shooting the heist scene, when Tom was hanging from his wire and we had to let go and catch him just before he hit the ground. It was very difficult to get right. Tom was very patient even though he was dangling in a very uncomfortable position. And I love the spins he does on the roof of the train at the end.

Did you cut many scenes? In the trailer we see Tom Cruise and Emmanuelle Béart kissing, but that scene isn't in the film.

I don't remember. Tom had a lot of problems with Béart, though I never quite understood why. I suspect that he felt the way Cliff Robertson felt about Geneviève Bujold on *Obsession*; he thought she was so good that she might steal the limelight. In the baggage compartment scene at the end he wasn't very nice to her, which annoyed me because she was doing a good job. Tom, Robert Towne and I argued over that scene because at first they didn't want to do it, and the tension between Tom and Emmanuelle didn't help. It was a tricky shoot.

It's strange that Cruise felt that way, because Béart's character isn't that important in the film.

I know, but that's what happened.

How long did you work on Mission: Impossible?

I started in January 1994. We began shooting in March 1995 and I finished the film a year later in the spring of 1996. It was endless.

The whole process of creating the special effects at George Lucas' ranch in California seems to have been especially difficult.

I was with George the first time he went to the ranch in the mid-Seventies. There was nothing there. I lived there during *Mission: Impossible*'s post-production. It was the first time one of my films required such extensive special effects work.

Was that boring for you?

Not at all. I enjoyed it. The people who work for George are talented computer geeks, and I got along with them. I understand them because I have the same background. On the other hand, working on special effects can be a bit tedious. It's a case of "Add a little reflection here. Not too much or the texture will change…" You have to start over again and again.

When did you first meet George Lucas?

In 1969 or 1970, at a party. I remember Martin Scorsese and Irvin Kershner were also there.

Did the success of Mission: Impossible *change your status in Hollywood?*

Completely. I hadn't had a real hit since *The Untouchables*. *Raising Cain* made a bit of money, but not enough for Hollywood.

Did Paramount executives see Mission: Impossible *as a Brian De Palma film and not just a thriller tailor-made for Tom Cruise?*

The best answer to that question is *Snake Eyes*, which David Koepp and I sold to Paramount for $11 million.

Were you in demand?

Yes, that's how it works in Hollywood. Nobody tries to understand exactly who did what. Paramount knows better than anyone what really happened during the production of *Mission: Impossible*. The executives, Sherry Lansing and Jonathan Dolgen, knew how committed I was. I felt responsible to them because I was spending their money. When I was concerned about something I would call them and ask for this or that, and they supported me.

What do you think of Mission: Impossible *today?*

It contains some of the best stuff I've ever done. I spent so much time planning certain sequences, getting them done, fighting for what I really wanted. I had to let some time go by before watching the film as a regular viewer – and then I was amazed. Of course when the film came out the critics didn't like it. They didn't understand the story. As usual, it was underrated.

The story of Mission: Impossible *makes active use of the Internet. What is it about this new mode of communication that you find so interesting?*

All new media interest me – video games like *Myst* or *Riven* in particular. I've followed their development closely since the early Eighties. They have opened new storytelling pathways by taking us into virtual environments that can be perceived subjectively. There was nothing like it before; it's the closest thing to the way we experience life. *Myst* and *Riven* also tell stories in a non-linear way. Clues are offered and you discover the story little by little, like an archaeologist. You can read a book or go open that cupboard, where there's something waiting for you. You can walk into a room and learn about your character. Unlike the usual narrative forms, where the director takes you from point A to point B, there's a much more varied range of paths available to you, each of which is an interactive way to discover the story. This is very interesting for the person telling the story, as it multiplies the possibilities. How does knowing that you can tell your story in so many different ways dictate how you direct the player's view as he moves through a space? What might push players in one direction and not another? It's really a completely new medium, in many ways similar to the novel, because both can be created by a single individual working from home.

Spielberg is developing a revolutionary new game at DreamWorks which allows you to manipulate objects directly in the virtual environment. Your perception of space will always be subjective, but you'll have a hand that will allow you to put something in a certain place. You can throw a stone, take a gun, stack boxes on top of each other, and climb them to reach something. It's a revolution, because before, in so-called interactive games, you would go through environments, a monster would appear, you had to kill it, then you took a key to access a new level – that kind of thing. Today the visuals are more elaborate and the artists who create them are more skilled. It's all moving way beyond the games we used to play, mostly bad imitations of *Star Wars*. It's really the future for me. The amounts of money being invested are huge. Artists have always followed the money.

The video game, as you describe it, is a solitary, isolating experience.

Not for me. A game designer is no more cut off from the world than a writer is from his typewriter. We're dealing with a totally new medium that I can't exactly define because it's constantly evolving, which is why I'm always buying new games to keep up with what's going on. It doesn't have much to do with the game itself anymore; it's like going into a parallel world. Just think! In some you can even go to the bathroom.

When we said that the game isolates you, we meant the player.

I understand, but the writer is also alone.

Seeing a film in a cinema is a shared experience.

Not necessarily. I generally go to the movies at the noon showing because there's no one around at that time of day. I don't like to see movies with a lot of people or in a crowded theatre. Their reactions get in the way of my own thoughts and feelings. For me, the movie experience is best done alone. But I'm also not the kind of person who has a movie theatre at home. I've never understood that – inviting people to your house to see a movie. Noon shows are heaven for me. I also like test screenings. Previews not so much.

The Internet experience is ironic in that it opens you up to the world, yet isolates you at the same time.

When it comes to a dumb teenager chatting with prostitutes online, I agree with you. He's chatting with a hooker in Taiwan, he's chatting with someone who-knows-where in the world. There can be up to six of them at once. Believe me, that kind of stuff exists. But I'm not interested in that. I've been in a few Internet chat rooms. They're pretty silly.

Do you visit chatrooms under your real name?

Yes, but nobody thinks it's me! One day a guy tested me see if I was really Brian De Palma – and he stuck it to me! He said, "You're not Brian De Palma!" I told him I was, and he asked me some question about Dennis Franz in *Dressed to Kill* which I couldn't answer. You should have seen my face! The guy laughed. "You don't know! What did I tell you!" You might think I'm a celebrity but I rarely get recognised. I can move about without anyone bothering me. I live not far from New York University, and from time to time film students come up to me and say, "Holy cow, you're Brian De Palma!" But most of the time I go incognito. Unlike my friends I'm rarely interviewed on television. Nowadays everybody recognises Steven, Marty or George. Francis isn't quite as well known because he isn't in the public eye as much these days, but of all of them I'm recognised the least.

There are several websites about you.

We filmmakers will live forever thanks to the Internet. The guys who run those sites are unbelievable; they know more about me than I do and are always finding new things to write about. They're much more interesting to read than mainstream critics.

Snake Eyes *reminds us of* Phantom of the Paradise.

Do you think so? In what way?

In both films there's a physical environment as important as any character, a violent attack in broad daylight, an innocent woman who becomes involved in a fight to the death between two heroes, and videotapes that reveal a secret and whose deletion prefigures the death of the person recorded on them. At the end of Snake Eyes, *when Nicolas Cage is bruised and wounded, he looks a bit like the Phantom – as if the evil in him…*

…was suddenly painted on his face. That's exactly right.

What are the origins of Snake Eyes?

After *Mission: Impossible*, David Koepp and I wanted to make a film together. David had the idea of a crime that's observed from several points of view. I'd been thinking about that idea too, so we started from there. I added things I got from all the reading I was doing about Howard Hughes. To sell more planes, when he went to Las Vegas to negotiate contracts with the guys from the Department of Defense, he would take them to endless parties. That inspired the villain of the story, Powell, played by John Heard. And having grown up on the New Jersey shore, near Ocean City, I know Atlantic City, which, before the casinos were built, truly was heaven on earth. With the arrival of all the casinos, it became hellish; everything that was beautiful just vanished. I witnessed all of this first hand, and always knew that one day I would make a film about it. Atlantic City is very different from Las Vegas, which was built from scratch to be a gambling capital. Atlantic City was disfigured for that same reason. The real Atlantic City isn't there any more. The casinos are a blight. Who cares how much money they make for everyone?

Have you seen Louis Malle's film Atlantic City?

Of course. It's great. Anne Pritchard, who worked on *Obsession* and *Snake Eyes*, was the set designer.

Structurally, Snake Eyes *reminds us of Kurosawa's* Rashomon.

Maybe, but that's not how I see it. If I remember correctly – because the last time I saw that film I was probably in high school – there's a rape in *Rashomon* followed by three or four accounts of what happened during the crime. Each version is different; the way the narrative plays out changes from one to the other. The characters too. That's all very different from *Snake Eyes*, where the three flashbacks fill in gaps in the narrative until the puzzle is solved. The problem when it came to filming was that we had to shoot the same event differently each time. The flashbacks are subjectively filmed. The opening Steadicam shot, which introduces the character played by Nicolas Cage, focuses only on his reactions and never shows the audience what he's looking it.

How did you work with Koepp?

I would email him in California from Manhattan. Those emails laid the foundation for the story, then David wrote the script.

Koepp wrote three of your films. It's the most sustained collaboration you've ever had with a screenwriter.

I really like working with him. As soon as I met him there was an immediate connection; I knew he was someone I'd be working with for a long time to come. Most of my collaborators are old friends I've known for years. Koepp is younger than me, but I enjoy spending time with him; we share the same sense of humour. I first met him through Martin Bregman and Al Pacino, who had commissioned him to write *Carlito's Way*. Throughout my career I've worked with the best American screenwriters: Paul Schrader, David Rabe, David Mamet, Oliver Stone. But I haven't been able to develop an ongoing collaboration with any of them. Oliver gave me a hard time on *Scarface*, writing a letter to the producer and Pacino after the first cut, detailing everything he thought was wrong with it. I ignored him and hung in there. I have to admit I've never really been convinced by his directing. I enjoyed working with Michael Cristofer on *The Bonfire of the Vanities*, but the film was a disaster. He also went on to direct.

What about Robert Towne?

Robert Towne is considered the greatest of American screenwriters, but there's no question that Roman Polanski and Jack Nicholson added a lot to his *Chinatown* screenplay. I've worked with Bob Towne and know what he's capable of. The truth is, he isn't a great screenwriter. His talent may have declined over time, but still, on *Mission: Impossible*, for him to rewrite a scene, I had to talk him through it. Towne is a former actor who has acquired a certain aura over the years, but basically he's a script doctor, a guy who rewrites other people's work, which he's very good at.

Mission: Impossible and Snake Eyes are constructed in the same way. In the first part some big drama occurs, as witnessed by the main character. Like him, we believe what we're seeing. But then, in part two, you show first that it was all an illusion, then reveal what really happened.

Mission: Impossible and *Snake Eyes* are about the deceptive power of the image. Once again, cinema is a lie twenty-four images a second. This is particularly true of television, where images can be made to mean anything. The truth and its opposite.

You seem to think that we should be more wary of images than ever, all the more so at a time like ours when people tend to believe everything they see on television.

The investigation into Kennedy's murder has probably brought together the most eyewitness accounts in the history of mankind, not to mention amateur film of the assassination itself, shot by Abraham Zapruder. And in the end, what was the result? Nothing more than a succession of hypotheses. It's ironic, to say the least. We have forever been in search of truth, but the irony is that the truth doesn't exist. We all hope that a sufficiently thorough investigation can provide the key to a mystery. As with many narratives, the confusions in *Snake Eyes* are ultimately laid to rest, but generally speaking, in life, the more information you amass, the less you know. That's another lesson from the Kennedy investigation, where a proliferation of information didn't help solve the puzzle. If I make films about puzzles that are solved, it's because this kind of thing lends itself to storytelling. But it doesn't reflect my deepest convictions about the world.

Why did you set Snake Eyes *in a casino?*

What fascinates me about casinos is that everything, from top to bottom, is under surveillance. There is no place more controlled. On the other hand, it's a vision of hell on earth, because the casino's ultimate goal is to destroy you. The moment you walk in, you're a dead man. You lose all sense of reality. There are no windows, you don't know if it's day or night, there are lights everywhere. The employees all serve you with a smile, but they do so with the intention of stripping you of everything you own. The casino always wins. And to do that they beguile you into believing that *you* can win. Walk into a casino and the first thing you hear is the sound of slot machines. But the concept of a slot machine defies logic. Putting money into a device that electronically determines a combination, in the belief that you'll be able to break that combination, is a complete delusion. And yet slot machines are the biggest money-makers in casinos. It's all one enormous lie.

Are you a gambler?

Absolutely not. If I happen to walk into a casino and win a little money, my first instinct is to get out of there fast because I know that in the end I'll lose everything. That's also how I see life. What saves me is that I'm completely indifferent to anything that society can offer me in terms of fame or celebrity. I'm not materialistic. I've lived in the same apartment for twenty years. I have two little girls that I love, plus my computers. What more do I need? I'll probably die in my apartment.

Were you like that as a teenager?

Yes, and I can't imagine I'll ever change.

Nicolas Cage is called Santoro in the film, which is also Joe Pesci's name in Martin Scorsese's Casino.

I had forgotten that. Marty's film depicts the casino in a much more analytical way than mine. In *Snake Eyes* what interested me was the out-of-this-world aspect of the place.

Snake Eyes isn't really about casinos or Atlantic City. At its centre is the storm raging inside Ricky Santoro.

That's certainly true. He's an angry, bitter guy, forced to make a moral choice about whether or not he should turn in his friend Kevin Dunne, played by Gary Sinise. If he does turn him in, Kevin will die, that's for sure. Ricky may be corrupt, but there's a line he won't cross. It's even harder for him because he loves his life in Atlantic City. He's like a pig in shit – but he sure loves it. Being in that kind of hell is a blast and it's hard to walk away from. People who have sold their souls to the devil always seem so sinister on film, but nothing could be further from the truth. There's nothing more fun than becoming a degenerate. Ricky is like Tony Montana, who might be a monster, but also has a line he won't cross. He won't kill kids, which is what ends up destroying him. Do one good deed in hell and you're finished. To survive in a corrupt universe, you have to turn your back on all of humanity.

Greetings was overtly political, unlike Snake Eyes.

Yes, but Ricky Santoro still reflects the deep cynicism of our times. When I made *Greetings*, cynicism was reserved for the politicians. Today it's deeply embedded in everyone. Santoro isn't interested in truth. What he cares about is one day becoming mayor of Atlantic City. That's why Gary Sinise is so surprised by his about-face.

The first sentence Ricky utters in the film is "I'm on TV!" He could also have said "Hi, Mom!"

Ricky has the same dream as millions of Americans. If you're on TV in this country you're a big deal and can get away with anything. The most famous and respected woman in America is Oprah Winfrey. There's nothing remarkable about her except that she hosts a television talk show. Millions of people see her as a god. For them, something is real only if they see it on TV. That's the irony of *Snake Eyes*. Ricky has to watch a film of the events to understand what really happened. The irony is that at the end he flees from the cameras after being indicted for corruption. He wanted to be on TV, but ends up having to run from that world. His final sentence echoes his first: "At least I got to be on television." But he says it with bitterness.

After having created memorable long takes in The Bonfire of the Vanities *and* Raising Cain, *why another at the start of* Snake Eyes?

It provides the audience with a lot of information without boring them. It's useful for a scene where you have to deliver up a lot of exposition about the main character. It also allowed me to capture what the atmosphere of a boxing stadium is like in the twenty minutes before a fight starts. I don't know if you've ever been to a big boxing match, but at first there's a faint background noise which gets louder and louder as the excitement builds. In the end you can't hear your own voice. That long shot allows me to take the audience through that experience. But I'm not the only one who does that kind of thing; Scorsese used the same technique in *Raging Bull* and *Goodfellas*. The inspiration for us all, of course, is the opening shot of Orson Welles' *Touch of Evil*. I paid tribute to Welles in *Phantom of the Paradise*, with the sequence where the Phantom places a bomb in the theatre. My version is a long split-screen shot, which was wildly difficult to do because there was no Steadicam at the time. The cameramen were on big dollies and made superhuman efforts not to catch each other in shot.

If the first part of Snake Eyes *is very fluid, with the Steadicam shot, the second part is very different. It's more cut up and more of a mix of genres.*

It's like silence; you don't really become aware of it until it's not there. What follows that long opening shot is something much more traditional – a girl trying to escape and the audience wondering if she'll get away. There's nothing wildly innovative about it, but it works because it's so different from what came before it. Every cut makes an impact because of the long shot that opens the film.

Would you ever push your use of the Steadicam and make a film with a single shot, like Hitchcock's Rope?

That would just turn it into a gimmick. The long take is a discipline, and it works only when you don't push it too far. Try to pack a film with those kinds of things and it falls apart. I'm always trying to find the best possible way to film something, using the extensive visual grammar – split screen, long shots, jump cuts, that kind of thing – that I've been working with for so many years. I'm very familiar with the effect of each technique on the audience, which allows me to take a primarily visual approach to the material.

We first see Gary Sinise in the middle of that opening long shot via a quick pan from Ricky. Did you do that in case Sinise made a mistake, so that you could cut into the shot and not have to start from the beginning?

No, it was designed to show what Ricky is pointing at. I did think about having other quick pans so I could cut into the long shot if need be. The long take made Nicolas and Gary nervous; they had never done anything like it before. But they're very good actors and were excited to take on the challenge.

How many takes did you do for the opening sequence?

Five or six. The sequence is actually four shots stitched together, though you'll never notice where we cut. The opening of the film was the most difficult part to shoot.

Another challenge was to find a different tone for each flashback.

I try to be as expressive as possible, and in the case of the flashbacks, each is subjectively presented. When the boxer tells his story, I focus on his point of view. There are some objective shots but it's more or less his version of the fight. Then we switch to Dunne's point of view, again a subjective shot, but this time it's a lie. I can't think of another instance where a subjective camera has been used in this way. It's a technique generally reserved for truth-telling. Because the lies are filmed subjectively, they're more believable. Following that, the split-screen sequence makes clear what *really* happened.

Carla Gugino seems to be the only Hitchcock reference in Snake Eyes. *With her blond wig and white outfit she reminds us of Kim Novak in* Vertigo, *but also Angie Dickinson in* Dressed to Kill.

It's possible; I hadn't thought of that. If anything, you're in a better position to say whether it's a Hitchcock reference or not because by now you've watched my films so much that you know them better than I do. I figured she should be in white because she would be easier to spot in the crowd, and I made her blonde for the same reason. I wanted her to be in disguise, so I decided to give her a wig. We looked at a lot of them before we found the right one. Carla tried one on which I liked and that made her look like Marilyn Monroe – and now you're telling me it's a Hitchcock thing… Perhaps it's reminiscent of *Marnie*, but that was never my intention. That's not how things work.

You know Ingmar Bergman's comment about the last shot of *The Seventh Seal*? He was asked why one of the important characters in the film wasn't in the final shot, when Death leads them up the hill. "Because the actor was sick that day," explained Bergman. The critics racked their brains trying to justify why the character survived when in fact the actor simply wasn't feeling well. That's how filmmaking works; some things are under your control, other things are accidents. It's important to stay open and pragmatic.

Your films are so meticulously prepared that it's hard to believe that you leave anything to chance.

It's true that I prepare everything very carefully, but what guides my decision-making isn't my previous films. I try not to draw inspiration from them. How did I come up with the staircase scene in *The Untouchables*? Well, first you have the character of Eliot Ness, who loves kids. What would his reaction be if all of a sudden, in the middle of a gunfight, someone threw a baby at him? And what if we took the image from *Battleship Potemkin*, of the baby carriage going down the stairs? An image in your head – that's all you need, just a good idea, like a baby carriage in the middle of a gunfight. It worked in *Battleship Potemkin* and it works in *The Untouchables*. People imagine that I watched *Potemkin* frame by frame, then decided how to cut the train station sequence together, but the opposite is true. I'm interested only in good ideas. When I take an actress like Carla Gugino, who's a brunette with short hair, and I need to completely transform her appearance, I dress her in white and put a blonde wig on her. The fact that Hitchcock discovered in *Marnie* that you can completely alter someone's personality by changing the colour of their hair may have influenced me – but only unconsciously.

Snake Eyes is a very Langian film. The moral of Lang's film Fury *is "Never believe what you see." Do you like that film?*

Is that the one with Spencer Tracy? I don't really remember it.

Fritz Lang, like you, spent his career questioning the power of images. But he didn't have the same technical means as you, and at the time images weren't as ubiquitous as they are today, which is why is seems to us that your work is more relevant than ever. It's odd that people aren't more receptive to your approach.

Hitchcock went through that too. Before the French critics took an interest in him and told the world that his films were far more complex than anyone could imagine, in America he was considered nothing more than a clever technician and a showman. By the time people finally came around he was sixty years old. It's kind of the same thing in my case. What I want to say with my films seems clear and readable to me, but everyone always throws out the same clichés when talking about my work. Most of the reviews of *Snake Eyes* criticised me for revealing the identity of the villain before the end, because from that moment on, they said, the film was no longer interesting. But I wasn't making a whodunit. *Snake Eyes* is about the moral dilemma Ricky Santoro finds himself in. To make that clear, early on I had to let the audience know that Gary Sinise is a traitor. The film is about someone who suddenly finds out who he really is and what he has to do to keep from going the way of the bad guys.

American critics found the film to be primarily an exercise in style. There appears to be an obvious disconnection between what people expect from you and what you give them.

That's true.

But that wasn't the case in the Seventies. What changed?

I don't think there's anything left to expect from critics in the United States. There's no one interesting to read anymore. The good ones usually write in marginal publications and the most widely read ones aren't any good.

Presumably you enjoy talking to colleagues about cinema?

Absolutely. I talked about *Snake Eyes* with Spielberg, who understood it all. I'm a director who likes to please other directors. A few smart critics understood the film, but the others... I don't even know if you can call them critics anymore. They don't talk about what's on screen. It all just seems to go over their heads.

It's as if they were writing about an opera by focusing on the libretto alone.

Exactly. Or they make a big deal about Steadicam shots, which is the kind of thing they really adore. "What a great shot! But why did you do it that way?" For me it's obvious. I try to show the space; it's my way of understanding the universe in which the characters live. I try to show things as they see them. It's not about creating some cool shot by keeping the camera rolling as long as possible. Look at *Dionysus in 69*, where I was already showing the space in which the theatrical performance took place. I let myself be guided by what's happening.

Critics and the public seemed to expect Snake Eyes *to be an action movie, like* The Rock *or* Face/Off. *They were even more disappointed because Nicolas Cage's character is passive, the opposite of an action star.*

Nevertheless, from that point of view the film's trailer was spot on. *Snake Eyes* isn't an action movie; it was sold as a police investigation with a puzzle to solve, and in the trailer you can't tell who committed the crime. I think the film wasn't successful because it has a film noir feel to it, and that kind of cinema isn't very popular with audiences because it offers a dark view of humanity that Americans generally don't want to deal with. They prefer to see Eliot Ness win at the end, and also aren't too wild about the hero going to jail. *Snake Eyes* made about $56 million dollars in the United States; it's the fourth highest grossing film of my career. "We're disappointed," the folks at Paramount said to me. "The film didn't do what we hoped."

We heard that you wanted a different ending.

Not true. Originally there was a wave that washed Gary Sinise's character away. We tested that version but audiences felt that it came out of nowhere. You see those kinds of things all the time on the boardwalk during storms, but the public, who have seen dozens of disaster movies, took it for a tidal wave, so I cut it and shot the scene where Gary commits suicide, as filmed from the point of view of the news camera.

That's a shame, because the wave would have given the hurricane a reason to exist. In the current version it has no dramatic role.

You can look at it that way, but I thought long and hard about the problem. In my first version the bad guy is punished by divine justice. God creates a wave that punishes Gary Sinise. The problem is that today in America nobody believes in God or the Burning Bush. A movie I like a lot, Paul Thomas Anderson's *Magnolia*, was criticised for its ending, where millions of frogs fall from the sky. But I like it.

Snake Eyes *is full of biblical references. The hurricane is called Jezebel and Atlantic City is compared to Sodom and Gomorrah. It's certainly no coincidence that the theme song at the end is called "Sin City."*

Clearly you come from a very Catholic country where such things still have meaning, which is no longer the case in America. The wave certainly made sense to me, which is why we wrote the scene where Gary tells Nic that he saw the sailors drown. He knows that's his own fate. As it is in the film now, the hurricane puts Gary in a situation where he's forced to kill himself. The news camera is pointing right at him when he tries to kill Carla and Nic. That's what pushes him to suicide. It's less contrived and less symbolic than God descending from Heaven in the form of a wave to sweep away the bad guy. God still intervenes, but in a more subtle way.

But your world is a world without God. The characters think they're God.

Yes, but in *Snake Eyes* the forces of nature intervene to purify the corruption that plagues the world of the casino.

It's true that in your films, storm scenes often accompany a denouement or a revelation. In Dressed to Kill, *Peter uncovers Dr. Elliot's secret during a storm. In* Casualties of War, *the rape takes place in the rain, and in* Mission: Impossible *it's pouring when Tom Cruise goes to the train station to meet Jon Voight. The tornado in* Mission to Mars *precedes the appearance of the humanoid figure.*

Yes, that's very true. For me, it's a bit like the intrusion of a divine force in the corrupted world of humans. These deluges are often inexplicable; they defy logic and help morality triumph. I really believe in that.

Ryuichi Sakamoto did the music for Snake Eyes. *Was it his score for Nagisa Oshima's* Merry Christmas, Mr. Lawrence *that first drew your attention?*

No, it was his work on Bertolucci's *Little Buddha* that really intrigued me. I listened to it endlessly at the time; he really did some wonderful things there. I have lots of his music. He's very imaginative and hard-working, plus he lives close to me in New York. Like most contemporary composers, Sakamoto works on a computer. In the old days you had to go to a studio; that was especially the case with Bernard Herrmann, who never let you hear anything ahead of time. I would go see Sakamoto and he would play things directly from his computer, and by the time we got to the studio, I knew the music by heart.

Why did you use a pop song for the end credits?

I wanted the ending to bring us back to today's world. As the final shot is very long, a song seemed to fit nicely. As with the end of *Casualties of War* I wanted to suggest that after having lived through hell, the hero has redeemed himself. He's paid the price. Life goes on.

The lyrics of the song are somehow connected to the story of the film.

That's right, but the tone of the song is much lighter than Sakamoto's music. The instrumentation brings something very rock-like and contemporary into the film; it's a breath of fresh air. It was ideal for the ending, which is the only daytime exterior shot in the whole film. It helps round out the story.

How was the shooting of Snake Eyes *in Montreal?*

I loved shooting there; it's a great town. We set up in the old Forum, which is huge, and built our sets there. Nicolas Cage couldn't have been nicer. He works hard and is always focused. Gary Sinise too. The other actors were good too. Everything went well. I love working in Canada and went back there for *Mission to Mars*.

A question about the cinematography. We read that you lit the stage of the boxing stadium so that some parts of the stands were in complete darkness.

We had to make it look like there were fourteen thousand people in that space, even though we only had two thousand extras, so we spent time moving them around according to where the camera was.

Gary Sinise was the last actor hired. Initially you thought of Al Pacino.

We developed a script for Al, but in the end we decided that these two characters should be the same age; we weren't interested in the little brother-big brother thing. Gary Sinise was available, and since he's a very good actor we said to ourselves, "Why not him?"

Have you seen his films as a director? Miles from Home *and* Of Mice and Men?

Yes, he's talented.

Is there a difference in the way you work with an actor who is also a director?

He brings you ideas and understands what the camera sees. He doesn't necessarily need to discuss everything with the director. Gary is a smart guy and we both worked hard to give some depth to his character. He was very much against being swept away by the wave at the end, and was right to be so insistent.

Carlito's Way, Mission: Impossible *and* Snake Eyes *form a trilogy about betrayal. You seem more pessimistic than ever about human relationships and friendship.*

True. And yet nobody has ever betrayed me; I have the same friends I did thirty years ago. Why am I more cynical these days? I can't answer that question. For me, betrayal in these films is something symbolic; it's a reference to Judas and Christ. To tell you the truth it doesn't reflect my personal life at all. In my professional life, on the other hand, I've been in constant contact with betrayal. You're with a colleague, you work with him on a script, he swears he's committed to the project, and then he meets someone who offers him a lot of money to go work with him instead and he bails on you, only to realise that he's made a terrible mistake and that this other project isn't going anywhere. He sold out because of pure greed. I have a lot of empathy for the kind of character who gets destroyed by temptation. Hollywood is built on the myth that one day someone will make you a star or buy your script for a fortune. But that's mostly an illusion.

Another director had just withdrawn from Mission to Mars *when you were hired for the job.*

My agent sent me the script when I was struggling to find financing for *Nazi Gold* and *Mr. Hughes*. I was told that the first director who was offered the script, Gore Verbinski, backed out due to artistic differences with the studio. Apparently he wanted to shoot the entire film in the desert, but with a budget of $130 million, and the studio got cold feet. "Sorry guys," Verbinski told them, "it can't be done any other way." Then he quit. I liked the script and thought it was a good story, so I jumped on board.

Are you interested in Mars?

Not really, but the story was exciting. It kept me on the edge of my seat and I wanted to know what was going to happen at the end. The producer was happy that I signed on when I did because the studio had given a green light and the design team had been hired. All they needed was a director. When I showed up everyone was looking to me to get it off the ground, and on my very first day I started storyboarding. We were full speed ahead and finished two weeks ahead of schedule.

Did the story remind you of the science fiction novels you loved as a child.

Yes, especially *Red Planet Mars*. I was crazy about those kinds of books. My brothers too.

Why did you wait so long before getting into science fiction?

There are actually two sci-fi projects I've always wanted to do. The first one you know about – an adaptation of Alfred Bester's *Demolished Man*. I never got around to that. The second is a remake of *Forbidden Planet* by Fred M. Wilcox. The invisible creature is such a great idea for a monster movie. Other filmmakers have done it, more or less, with films like *Sphere*, *Predator* and *Solaris*.

Mission to Mars *is highly realistic in terms of equipment and technology.*

The production had already done a lot of work in conjunction with NASA's Jet Propulsion Laboratory. A lot of books have been written about Mars, and the people I was working with were familiar with them all. Since the film's mission is a NASA one, we had to be as realistic as possible. NASA wouldn't have allowed us to put their logo in the film otherwise, and all the designs – rovers, ships, everything – came out of the NASA design office. We added a few details, but the essential elements were based on real-life plans. In the script, mission control was at Cape Canaveral, but I moved it to the space station.

You've said that unlike Kubrick or Spielberg, you aren't too comfortable designing imaginary worlds and that you prefer shooting in real settings. This film proves the opposite.

It's true I like working in environments that actually exist, certainly where there is interesting architecture, but in the case of *Mission to Mars* I got my feet wet to see what would come of it. Apart from the barbecue scene at the beginning, everything in the film was shot on a set. I realise today how remarkable George Lucas' work is. There's nothing more difficult than creating a believable universe from scratch.

Did you make any changes to the script?

Not many. The funny thing is that Ted Tally, the screenwriter I worked with on the rewrite, didn't get a credit, even though he wrote my favourite draft. After that a new version was written but I didn't like it, so we went back to Ted, who fortunately was available. He and I worked on two or three drafts, essentially reworking the characters, Gary Sinise's inner journey in particular. But the core of the story never changed.

Was the scene of Woody Blake's death in the script you were given?

That's a powerful scene. Yes, it was always in there.

It's a typical De Palma scene. Someone is going to die and no one can save him.

True. When I'm not making up scenes like that I find them elsewhere.

The moment in Alfonso Cuarón's Gravity, *when George Clooney sacrifices himself to save Sandra Bullock, reminds us of* Mission to Mars. *It's as if Cuarón decided to build an entire movie around the best scene in your film.*

Perhaps, but *Gravity* is completely unrealistic. It's fun to watch, but it's complete fiction. On *Mission to Mars* we needed NASA's approval and had real astronauts on set every day. We couldn't have shown just anything. But you're probably right... Alfonso Cuarón must be a fan of my films.

What's unusual about the film is the abrupt transition to Mars. You start with the barbecue scene, which introduces all the characters, then you jump to Luke, played by Don Cheadle, at work on Mars. Other filmmakers would have shown the moment when man first steps onto the Red Planet.

I wanted to avoid the clichés, like a rocket launch or the trip to Mars, and especially the spaceship landing, which we've seen in so many movies. After the barbecue we jump directly to Mars; I wanted that abrupt transition because I wanted the audience to be struck by the enormity of the environment. As you say, the first scene, on Earth, is there to establish the relationships between characters. I wanted the camera to move and set a fast rhythm so that we feel that all these characters – including Gary Sinise, the one who doesn't go with them – are united by a common project. The funny thing is that Gary had already played an astronaut who stayed down on Earth in *Apollo 13*. He stares at a child's drawing and then – *wham!* – we're on Mars. I also wanted to be sparing with the Martian landscapes. The rarer that kind of shot, the stronger the impression it makes, which is why it's important to start with an especially powerful image which sets the scene. From there you can move into the story. There are four essential settings on Mars: the great canyon of Cydonia where the robot evolves, the place where we find Luke working, the mound that covers the Figure of Mars, and the spot where the astronauts' settlement is located.

Where did you shoot the Martian scenes?

In Vancouver, where a large cement pit was transformed into the surface of Mars. We had to hope it wouldn't rain. The very first scene on Mars was filmed in Jordan, in Aqaba, by Eric Schwab, my second unit director, based on my storyboards.

Since Mission: Impossible *you seem to be increasingly attracted to confined, sanitised and artificial worlds.*

That's just a coincidence. If I had directed *Nazi Gold* or *Mr. Hughes* you wouldn't have said that. But it's true that thanks to digital imaging it's now possible to create interesting universes from scratch, which is always exciting for a director, especially when you're working on a spy movie like *Mission: Impossible* or on *Snake Eyes*, where you have to make an entire universe come to life inside a casino. *Mission to Mars* is set on Mars and in space, so I didn't have a choice.

What these three films have in common is that they explore psychological spaces. Mission to Mars, *after all, ends inside of a huge artificial head.*

They're artificial spaces reflecting the souls of the characters who inhabit them. But it's all somewhat dictated by circumstance. No filmmaker can make a career change and say, "From now on I'm only going to film psychological spaces."

The huge humanoid head on the surface of Mars is one of the film's most striking images.

I didn't invent anything; it's all part of the mythology of Mars. For more than twenty years the images taken by probes have highlighted a gigantic formation that looks like a human head. Its nickname is "The Face on Mars." If you do an Internet search for "Face on Mars" you'll get dozens of sites dedicated to it, not to mention books. In the original *Mission to Mars* script there was no mention of this figure; it was just a dome. I brought the idea up during the rewrites, then asked my art director to make it look like a sleeping goddess. I also came up with the idea of the energy field, the tornado that sucks up the astronauts on the first mission. In the script all we wrote was that something was throwing them to the ground. To tell you the truth, I really liked this theory of the figure. I find it believable. If you belonged to an extra-terrestrial species, if you had fled your planet and wanted to leave a trace of your journey to other species, what would it be? A monument in the shape of a humanoid head. It's very logical to me.

How did you design the creature that the astronauts meet in the planetarium?

I wanted it to have human form but at the same time be different from us. What inspired its appearance was the primitive warrior from the movie *King Solomon's Mines*; I liked his angular, elongated face. I also wanted the creature to be purely digital, like the planets in the show they're watching. After all, these astronauts are watching a virtual planetarium show, and this creature, also virtual, is their guide. I didn't want to use a puppet, like they did in *Star Wars*. I also wanted her to be a woman. It was something different.

Did you know that "Mission to Mars" is the name of one of the first attractions at Disneyland?

I didn't know that. But then again, "Mission to Mars" is a much-used term. Type it into your search engine and you'll get dozens of hits.

You're famous for not liking expository dialogue, yet the script for Mission to Mars *is full of it.*

Not really. There's a lot of talking in the opening scene at the barbecue, but it introduces the characters, which makes sense. The rest of the talking in the film is mostly scientific gibberish. The action is by no means conveyed exclusively through dialogue.

It was the second time, after Mission: Impossible, *that you used special effects shots. You told us you were exhausted by your stay at George Lucas' Skywalker Ranch in 1996. Was it the same thing this time?*

It was worse actually, which is why I left as soon as the job was done. I couldn't stand looking at those images any more. I watched the first scene on Mars, with the robot going through the canyon, for a whole year. There are six hundred special effects in the film, which had a budget of $100 million. When you know that George Lucas' *Phantom Menace* had more than two thousand of them, you understand why Lucas is the only one who can make the *Star Wars* movies. No one else could afford it. ILM [Industrial Light & Magic], Lucas' special effects company, was created by George to work on his own films.

Tim Burton says that computer-generated imagery doesn't have the same emotion as live action.

I disagree. The technology was created for artists to use however they want. You can use it to make hyper-realistic movies like mine, or fantasies like *Mars Attacks!*

Were the actors already cast when you became involved in the film?

Gary Sinise and Don Cheadle were under contract, which was good news for me. I cast the other actors fairly quickly. I knew Tim Robbins because I had met him during the preparation of *Snake Eyes* and for a while thought about giving him the role that Gary Sinise eventually played, but ended up suggesting him for the role of Woody. I had seen Jerry O'Connell in several films; he was one of the first to sign on. For the role of Terri I went to Monica Potter, who ended up skipping out on us, and at the very last moment we found Connie Nielsen. Armin Mueller-Stahl was also my suggestion.

You reunited with Ennio Morricone for Mission to Mars.

I had wanted to work with him again for years. I love the piece he composed for the astronauts entering the planetarium, and was very moved when I first heard it. It's one of my best memories of the film.

What did you think of George Lucas' Star Wars: The Phantom Menace?

I thought it was amazing. These days I'm better able to really appreciate it. It's a shame that George never gets credit for the extraordinary visuals he creates for his films. He and I get the same kind of criticism for our films, but what people don't understand is that you have to look at *The Phantom Menace* and *Mission to Mars* through the eyes of a child. George's film is clearly a children's film, unlike the first *Star Wars* film, which was geared to an older audience and full of wisecracking characters. *The Phantom Menace* and my film aren't in the least cynical; they're full of innocence. You have to leave your prejudices outside when you watch *Mission to Mars*. If you aren't able to buy into it – and most critics weren't – you won't enjoy the film.

Mission to Mars is more oriented towards adults than The Phantom Menace.

That's what French critics have told me. American critics don't even see what's in a movie anymore. If they know it's one of mine, they roll out their usual stuff: "De Palma has stolen this time from so-and-so." I want to say to them, "Look at the film for God's sake! It has nothing to do with *2001*!"

Some scenes do evoke the visual universe of Kubrick's film. The interior of the ship, in the shape of a centrifuge, reminds us of the Discovery from 2001 *and the end, set in an immaculate white space, recalls the white room in which Keir Dullea sees himself. When the door of the planetarium opens, it's as if a black monolith appears.*

Why did I also use a centrifuge? Because, quite simply, it's boring to shoot actors in an actual zero gravity cylinder, like they did with *Apollo 13*. And the result isn't very visual – at least I don't think so. Can you imagine the explanatory scenes in my film, all that dialogue about the Figure of Mars, if the actors had spoken it in zero gravity? It would have been ridiculous. As for the monolith, the one in *2001* is a very specific concept. We see it the first time standing in the middle of a group of apes, and it's precisely this incongruous juxtaposition that makes the scene so special. I didn't do anything like that in *Mission to Mars*. Again, I took the existing mythology of Mars and the Figure, and imagined that inside the Figure was a large dome. The pristine white room you're talking about is the antechamber of the planetarium. I was forced to shoot fast and the set design team didn't have time to build me the set that should have been in that antechamber, so I told them just to paint it white. It was the easiest thing to do.

Was there pressure to release Mission to Mars *before Anthony Hoffman's film* Red Planet?

Yes, but it was always going to be released before that film. Forcing me to be ready for a March 10, 2000 release was ridiculous.

Do you agree with the film's thesis that life originated on Mars and was brought to Earth?

Absolutely. The script was inspired by serious theories.

It's also what L. Ron Hubbard, founder of the Church of Scientology, believes.

Really? I'm glad to know I'm on the same wavelength as the Scientologists... I've learned something.

What's new in Mission to Mars *is all those genuinely decent characters.*

That's another reason why I made the film. I was getting a bit tired of the cynicism that my previous films were full of. Do I really want to dig ever deeper into the corruption of the world? I mean, is it possible to be any more cynical than *Snake Eyes*?

You might just manage it with the Howard Hughes story.

Perhaps. In any case, *Mission to Mars* is a feel-good movie, and the portrayal of the astronauts couldn't have been any more accurate. When you talk to people who have come back from up there, they all have the same glint in their eyes. You really believe that they saw God. They've seen things that you and I will never see, which makes them very spiritual. I was fascinated by these elements and was relieved to finally be able to make a film that shows man's triumph over his environment.

Mission to Mars *is your twenty-fifth feature film. Among the filmmakers of your generation, you're one of the most prolific.*

Yes, but look at the generation that came before us. Hitchcock made about sixty films! When it comes to filmmaking, practice makes perfect. You should be constantly working, trying out new things, seeing what works and what doesn't. That's how you grow and develop. What amazes me is seeing critics applauding the way Terrence Malick or Stanley Kubrick work. Malick made some interesting films in the Seventies, but you get the impression that it's those twenty-five years when he *wasn't* making films that made him a living legend. Not making films will never make you a better director. Hitchcock or Ford were always shooting; that's what made them so good. You don't become better by doing nothing.

I know Malick well. Terry was teaching philosophy at MIT when I was promoting *Greetings*, and he told me later that it was seeing me speak to students on campus that made him want to become a filmmaker. That must have been in 1968. His first film, *Badlands*, was extraordinary, but the next one, *Days of Heaven*, wasn't nearly as successful, at least as far as I'm concerned. Say what you want about *Days of Heaven*, it just doesn't work for me. I felt that way even when I saw it for the first time, when it was released. And let's not talk about *The Thin Red Line*, which was extremely tedious. *Badlands*, though, is a masterpiece. Do you know it took more than a year to shoot? At one point they started all over again. To have that much time is a rare thing for a director.

Give me a year to shoot my film, like Stanley Kubrick did with *Eyes Wide Shut*, and you'll see what I come up with. I don't know if I would need a whole year… No, I really don't think it's a good thing for a director to have that much time. None of our elders worked under these conditions, except maybe Erich von Stroheim. Real directors don't work that way. Their careers, the rhythm of their films, evolve over time. That's the usual way things happen. What happened with *Days of Heaven* was that Malick suddenly had to work for a studio with a real schedule. He couldn't shoot seven days a week for a year; he only had six weeks. But he wasn't able to function that way. It shows in the film.

Which directors working today do you admire? A few years ago you said that one of your favourite films was Bertolucci's Last Tango in Paris.

Really? I said that? Today I would say *Run Lola Run* by Tom Tywker or maybe *The Ice Storm* by Ang Lee, which was brilliantly written and directed. Both are great films. It's becoming rarer to see such a well-constructed story. Other than that, it seems that cinema has come to the end of its rope – in its current form anyway. It's been on the decline since the 1940s. Since the group I was in that emerged in the Seventies, there hasn't been a comparable burst of talent. Every year there are a few isolated cases: Tarantino, the Coen brothers, *American Beauty*, *The Sixth Sense*, *Magnolia*, all of which I really liked, but those are exceptions. How many of our films will remain? Today, fortunately, we're able to preserve them, and with DVDs we can watch them anytime we want. The big question is whether we watch films today that decades ago were hailed as unmissable masterpieces. I have a small film collection, and the ones I watch most often are from the Forties and Fifties. I rarely watch films made in the Seventies or Eighties.

Why is that? Are they too much like yours?

I just don't think they're on par with Billy Wilder. Is there a better film than *Sunset Boulevard*? It's perfect. Cinema doesn't get any better.

At the time of Sisters *you cited Roman Polanski as a key influence.*

Polanski made his best films in the United States. When he left – like John Boorman – he let his obsessions take over and from that point on nothing he's made has been as impressive as *Rosemary's Baby* or *Chinatown*. Polanski was never better than with a Robert Towne script in his hands, produced by Robert Evans and starring Jack Nicholson. And yet, you can't imagine a more dangerous lion's den. Those guys are real snakes, and among the most venomous. They're all absolute vampires, manipulative doubledealers, but very talented too, among the best Hollywood has ever produced. Between the four of them they made *Chinatown*, which is an extraordinary film. Unfortunately you won't see them together again anytime soon; that kind of lightning strikes only once. I can't imagine what it must have been like to make that film, which is a masterpiece. Credit to Bob Evans, who had to referee all the time, because the others spent their time sabotaging each other with dirty tricks. That didn't stop them from making the most perverse, most degenerate film in the history of cinema. There is no darker, crazier or more desperate film than *Chinatown*. And there never will be.

CHAPTER NINE

FEMME FATALE – THE BLACK DAHLIA REDACTED – PASSION

How did Femme Fatale *come about?*

I had wanted to make a film noir for a while, something like Fritz Lang's *The Woman in the Window*, but with a happy ending. In my first draft the heroine takes part in a robbery on a floating casino; I had visited one of these rather incredible huge boats during a trip to Florida. After the robbery she's on the run across the country and ends up in a small town, where she meets her double. Then she sees a report about some young Silicon Valley buck, and like a shark honing in on its prey, thinks, "That's where I should go," so she seduces a Bill Gates-type tycoon and marries him.

In March 2000, I left America for Paris and was living in a hotel near the Champs-Elysées. Little by little, the idea took shape and I wrote the script pretty quickly. I ended up staying in France longer than I had planned, and as I travelled around and visited different places, I realised that it was the perfect setting for the film. I knew I could make it work there. You don't have floating casinos, but I knew I could find casinos on the French Riviera. Then I went to Cannes in 2000 for *Mission to Mars* and found myself, like every guest does, climbing the famous steps. My companion, Elli Medeiros, was wearing diamonds lent to her by the jeweller Chopard, so we were escorted by bodyguards, and I got the idea of the hold-up that opens the film, where the heroine helps to steal a piece of jewellery worn by a young woman at Cannes. My Silicon Valley billionaire was transformed into a diplomat who becomes the next U.S. ambassador to France.

How long does it take you to write a script?

When I'm on a roll, I can do a first draft in eight or ten days. Paul Schrader was great at that, writing 110 pages without interruption. *Dressed to Kill* was also written that way.

Would it have been possible to find financing for Femme Fatale *in Hollywood?*

Perhaps, but I didn't want to deal with the stupid way movies are made there these days. I didn't want to have to deal with ten agents, twenty PR people and thirty lawyers. The best American films today, like Christopher Nolan's *Memento* and David Lynch's *Mulholland Drive*, are made outside the system.

How did you choose the Paris locations?

When I arrived in Paris I walked around the city, as I usually do, pinpointing places I liked. I even rented a scooter to get around more easily. I went everywhere. For Nicolas Bardo's photomontage I was looking for somewhere that was photogenic and characteristic of the city. One possible location I looked at turned out to be too much like a picture postcard. Then Elli Medeiros suggested the neighbourhood where she was living at the time, near Place Maurice-Chevalier. That's how I found the church. Nicolas Bardo's apartment in the film is actually Elli's former sister-in-law's apartment. I liked the area and its diverse community. In the original script I had a motel, the kind you find near an airport, but I knew it wasn't quite right. Then Régis Wargnier told me about the Sheraton Hotel at Roissy-Charles-De-Gaulle, and the second I saw it I knew it was the place.

Laure had to fall from high up, then be found by the couple who take her in. I proceeded as I always do, finding settings that inspire me and then devising sequences I could shoot there. The hotel inside the airport was unlike anything I'd ever seen. I could talk about the Centre Pompidou in Paris in the same way; it's a marvel, and every time I go there I'm always thinking how much of a perfect setting it would be for a thriller. I'd love to shoot there; it's so surprising that no one has. For *Femme Fatale* all the settings had to be used twice, for the real scenes and the dreams, so I had to choose places that were immediately identifiable in order to give that sense of déjà vu that Laure experiences.

You filmed Paris very differently from the way you filmed Florence in Obsession. *You show us very little of the city.*

That was intentional. I wanted very specific exteriors. I don't like films where characters drive around endlessly; it ends up confusing things. I wanted the Parisian exteriors to look like surrealist paintings. The same ideas return again and again, even if the locations are different. It's a bit like all my films. They have different actors and different settings, but the themes, and my obsessions, are the same.

It's similar to Obsession, *which also had a sense of déjà vu and repetition of the same events several years apart.*

That's something I always seem to come back to. My initial idea was a girl on the run, someone who had done something bad and finds herself in a small town where everyone looks at her funny. When everyone takes her by the hand and says how sorry they are, she realises that she's being mistaken for someone else – her double – who eventually she meets and whose identity she assumes.

Since Sisters, *the theme of the twin has been important to you, but you've never dealt with it in such a direct way as in* Femme Fatale.

In 1987, in Florence, I met a man who was in every way the spitting image of my late brother Bruce. Since my mother's family is from that part of Italy, this guy might have been a distant relative! I can't say for sure, but it was definitely weird to see my brother's twin. From then on I became increasingly obsessed with this idea of twins, but in general I would say that a film like *Femme Fatale* comes mostly from my subconscious. The twin idea inspires and appeals to me because it's visually so powerful. As I said, *Sisters* was inspired by a picture of the Russian Siamese sisters Masha and Dasha from *Life* magazine. Likewise, this Bruce look-alike living in Florence, where I shot *Obsession*, haunted me and ended up inspiring a story.

The notion of falling is important in the film. Laure falls three times at three key moments. The first, at the Sheraton, is the end of her escape and the beginning of her entrance into Lily's world. The second is a dream where Black Tie and Racine throw her from the Debilly footbridge, ending the dream. And the third, when the truck appears, is the end of her problems and perhaps the beginning of a new life with Nicolas Bardo.

That's true. Falling must be something I associate with the phoenix. It represents a symbolic death and rebirth.

The central part of Femme Fatale *is a dream that Laure has in the bathtub, at Lily's house, which is filmed just like the rest of the film, though there are small details that make it clear that something is awry.*

Laure falls asleep at 3:35pm in the bathtub, and every clock in every location – the church in Paris, the police station – stops. The water in her bathtub overflows just before she dozes off, and when Lily arrives to commit suicide, the water in her aquarium overflows. This doesn't prevent the characters from behaving normally, because in a dream, even if strange things are happening, we usually don't pay attention to them. Everything seems quite normal, which is what happens in the film. I didn't want to shoot Laure's dream in black and white and or use fancy fades or slow motion, the kind of thing we see in lots of films. I wanted the whole sequence to look like a film noir dream. That's why the cinematography occasionally uses techniques of the genre and why Laure behaves and speaks like a character out of a film noir, like the heroine in *Double Indemnity*, the film she's watching in the opening scene.

Weren't you concerned that at the end audiences would think it was all just a dream?

It makes sense that she's dreaming, because emotionally, she's already in a dream-like state. She's being chased and has to escape. It's an image that comes up a lot in our dreams, when someone is out to get you and you wake up right as it's happening. Since she's already in a dream-like state, it seemed logical to me that the dream she has anticipates reality; in a way, it's an ominous dream. I then tried to divert the flow of things and show that this dream could be a way to change her life, and to change the typical, unhappy film noir ending. When she wakes up and sees that things are happening just as they were in the dream, she thinks that if she can stop Lily from killing herself she might have a chance of escaping her destiny, which is what happens.

But I agree with you – there's nothing more touchy for a filmmaker than that moment when the character wakes up and the audience realises they've been taken for a ride and the whole thing was just a dream. Most people really resent it. The reason it works in *Femme Fatale* is that the audience absolutely doesn't expect it. When the two bad guys throw her into the Seine and we make the connection with Laure waking up in her bathtub, audiences are completely taken by surprise, like the hand coming out of the grave at the end of *Carrie*. The most important thing was to deal with what happens after she wakes up and gives her twin, Lily, the will to live, as opposed to what she does in the dream, where Lily committing suicide triggered only one idea: "I have to take her identity!" I think Rebecca Romijn-Stamos is very good in the scene, which wasn't easy to pull off.

Laure has the possibility of intervening, unlike the dying Carlito, who sees his life flash before his eyes without being able to do anything about it.

Exactly. I've never made anything like *Femme Fatale*. It's the first time I've made a film and only afterwards noticed things in it that I was unaware of when we were filming, as if a piece of my subconscious was speaking. David Lynch's *Mulholland Drive*, which I really like, functions on a similar level. I was amazed at how much his film has in common with mine. I originally planned that the film they watch during the jewel robbery at the beginning would be *Mulholland Drive*, but David wasn't available for the three days I needed him and in the end Régis Wargnier took his place. I only recently watched *Mulholland Drive* and realise now that if David had been part of *Femme Fatale*, the irony would have been even more pronounced.

We know when the dream begins and ends in Femme Fatale, *which makes the film more linear than* Mulholland Drive.

Yes. *Mulholland Drive* is more complex – at least the dreamlike part. Scenes don't always follow each other logically in a Lynch film. But I didn't want audiences to be lost. The problem with "dream" films is that too often they're impressionistic and don't fit into any classic narrative mold. They have an internal logic unique to the author, which is why there's nothing more boring than someone telling you their dreams. For them it makes sense, but for you it's tedious nonsense. I also wanted the film noir aspect of *Femme Fatale* to disguise the fact that it's a dream. I did the same thing in *Carlito's Way* when I showed his death during the opening titles and stylised it as much as possible with music, in slow motion and black-and-white imagery, so that the audience forgets that it's watching a flashback and is taken by surprise when Benny Blanco shoots him on the platform at the end of the film. I always prefer to place dreams in some kind of specific framework.

I remember a screening of *Out of Sight* that Steven Soderbergh did in Manhattan which turned into a bit of a mess because the film wasn't quite finished and journalists had been invited. There was a dinner after the screening. I felt that the film had structural problems, but I didn't say anything because the press was there. There's a dream sequence in which Jennifer Lopez is in a bathtub. We know where the dream starts but it isn't obvious where it ends, and I told Soderbergh that he needed to let audiences know this. "That's what *you* would do," he said. "But not me."

How do you explain the photomontage that Nicolas Bardo is working on?

It's a puzzle, just like the film. Between the first photo of Laure that he takes on the steps of the church and the last one, when the truck appears, seven years go by. He helps put Laure's adventures into perspective. In a literal sense, she's a woman involved in a jewel robbery, a woman who meets her twin, and an accomplice chased by two thieves. From another perspective she's just a pawn in Nicolas' gigantic collage, which makes her trajectory even more ironic. All the dramas she has dreamt or lived are used to fill spaces in the photo collage of a man she barely knows. It's like the end of *Blow Out*, when the whole experience with John Travolta and Nancy Allen culminates in a B-movie shriek.

The finale is also the first real encounter between Nicolas and Laure. You took them, and us, through a wildly twisted story, all so that a man could approach a woman in the street.

Exactly right. Maybe the whole story exists only so that Nicolas meets Laure. It's like Kurt Vonnegut's *Sirens of Titan*, a book I've always liked. But for me what's most important is the optimism of the epilogue, which doesn't happen very often in film noir. *L.A. Confidential* – a brilliant adaptation of an extremely dense novel – comes to mind.

Did you have trouble finding the actors for Femme Fatale?

Antonio Banderas was hesitant at first, to the point that after reading the script he came up with a lot of ideas to flesh out his character, which he didn't find very interesting on the page. I listened to him calmly, then said no to all his suggestions. He wasn't too happy about that, but the good thing about Antonio is that he trusted me. "OK," he said, "I'm going to do exactly what you want. I think you're wrong, but I'm willing to try to be a means to an end." When he saw the film his doubts went out the window. The same goes for Rebecca Romijn-Stamos, who during filming said that she didn't really understand the script, but that didn't stop her from giving it everything she had. She plays on several levels, which isn't easy to do, but she's very believable in the role.

The first person I thought of was Uma Thurman. I've known her for a long time and thought about giving her the role that Melanie Griffith played in *The Bonfire of the Vanities*. When I suggested *Femme Fatale*, Uma had just signed on to play the lead in Quentin Tarantino's next film, *Kill Bill*. Then Tarantino's film was delayed by an actors' strike and Uma got pregnant. I auditioned lots of known and unknown actresses until, at the last minute, I found Rebecca. Before I cast her I had three girls in mind: one English, one French and one Spanish. The problem is that the film is called *Femme Fatale* and I needed someone with the right look – someone fascinating, like Rita Hayworth, someone you could lose your mind over. It didn't matter if she was famous or not. A girl like that doesn't come easy, believe me. Rebecca has several different looks in the film. There's the Grace Kelly look at the beginning, at Cannes, then the brunette girl, the blonde girl on the barge, the depressed brunette and the blonde girl in the last scene, which is yet another look. She had to be alluring at all times – and she certainly was.

Did you audition many actors before deciding on Edouard Montoute and Eriq Ebouaney?

I don't remember if those roles were written specifically for black actors, but Edouard and Eriq were great. Eriq, in particular, reminded me of a black Marlon Brando. And there are so few roles written for actors of colour anyway.

The jewel robbery sequence at the Cannes Film Festival is one of the most exhilarating you've ever filmed.

It took us three nights. I had a good Steadicam operator on the film, but in order to get that long take done fast, I flew in my favourite technician, Larry McConkey, from the U.S. I wanted the sequence to look like *Mission: Impossible*, so that the change in tone would be even more notable when Laure meets her twin and another kind of story starts. This shift is also reflected in the soundtrack. The credits use Miklós Rósza's music from Billy Wilder's *Double Indemnity*, which she is watching on television; then there's the Ryuichi Sakamoto piece that accompanies the jewel theft, interrupted from time to time by Patrick Doyle's music for Régis Wargnier's *East/West*, which is projected in the Palais. And there's the Elli Medeiros song that the two girls listen to when they're fooling around in the bathroom, and even Saint-Saëns, the intro from *Carnival of the Animals*, which is the anthem of the Cannes Festival.

Sakamoto's music for the scene in Cannes delicately distinguishes itself from Ravel's "Bolero." Laure was originally going to be listening to "Bolero" on her Walkman. Sakamoto had composed a long *Mission: Impossible*-like piece to accompany the jewel robbery and corresponding action. It was a huge job that took him months, and I was extremely embarrassed when I told him it didn't work. The scene is about seduction, so the music had to establish some kind of sexually infused atmosphere. The diamond robbery is secondary; it's not what the music should primarily communicate. It was me who thought of using "Bolero," and it worked immediately, because not only does it fit the images perfectly, it also shows that the film is about to move in a different direction. I asked Sakamoto to compose a variation, and he did a great job. It's a long piece, more than ten minutes. You have to listen to the whole thing to grasp just how subtle it is. I used it again for the end credits because I thought it was a shame to use only parts of it during the robbery scene.

The music ends when the power in the Palace cuts out.

The worst nightmare for a director – a power failure during the screening of your film! I witnessed this very thing while watching Jean-Jacques Beineix's *Mortal Transfer* at the Viennale. A blackout on reel two.

Was Ryuichi Sakamoto your first choice for Femme Fatale?

Originally I wanted Eric Serra, but he was busy with *Rollerball*. He really wanted to do *Femme Fatale* and I would have loved to have him, but he couldn't do both. Then I went to Patrick Doyle, who liked the film but couldn't compose the music in the time frame I wanted because he was recovering from a serious illness. There was a lot of work to be done, so I was lucky Sakamoto was available. He spent four months on the job. It helped that we knew each other and had worked together before, because I can put off a composer who meets me for the first time. I'm very demanding.

Femme Fatale *is more sensual and erotic than your last films, where the female roles were secondary.*

I like to film attractive women. What's more beautiful than Rie Rasmussen walking? She's so sexual. Once you start looking you can't take your eyes off her. Even the way she walks is incredible. Same thing for Rebecca in the striptease scene, which was her idea. She rehearsed with choreographer Mia Frye, without me interfering, and then showed me what they had done. All I did was film it. This isn't the first time I've filmed a woman dancing sexually, but no one comes close to Rebecca in that scene.

Hiring a French director of photography, Thierry Arbogast, presumably wasn't a decision taken lightly.

Arbogast came highly recommended. He's one of the best in Europe and shot a lot of films that I like, Besson's in particular and *The Apartment* by Gilles Mimouni. He has a great team. We had some focusing issues at the start and I wanted to fire the technician responsible, but unions are so strong in France that I wasn't allowed to. I did eventually manage to get rid of him and his crew stopped working for a few hours, which was very annoying. But apart from that, everything went smoothly. Arbogast works fast, which is important to me. We shot the film in ten weeks, on time and within budget.

Nicolas Bardo in Femme Fatale *says that after his divorce, he left home and came to France to start a new life and "reinvent" himself. We could imagine you saying the same thing.*

Absolutely. It's important for an artist to change his habits and explore new places as he gets older. I'm happy that I got out of the American system for a while after shooting several big films there in a row, which was exhausting. With *Femme Fatale*, I felt like I was back in my *Blow Out* days: a no-holds-barred script I had written myself, followed by meticulous preparation, like all that location scouting in Philadelphia and set construction.

Quentin Tarantino borrowed the seduction dance sequence from Femme Fatale *for* Death Proof.

That scene was created by Mia Frye, the extraordinary French choreographer who also directed the dance scene in the lesbian club in *The Black Dahlia*.

One of the challenges of Femme Fatale *was to avoid clichés when filming Paris, which is by no means easy, given that it's the most filmed city in the world.*

As much as I admire a lot of French directors, you have to face facts: most of French cinema is two people talking in a café or walking down a street. I know what I'm talking about; I've lived in Paris. I say that, and yet there's a shot of the Eiffel Tower in *Femme Fatale*.

James Ellroy's Black Dahlia *seems like the ideal story for you. There's a gruesome crime, an obsessed hero, and a woman who reminds him of someone else. It covers all the bases.*

I discovered the book – my first Ellroy – while promoting *Carlito's Way* in December 1993 and thought it was great, and immediately wondered what kind of a film could be adapted from it. In the Virgin Islands during the Christmas holidays that year I ran into Art Linson; I had worked with him on *The Untouchables* and *Casualties of War*. We talked about the book, which he had also read, but at the time neither of us thought we would ever actually work on an adaptation. Then, in 1997, Curtis Hanson's *L.A. Confidential* was released – a very intelligent adaptation of a complex book. Ellroy's polyphonic structure and dense plot might have been big obstacles for the big screen, but Hanson's film showed me how *The Black Dahlia* could be done. The film took three years to make. I don't think anyone wanted to finance such a dark story. Twice the money fell through, and after considering Germany and Italy, we decided to shoot in Sofia, Bulgaria because we could recreate the Los Angeles of the 1940s on a relatively small budget. Only a few exteriors were shot in Los Angeles because we couldn't rebuild everything.

Do you like Josh Friedman's script?

As you know, I was much criticised for deviating too far from Tom Wolfe's book when I made *The Bonfire of the Vanities*, both in terms of the adaptation and casting, so with *The Black Dahlia* I decided to stick as closely as possible to the novel, which isn't easy because it's a complicated story, full of subplots that aren't easy to follow. We simplified it quite a bit, but it's still quite convoluted.

The average moviegoer isn't used to that kind of elliptical narration.

It's true that audiences don't like being confused. My problem was working out how to visually reveal the characters' obsessions, which in the book aren't very dramatic. I remember saying to Linson that some of the characters Ellroy talks about don't physically appear in the story. Everyone kept asking me, with a worried look, when Bobby De Witt, who plays a key role in the Dahlia puzzle, would show up. I spent my time reassuring Linson. When De Witt arrives, things certainly get clearer.

David Fincher worked on the adaptation of Ellroy's novel with Friedman before you did. Was any of that version retained?

Nothing. I don't know anything about his script. Art Linson, who produced *Fight Club*, Fincher's fourth film, told me it was all over the place and wasn't usable as a starting point.

Fincher later directed Zodiac, *a film similar in tone to* The Black Dahlia*. As with the murder of Elizabeth Short, many people are obsessed with Zodiac's unsolved crimes.*

A murder story in which the culprit isn't named is always problematic. Audiences find it frustrating.

It's been said that one of the reasons why Fincher abandoned the project was the length of the film. He imagined a three-hour adaptation. Your film is a little over two hours.

No one forced me to make any changes. I did cut one scene, but I don't see the point in making a three-hour film. Ellroy's novel moves from one testimony to the next, but they don't actually go anywhere. We had to tighten things up, trim them down, and not get lost in digressions.

In addition to Art Linson there are twenty-one producers credited. Which of them did you really work with?

Art Linson, of course. The other names you see in the credits are there for show. There was a time when studios provided all the financing for a film and the producer made a film with the executives. Today, a producer has the control because he works mainly with bankers who like to drop by the set and be photographed with famous actors.

How was James B. Harris, the producer of Stanley Kubrick's Paths of Glory *and* The Killing, *involved?*

He was there from the start; I think he wanted to make the film himself. He had already adapted another Ellroy novel, *Blood on the Moon*, which became *Cop*, starring James Woods. Harris had a script of *The Black Dahlia*, but could never get it financed.

Formally speaking, The Black Dahlia *is the most traditional of your late films.*

What interested me was the wildly complex story. My main concern was being able to recreate it on film.

Did it take long to cast?

I auditioned a lot of actors for the role of Madeleine Linscott, including Eva Green, but Mia Kirshner made the strongest impression on me. I liked her a lot in *The L Word*. She was also originally supposed to play the role of Madeleine Linscott, but in the end I couldn't convince the producers. Since I wanted Mia to appear in the film I put her in the film as Elizabeth Short, who originally wasn't even in the script. Having her was a good choice for the film.

And Hilary Swank?

I knew her because I often saw her in New York. Hilary is too often cast in tomboyish roles, like the boxer in Clint Eastwood's *Million Dollar Baby* or the transvestite in *Boys Don't Cry*, even though she's brimming with femininity. I convinced her to explore this part of her personality openly. For the role of Lee Blanchard we had an agreement with Mark Wahlberg, but the financing stalled for six months, and when we finally got the money he wasn't available, so we had to find someone else and went to Aaron Eckhart. Josh Hartnett was already part of Fincher's project. Art asked me to meet with him and I decided to keep him. We were an independent production and it was hard to get bigger stars because we weren't able to pay their usual fee, which is why their agents didn't even bother them with our offers. They would have acted very differently if the offer had come from Warner Bros.

Which were the most complicated scenes to film?

Boxing sequences are never easy. I had to find a way of shooting the boxing scene differently from the one in *Snake Eyes*. Directing actors in the ring is like staging a ballet. There's a complexity to it; you have to watch everyone's movements very carefully at all times. At one point Aaron Eckhart almost knocked out Josh Hartnett.

How was it filming in Bulgaria?

Very good, very easy. I relied a lot on my director of photography Vilmos Zsigmond, who I hadn't worked with since *The Bonfire of the Vanities*, and also Dante Ferretti, an exceptional set designer.

The Black Dahlia *was your final collaboration with Zsigmond, who died in 2016.*

Our work together on *Obsession*, *Blow Out* and *The Bonfire of the Vanities* always went very smoothly, but by the time of *The Black Dahlia* Vilmos had changed and was doing things on his own, sometimes without letting me know, which created tension between us. For one shot with a crane he used a second camera, which as you know is something I never do, so I asked him to get rid of it, which led to an argument. His work on *The Black Dahlia* is still great, but he wanted to do things on his own, which doesn't go down too well with me. It's like when Robert De Niro didn't learn his lines for *The Untouchables*, even though we were paying him a fortune. I remember preparing a shot where I had to get very close to him with the camera. I didn't want to cut the shot when we were editing, but because he didn't know his lines I was forced to use a cutaway.

What do you think of De Niro's recent career choices, like Dirty Grandpa?

I don't get it. It's not as if he needs the money. He must be bored and just wants to keep working, whatever the role. Pacino's the same. But why waste talent like that? It would be like me directing a commercial. What's the point of using your skills just to make money? Apart from that incident on *The Untouchables*, I've always had a good relationship with Bob. It goes wrong when actors start directing other actors for you, like Bruce Willis during *The Bonfire of the Vanities* or Cliff Robertson in *Obsession*. It can happen with screenwriters too. On *Scarface*, Oliver Stone would come to the set and talk with Al, and in the end I had to get rid of him. You never want to let that happen because you can lose control of the film, which is what happened to me with *Get to Know Your Rabbit* with Tom Smothers, who didn't trust me.

You've worked with a number of actor-directors: Orson Welles, John Cassavetes, Robert De Niro, Sean Penn, Keith Gordon, Tim Robbins, Gary Sinise. Are they difficult to handle?

Quite the opposite; I find it easier. An actor who directs is aware of the problems I might be dealing with, which can make things smoother for me. Keith Gordon hadn't yet directed anything when I directed him, but he already understood what I was doing.

More so than L.A. Confidential, *the reference for* The Black Dahlia – *which is about a corrupt city and is based on a true story – seems to be Polanski's* Chinatown.

Absolutely. We're talking about an era when there was staggering corruption in the LAPD. The quintessential Ellroy character is concealing a dark side. This is pretty typical in the contemporary American noir novel, where everyone lies to everyone else. Kay, the character played by Scarlett Johansson, is a lying machine. We never know what makes Lee Blanchard, played by Aaron Eckhart, so crazy. The only honest person in the film is Elizabeth Short, which I why I beefed up the character. Everyone else is a cheat and a liar.

As with Jack Nicholson's private eye in Chinatown, *Bucky Bleichert is taken for a ride for much of the film.*

Bucky doesn't understand what has happened until the end of the movie. Like Nicholson in *Chinatown*, it's a woman who provides him with solutions to the puzzle he's confronted with.

Universal distributed the film in the United States. Did they try to meddle with your edit?

Of course. They asked questions like, "Why doesn't Bucky understand what's going on with the Black Dahlia right away?" That's actually a good question. But it has nothing to do with the novel or the movie. Bucky first thinks of how certain people could politically take advantage of the murder of the Dahlia. But after the murder of Lee Blanchard, it's the love triangle he forms with Kay and Madeleine that preoccupies him.

Billy Wilder's Sunset Boulevard, *one of your favourite films, seems to have been another of your influences for* The Black Dahlia. *The scene where Bucky meets Madeleine Linscott's family is like William Holden entering Norma Desmond's home.*

That's in Ellroy's novel, but it did make me think of William Holden's first meeting with Norma Desmond in *Sunset Boulevard*, when she mistakes him for the person in charge of her chimp's funeral. With a scene like that, audiences immediately realise that this is a complete madhouse. I wanted the Linscotts' home to have the same effect on the viewer: you're entering an insane asylum. I like the way Ellroy describes this passage in the novel; it's a real comic opera and not easy to render on screen. That's when I had the idea of filming the scene with a subjective camera, so that audiences, at the same time as Bucky, have the impression of being stared at by crazy people. Mrs. Linscott staring at him as if he were a moron, a stuffed dog with a newspaper in his mouth, and Hilary Swank talking about the weather. Bucky has entered an asylum where the residents think insanity is the norm.

You know dysfunctional families so well, it's no wonder this scene is one of the best in the film. Fiona Shaw, who plays the mother Ramona Linscott, is extraordinary.

I had seen Fiona in various films, always in secondary roles. She's a great actress but is relatively unknown. Originally she didn't even come to audition, but I wanted to hear her speak Ramona's lines, and when she finally did, the text suddenly shifted, as if her presence had woven itself into every word. Not only was Fiona the best person for the part, she was willing to listen to my suggestions and make improvements. I had the same feeling with Vanessa Redgrave on *Mission: Impossible*, who just wanted to listen. Fiona Shaw's task in *The Black Dahlia* is complex, because she has to convey vital information about the investigation in such a grotesque way, and through a flashback as well. She does it remarkably well.

The only issue we have is the dinner scene with the actor playing Emmett Linscott. We imagined more of a father figure, like the one played by John Huston in Chinatown *– a much more recognisable face.*

John Kavanagh, from Ireland, is an excellent actor. That dinner is one of my favourite scenes in the film. The performances are all great.

A lot of people were disappointed by the film because they were expecting a film about the Dahlia. But your story is about a man's obsession with a dead woman.

I had to explain this to the executives at Universal, who kept telling me, "Can't we get to the Black Dahlia faster?" But this isn't a film about Elizabeth Short. They weren't too happy with my solution. But then it's not as if they ever read the book.

For James Ellroy, Elizabeth Short remains a corpse until the very end.

The book cleverly recounts how everyone was trying to make a career out of this corpse by unravelling the mystery of this woman's death. Ellroy had also apparently projected onto the Dahlia the memory of his mother, who was murdered when he was a child. I couldn't develop these aspects in the film, so I concentrated more on Elizabeth Short's world, the world of Hollywood. And Hollywood here is a nightmare. In an early version of the script all you saw of the Dahlia was her dismembered body. Everyone was talking about her, good and bad, but I didn't see how the viewer could identify with her and share Lee and Bucky's obsession if we didn't actually see her.

When she appears, she becomes an illusion. We already know that she's dead before she is actually murdered.

I thought of what Hitchcock created with Kim Novak in *Vertigo*, a kind of romantic illusion. Bernard Herrmann told me that he saw rushes of *Vertigo* and thought Kim Novak was incredibly sexy, so he asked Hitchcock if he could arrange a dinner with her, which Hitchcock did, and Herrmann spent an evening with her. The next day he went to see Hitchcock to explain that he couldn't believe how boring it was. "That's what happens when you fall in love with one of my illusions," said Hitchcock. *Vertigo* is so captivating because what it's really about is how a film director is able to successfully play on our perceptions and fantasies. It's why the auditions in *The Black Dahlia* are so intriguing, even though they were actually mostly improvised and shot in one take. It's like "Be Black, Baby," the Happening in *Hi, Mom!*, which feels so real. The drama doesn't artificially arise from the script; it's almost captured by accident by the camera. You feel like you're watching a documentary.

The voice of the director in the auditions is actually yours.

When Mia and I started shooting these casting sessions, I put myself in the position of an authoritarian, manipulative director, a kind of Otto Preminger character who sets out to destroy the actress in front of him. Mia perfectly understood the nature of that game. In the scene she's uncomfortable, but wants the role. One of the things I'm most proud of in the film is how she so brilliantly makes the audience wonder whether she's playing for keeps or expressing a deep sadness. Audiences find it upsetting because she's playing for real. I wanted to shoot with as few cuts as possible in order to convey this sense of truth, the feeling of genuine despair being played out right in front of us.

Looking back, are you happy with the performances?

I'm happy with what Hilary did, but it's an unusual role for her, not really in the style of a sexy femme fatale. But again, it should have been played by Mia.

That's singer k.d. lang in the scene at the Frolic Room, the lesbian club.

And the choreographer Mia Frye, who worked with me on *Femme Fatale*. Mia brought some wonderful French dancers with her, though most of the girls were recruited from classical ballets in Sofia. That was the last thing we shot in Bulgaria. Seeing k.d. lang coming down the stairs was quite something, and I remember saying to Vilmos Zsigmond, "We're going to shoot until the very moment the plane takes us home tomorrow." We filmed all night. I can't tell you how many takes we did, but we worked until the early morning, when the car took us to the airport.

There are plenty of theories about who killed Elizabeth Short. A French criminologist, Stéphane Bourgoin, wrote a book recently in which he points to a certain Jack Wilson as the culprit. Before him, Steve Hodel thought that his father George Hodel was the murderer.

It's like the Kennedy assassination; everyone has their theory and the debates are never-ending. And in this case we're in Hollywood, the land of illusion. The two cops in the film are obsessed in the same way that Robert De Niro is with the Kennedy assassination in *Hi, Mom!* Elizabeth Short found herself in the wrong place at the wrong time; it's a series of unfortunate circumstances. She was murdered, and it was only weeks later that her body was discovered on Norton Avenue, in an abandoned lot. Her murderer disappeared or was killed. We'll never know what really happened. I think it's the medical examiner's photograph of the dismembered girl and her aspirations to become an actress that kept the legend alive. It's such a strange story. All her life Elizabeth Short wanted to be a star, but she had to die, disfigured, to finally make that dream come true, without ever knowing that it did. I'm still very touched by the moment when Mia Kirschner turns to the camera and says, "I'm told that I'm very photogenic." It's an improvised line, you know, but I can't get it out of my head, because even though she didn't know it, nobody was more photogenic than Elizabeth Short. That's why I saved the image of her body until the end of the film, because I know that nobody who sees it can ever forget it.

You included references to Paul Leni's Victor Hugo adaptation of The Man Who Laughs. *In Ellroy's novel there's an allusion to Gwynplaine, the main character of Hugo's novel, and his terrible grin.*

I wanted to go back to the source. In Ellroy's novel, as you know, the key to the puzzle lies in a burlesque Keystone movie, part of which is filmed in a bedroom where the Black Dahlia porn film was also shot, but I wanted to come up with something more interesting, more disturbing, and landed on *The Man Who Laughs*, which I had never actually seen. I had a long discussion about it with screenwriter Josh Friedman, who questioned the whole thing, but I checked to see if the characters in the story might have seen Paul Leni's film. It turns out that there were indeed silent movie theatres in the Forties.

The silent film influence can be seen not only in the use of Leni's film but also in the way you film certain characters. William Finley, who plays Emmett Linscott's ex-partner Georgie, who reveals himself to be Elizabeth Short's murderer, has a very unique look.

It's comparable to Conrad Veidt in *The Man Who Laughs*. Once you've seen that face, it's impossible to forget. From *Dionysus in 69* to *Sisters* and *Phantom of the Paradise*, I always directed William Finley as if he were a silent expressionist actor. Everyone in *The Black Dahlia* talks about Georgie – who he is, where he comes from – and when he does finally show up, the audience is struck by what he looks like.

Are you happy with the soundtrack for The Black Dahlia?

Originally I wanted James Horner, but couldn't get him. I'm very happy with Mark Isham's music.

That trumpet is an obvious tribute to Jerry Goldsmith's Chinatown *score. Wouldn't you have preferred to work with Goldsmith instead?*

No. *The Black Dahlia* needed a trumpet. Mark Isham plays it himself.

How did you get along with James Ellroy?

He got involved during the release by coming to Deauville and Venice with us and saying good things about the film.

Today he's more critical.

At the time he seemed to like it, but maybe he was being insincere or has since changed his mind. I've had that kind of experience with screenwriters or writers whose work I've adapted.

Tell us about the novel you wrote.

It's a political thriller based on an idea I had for a screenplay. I wrote it with my partner Susan Lehman. I'm good at plot and dialogue, she's good with characters. Everything else we wrote together. We sent it to one of my agents at ICM who didn't know what to do with it, though I think it's very commercial material. Since I'm so liked in France I thought maybe I could get it published in your country. I sent the manuscript to a friend in Paris who recommended a French publisher, so we'll see. As you get older you always have ideas, but when you're as old as I am, it's harder to put them together, so it's easier to turn them into novels. Kazan had the same problem. Our novel is similar to *Blow Out*. The main character is a senator running for office. The antagonist is his evil campaign manager, and there's also a photographer who is hired to work on a film that's the French version of *Vertigo*. As you know, *Vertigo* is based on a French novel by Boileau-Narcejac. I had a lot of fun writing it.

After The Black Dahlia *you were supposed to make another film with the producer of* Femme Fatale, *Tarak Ben Ammar, a thriller called* Toyer *that in the end didn't happen. What was it about?*

It's based on a play by Gardner McKay, the story of a psychopath who confronts women in strange way. He doesn't kill or rape; he puts them in an induced coma, which means he somehow avoids prosecution. A neurologist and a journalist team up to stop him. The original play was set in Los Angeles, but my version takes place in Venice during carnival. At that time I was working with Steven Zaillian on *American Gangster*, but after a long while dropped out because the producers weren't going to give me final cut. In the end Ridley Scott directed the film, which wasn't good. I was very familiar with the story. Years earlier, while I was working on *Prince of the City*, I met several people who knew the real Frank Lucas, the heroin dealer in the film.

There was also talk of a prequel to The Untouchables, *which you were to supposed to make around 2007.*

Capone Rising centred on the relationship between Capone and Malone, the cop played by Sean Connery in *The Untouchables*. The script, which was rewritten by David Rabe, was excellent. Nicolas Cage was supposed to play Malone, but we could never find a young Capone. I suggested Sean Penn, who would have been great, but he's too busy directing. Good for him. He's carving out a career as a director, though it's time he realised that his real talent is acting, not directing.

A few years ago Penn played Mickey Cohen in Gangster Squad, *a sort of ersatz* Untouchables.

Not a great film. The idea of *Capone Rising* was to show Capone winning in the end. There was an assassination scene at the opera during a performance of *Tosca* that I would have loved to film.

How did you get involved in Redacted?

At the Toronto Film Festival in 2006 I met a producer from HDNet, Mark Cuban, who said he was willing to give $5 million to certain directors to make a film of their choice, the only condition being that we shoot in high definition. I found it an interesting proposition. I had never made a digital film, so I came up with a suitable idea. Soon after that I read in the press about the incident in Mahmudiyah, Iraq, similar to the one that had inspired *Casualties of War*: American soldiers had raped a fourteen-year-old girl, burned her body, and killed her family. I started to research it, mainly on the Internet, which is packed with all kinds of information about the incident. That's when I had the idea to make a film from material available online. There would be a soldier's blog, shot with a small digital camera, video tapes from surveillance cameras, others showing interrogations, Iraqi television reports, amateur videos of opponents of the war, images shot by Al-Quaeda...

Why, after Casualties of War, *did you want to make such a similar film?*

To show that what happened in Vietnam was also happening in Iraq. It's the same metaphor. Through the martyrdom of a young girl, the rape of an entire country can be described. The irony is that I couldn't really stick to the story or use actual conversations between soldiers that journalists had reported in the press because lawyers insisted that we would get in trouble if we did, so we had to fictionalise the whole thing, which pulled the film more towards *Casualties of War*, because I couldn't tell the real story as it actually happened. It was all pretty stupid.

Why couldn't you refer to the actual incident?

Because some of the soldiers had been tried and others hadn't. No matter how much I told the lawyers that there was no risk, that these guys were all going to be sent to prison in the end, they wouldn't listen.

You couldn't even make a documentary about it?

No, because we wouldn't have been able to insure the production, which basically means that insurance companies act as censors. This is also what led to the changes made to the photo montage at the end. I had final cut and could do whatever I wanted, but without insurance no film can be released. This led to a legal battle between me and the HDNet production company because they didn't respect my contractual right to final cut. I took them to court and lost, and as a result the film itself was redacted because they blacked out some pictures at the end.

How does your film differ from the real incident?

There aren't many differences. In reality the girl was fourteen years old; in our film she's a little older. As we see in the movie, the soldiers spotted her when she was crossing the checkpoint with her family. They also had the idea to raid her house after a drunken poker game. They're angry as hell because of one of their guys has been killed.

Was this the first time you had to deal with such significant censorship?

Yes, which helped me understand why there are basically no images of the war in Iraq. It's one of the big differences between Iraq and Vietnam, where there were cameras everywhere. The Pentagon learned its lesson. If there are no pictures, no one knows what's really happening over there.

This quest for missing images is a motivation for many characters in your films, including Blow Out, Mission: Impossible *and* Snake Eyes.

For my characters, yes. But in my case it was more a feeling of powerlessness that motivated me, because it's impossible to stop things like this from happening. There will always be someone willing to pay for wars like this, but no one to prevent them. That's why I'm so frustrated, and that's what I wanted to express in the film.

What are the other films produced by HDNet?

The only one I can remember is Steven Soderbergh's *The Girlfriend Experience*. Mark Cuban, who ran HDNet, made his fortune in software. People from the film industry convinced him to produce digital films, which worked great until he produced *Redacted*, at which point he was attacked by Fox News for making an unpatriotic film, and as a result he shut down his production company.

You would think that billionaires like Cuban would be taking over Hollywood.

And you'd be right. Amazon and Netflix are here now.

But they produce television, not cinema.

Whether the money comes from oil, food, cars or new technologies, all billionaires want to end up in Hollywood because that's where the girls are. That's what they're *really* interested in.

Some people also put their money into football or basketball.

True, but there are no girls in sports, only bodybuilders. It's girls they really want. I recently watched *The Neon Demon* by Nicolas Winding Refn, produced by Amazon, which is full of vapid, naked models. I couldn't believe it. A producer's dream film: beautiful girls everywhere.

You say that you did most of your research on the Internet. Did you also meet with soldiers who had fought in Iraq?

Yes. One of the young guys who's in the film had just returned from Iraq.

How did the pre-production of the film go?

Very differently from previous films. First of all, I had to use unknown actors, which was essential to make the whole thing believable, so I hired a casting director in New York. I had a clear idea from the start that everything would be done in long takes, whether it was Angel's blog, the poker game, the surveillance cameras, the interrogations. The only exception was the documentary about the checkpoint, which was filmed by Eric Schwab, the second unit director.

Why did you ask him to shoot it?

Because I wanted it to look different from the rest of the film. He shot it in five days. We know each other very well; I've been working with him since *Body Double*. He was the one who did location scouting in Thailand for *Casualties of War*. He also hired a casting director in Jordan to find Zahra Zubaidi, who plays Farah, the victim. Meanwhile, I was in New York rehearsing with the actors I had hired to play the soldiers. We rehearsed every scene until they got it right, then we went to Jordan and I shot the rest of the film in about fifteen days.

Why Jordan?

Most movies about the war in Iraq are filmed there. Jordanians are very hospitable and the hotels are comfortable. Steven Spielberg, who directed *Indiana Jones and the Last Crusade* there, still had contacts with the Jordanian royal family and he asked them to look after me. Things went very smoothly.

When you were writing, did you already know what form each scene would take – which would be Angel's diary or the surveillance camera?

At first, because I thought I would have total freedom, I imagined that I would decide on the form of the scenes as we went along, but because of the insurance problems everything had to be written in the script, down to the last detail. It was like writing a contract. I would work through the material with the actors. We would improvise some things together, much like I had done on *Greetings* or *Hi, Mom!*, changing the dialogue if necessary, and then I put it all down on paper.

Why did you film the scene after the rape, in which B.B. orders McCoy not to tell anyone about what he saw, with a surveillance camera?

Because there are surveillance cameras that monitor the perimeters of this kind of camp. That's what gave me the idea that they would be filmed without realising it. Once the position of the camera was determined, I staged the scene so that it would be most effective from that angle.

Did you shoot more material for Angel Salazar's blog than what appears in the film?

No. Because of my decision to shoot each scene in a single shot, in a single axis, from one take to the next, only the interaction between the actors changed. For example, I did 27 takes of the poker game; we worked the actors into a state of exhaustion. When I asked if they wanted to try something else, they said they couldn't take it any more. Enough is enough! I had fully prepared them before the shoot and they knew the scenes in great detail, so it was easy to try out all these variations.

In the Sixties, the reality effect came through television and handheld cameras. What about today?

Today it's reality TV and what we see on the Internet that sets new standards in this area. Kids don't watch TV anymore; they have their faces permanently glued to their phones. It's what they see there that becomes reality.

Before starting a film you usually have two or three very strong visual ideas around which the script is built. Was it the same for Redacted?

Again, everything was inspired by what I saw on the Internet. I knew that a soldier's diary would be the starting point. I added the idea that Angel Salazar's character was making it for film school. I thought of the Skype conversations between father and son the minute I saw them online. I also wanted to illustrate the point of view of the Iraqis, with pictures of the mines they planted in the ground and posted on the Internet every time a soldier stepped on them. The same goes for beheading videos. As for the documentary on the checkpoint made by a French team, I wanted to use it to convey the overwhelming feeling of boredom that soldiers often experience in the field, the endless, never-changing routines, day after day in the scorching sun – monotony that's sometimes broken by a flash of violence. I wanted to slow down time to show the tedium, which is why I included Handel's "Sarabande," which Kubrick uses in *Barry Lyndon* in much the same way. I couldn't show all that in the film because of the directorial choices I had made, which is why I needed the documentary. I wasn't trying to make fun of French documentary filmmakers, as has been suggested. The important thing for me was that it be a documentary made by foreigners. Since I've spent a lot of time in France, I made them French, but they could just as easily have been Danes or Germans.

In Angel's blog you show the soldiers reading one of your favourite books, John O'Hara's Appointment in Samarra.

It's a wonderful novel about how one decision, one action, can change a whole life.

What was the most difficult scene to shoot?

The rape, definitely, because it was so difficult for Zahra. When you're shooting with someone from a foreign culture, you sometimes have to ask them to do things that their community considers sacrilegious. But Zahra did a great job. When the film came out, people in her family and community gave her problems and it became dangerous for her to stay there, so she had to leave Jordan. I brought her to the United States and found a school for her. Eventually she got her green card, and I believe she's a citizen now. She's a brave and resourceful young woman.

It was a very different situation compared with Thuy Thu Le, who played the young Vietnamese girl in Casualties of War.

Casualties of War *was her first film and she never acted again. I think she married a French dentist. I never saw her again.*

By dealing with two similar incidents, Redacted *and* Casualties of War *highlight the similarities between the Vietnam and Iraq wars. What do you see as the differences?*

It was even more difficult for soldiers in Iraq. Unlike in Vietnam, there were no beaches or alcohol, no women to fool around with, no prostitutes or drugs, nothing to relax with or ease their frustrations. Iraq was deadly boring, plus all the problems of Vietnam, like a population that hated them but that they still had to interact with, an extraordinarily difficult climate, a language they didn't speak, a culture completely foreign to them. Imagine seventeen- or eighteen-year-old kids in that kind of hell. No wonder they go crazy; it's a complete nightmare. On top of all that, the kids who ended up in Iraq were mostly from poor families. They're lost kids with no future, most of the time psychologically troubled, which makes them quite dangerous. Why else would you want to go out there? The actors I hired did a great job of capturing the anger and madness of those guys.

It must have been strange to tell a story that you had already dealt with but in another country. As with Michael Courtland in Obsession, *was there a feeling of déjà vu?*

I didn't go so far as to remake my own film, like Hitchcock did with *The Man Who Knew Too Much*. What interested me here above all was this new form of narration brought about by digital technology and the Internet, which forced me to find new ways of telling a story. I've been working for two years on a film project that uses the same storytelling technique as the CBS crime show *48 Hours*, where the actual people involved in the incident re-tell it like a documentary. Those shows fascinate me. I've reached an age where I'm not interested in making the kind of big movies I did in the Seventies, Eighties or Nineties. I've done it all already, and they don't offer them to me anymore anyway. Today it's possible to make films much more economically, with new narrative forms. That's what I want to do, a bit like at the beginning of my career when I did *Greetings* or *Hi, Mom!* Telling the same stories – but differently.

Which films of this kind have caught your attention lately?

I wouldn't know how to answer that because I see so few, but not too long ago there were clever films like *The Blair Witch Project* and *Paranormal Activity*. The problem is that there have been dozens of less creative rehashes of them since, and as a result that kind of found footage cinema isn't very interesting anymore.

Why does the Iraq War inspire American filmmakers less than the Vietnam war?

Actually, I've noticed that there are more movies being made now about World War II, which, unlike Iraq and Vietnam, was a war where everything was very clear-cut. We were the good guys, the Nazis were the bad guys. There's clearly some sort of nostalgia for that kind of perspective.

You didn't storyboard any of Redacted. *That's a big change for you.*

Sure, but it wasn't a problem. It's like working from only one camera position.

Something else new for you in Redacted *is that there's no original music.*

There's a simple reason for that: when I discovered all these videos of the war on the Internet, there was no music to any of them. In addition to Handel, we hear a few chords from Angelo Badalamenti's score from Paul Schrader's *The Comfort of Strangers* and a piece from Puccini's *Tosca* over the final photo montage.

Does that montage of victims include staged images or are they all real?

All the censored ones are real. Only the final one – of the dead girl – was staged. A well-known photographer took it. After seeing similar montages on the web, I knew I wanted to end the film with something similar. Google "Iraqi war victims" and you'll see plenty. I asked my researcher to make a selection of the most shocking ones. Everything I used came from the Internet, where you can see them without any alterations.

Redacted *caused a big controversy when it was released in the United States. Were you expecting that?*

Absolutely. You aren't allowed to criticise the military in America, especially when you're at war. I had already experienced this kind of treatment with *Casualties of War*, but it was even worse this time because of cable TV channels like Fox News, which broadcasted bulletins day in, day out, blasting the film.

Gary Sinise, with whom you worked with twice, criticised you very harshly.

I had problems with him towards the end of filming *Mission to Mars*. He made my life so difficult that it ruined our relationship forever.

How did American critics react to Redacted?

Pretty well, but the critics kept talking about the amateurishness of the actors, which is unfair, because that's exactly how you and I would look if a friend of ours filmed us in hi-def video. There was a lot of improvisation. One of the big champions of the film was Manohla Dargis at *The Los Angeles Times*. Roger Ebert also wrote a good review. There are hardly any film critics left in the United States anyway.

Did Redacted *hurt your career in the United States?*

I've always been Hollywood's ugly duckling, so I'm used to being harassed by the media. By the time the movie came out I was long gone as a player, so I don't think people in Hollywood really cared what I was doing. The press onslaught meant that I couldn't get any similar projects produced. One of them was another story of rape in the army, based on documents I found on the Internet. The victim was a female soldier; many women were afraid to go to the bathroom at night for fear of being assaulted. Another was about Jessica Lynch, the American soldier who became a symbol of misinformation during the Iraq War. After she was injured in a car accident and saved by Iraqi soldiers and doctors, the Pentagon organised a phony rescue mission with heroic American soldiers firing blanks into a hospital where there were no Iraqi soldiers. All of this was done so that a staged rescue could be filmed, all for the glory of the American army. It turned Lynch into a war hero, when in fact she never fired a single bullet when she was captured. The whole thing was fabricated; they even made a TV movie out of the story. It was all a desperate attempt to create a hero of the Iraq campaign.

Passion *is a loose adaptation of Alain Corneau's* Crime d'amour. *When did you first see his film?*

The producer of *Crime d'amour*, Saïd Ben Saïd, sent the film to my agent because he thought it would make a good remake. I immediately saw what was wrong with it, most notably that they reveal too early that Ludivine Sagnier's character is the murderer. In *Passion*, you never know who murders the advertising agency director – played by Rachel McAdams – because of the way I shot the ballet sequence. Noomi Rapace's character is innocent until the last ten minutes, which makes for a much more interesting audience experience.

Also, I wasn't wildly convinced by Ludivine Sagnier's performance in Corneau's film; it's just not credible that this girl could turn out to be such a criminal genius. I *want* to believe she's such a manipulative character, but she never seems genuinely threatening. Don't forget that the script was originally written for Isabelle Huppert, who would have been perfect, and the ideal choice next to Kristin Scott Thomas, who is very good in the film.

But then it was decided that someone younger was needed, and they pulled Sagnier's name out of a hat. For the story to really work it has to be two actresses of more or less the same age. That was absolutely crucial when it came to casting *Passion*. There's this unreasonable competition between the two women, and for that to work they have to be peers. There are also endless, extremely boring scenes in Corneau's film, including the finale, which doesn't work at all, in which Sagnier does nothing more than lie down on a bed. What does it mean? Who came up with that?

In *Passion*, the puzzle begins to unravel only near the end. This is one of the reasons why Hitchcock hated "whodunits." The protagonist simply goes from one place to another, gathering information. Then, at the end, it's all nicely wrapped up, with a shot of someone explaining everything.

Like the epilogue of Psycho *that Hitchcock disliked so much.*

Exactly. It's the weakest part of an otherwise perfect film. That kind of explanation should be avoided like the plague.

How long did it take to get Passion *up and running?*

It took us a year to get the cast together – which is a long time. We made the same mistake as Corneau, which was to look for a mature woman and a younger one, but it was basically impossible to find an older woman who would attract investors. In New York I ran into a director friend, Steven Shainberg, who was in touch with Noomi Rapace. He had with him a DVD of Noomi that he gave me, and told me to consider her for the role. I had heard about the *Millennium* trilogy, though I hadn't seen any of them. I liked what I saw on that DVD and mentioned her name to Saïd Ben Saïd, who liked the idea. Noomi and Rachel McAdams were actually both represented by the same agent, so the whole thing became a series of chance circumstances. If I hadn't stumbled across Steven Shainberg, if he hadn't had a DVD with him, if Noomi and Rachel hadn't acted together in *Sherlock Holmes: A Game of Shadows* and loved shooting together, and if Paul Anderson, the lead actor in *Passion*, hadn't also been in the Sherlock Holmes film, who knows what would have happened?

I heard that you originally wanted Kate Winslet and Rachel Weisz for the two main roles.

We talked about them, but they either weren't available or weren't interested. Top of my list was Carice Van Houten, who starred in Paul Verhoeven's *Black Book*, but by the time we got the money together to make the film, she wasn't available.

Rachel McAdams usually plays uncomplicated blondes, very different from her vicious character in Passion.

I thought she was very good in Nick Cassavetes' *The Notebook*, and really excellent in Neil Burger's *The Lucky Ones* as one of three Iraq War veterans. She also surprised me in *Mean Girls* by Mark Waters, in which she's really quite diabolical. That's what I wanted for *Passion*.

Noomi Rapace has a very distinct kind of beauty.

That opaque face gives her a Sissy Spacek-like quality. There's a madness about her in the *Millennium* films that I found quite haunting; you really believe she's a killer. She's the female equivalent of Jack Palance, or an alter ego of Mercedes McCambridge – a girl you wouldn't want to sleep with.

You seemed to have made certain choices based on contrasting hair colours. There's Christine the blonde, Isabelle the brunette, and a little later in the film even a redhead, Dani.

Yes, played by Karoline Herfurth, who's a big star in Germany. She had a small role in Tom Tykwer's *Perfume: The Story of a Murderer*, which is where I first saw her. Her red hair made an impression on me. Her character blends in wonderfully in this snake pit of an office, because she seems to be the only person with a semblance of humanity.

Passion *contains classic elements of a De Palma film. There are twin sisters and cameras everywhere.*

In Corneau's film we aren't told anything specific about the work the two women do. We don't know what they sell, so the smartphone, which can be used to film anything, anywhere, was my idea. Christine's lover films himself having sex with Isabelle in London and later uses the footage to humiliate her. Today this kind of thing is even more insidious, and more realistic, because everybody films everybody. The commercial that Isabelle creates was actually inspired by a real ad which went viral on the web and is more or less the same as the one you see in the film. It was made by two girls who put their cell phones in the back pocket of their jeans and walked around Los Angeles filming men staring at them.

Before that I had another idea for the commercial; it was going to be a bit like Christopher Nolan's *Inception*, which is a film I like a lot. The idea was that there would be three levels of consciousness, the third level of which is symbolised by a safe that you open and in which you discover a cell phone. It was originally written like that in the draft of the script I gave to my director friends Noah Baumbach, Jake Paltrow and Wes Anderson. They liked it – everything except the *Inception* reference, which they thought was silly and completely unnecessary. I argued that commercials often parody movies, but they were having none of it.

How did you work with Natalie Carter, who co-wrote the original screenplay for Crime d'amour?

I met her through Saïd Ben Saïd, and we became good friends. During filming I had a big problem with Noomi Rapace, who asked that her character be largely rewritten, so I asked Natalie to join me in Berlin. In one week, in the middle of rehearsals, we rewrote the script.

Tell us about The Secret Cinema, *Paul Bartel's short film made in 1968, which somehow presages* Passion.

Paul Bartel's glorious idea is so unbelievably paranoid. Not only does the protagonist's life become a soap opera, she's also being constantly filmed without knowing it and her very existence is divided into short episodes and screened at the local theatre. She has no idea she's such a star and doesn't understand why everyone is staring at her as she walks through town. It was an astounding prospect at the time, except of course today it's all become true. Reality TV is the biggest thing ever. Look at *Survivor*; people mistake it for reality, but there are cameras everywhere and the characters follow a script like all actors do. There's nothing further from reality than reality TV. It's successful because it's so cheap to produce, mainly because you don't have to pay the performers. People will do anything to be on television. Ask someone to slow dance with a grizzly bear and they'll do it, so long as there's a camera pointed at them.

You use the phone in Passion *in a very particular way. It's a communication device, because everyone has one...*

...and also the thing that leads us into the final surreal dream sequence. Cell phones have changed everything. They're everywhere all the time, and we're always checking to see if it's our phone that's ringing. Coming back to the final scene, I'd just say that it has something to do with me personally. I usually wake up three or four times a night. Each time I can't be sure if I'm still dreaming or not. It takes me a minute to return to reality. It's the same thing at the end of the film, where we can't be certain of anything. Is Karoline Herfurth dead? Did Noomi Rapace kill her?

Christine steals the idea for the ad from Isabelle, which is also what happens in Phantom of the Paradise, *when Swan steals Winslow's music.*

Christine wants revenge on Isabelle, who slept with her lover. That's why when Isabelle comes back from London, she asks how the trip was. As for the theme of stealing someone else's idea, it does show up in *Phantom of the Paradise* – you're not wrong. *Passion* is also a return to the erotic thriller, like *Dressed to Kill* and *Body Double*. I had originally imagined the scene where the two girls make love as being very sensual, but Noomi Rapace explained to me that she wasn't a lesbian and so it should be filmed as a rape scene. I had to rethink everything. Just like with the ending of *Carrie*, with that hand rising from the grave, which came to me at the last moment, two days before we shot the scene with Noomi and Karoline Herfurth kissing, I had no idea what I was going to do.

Why the split-screen sequence with Isabelle attending the performance of Debussy's Afternoon of a Faun *on one side, and on the other Christine having her throat slit? It's the kind of striking set piece you love to put at the heart of your films, but in this case it very much challenges the way that audiences normally read images, because Isabelle being at the ballet means that she has an alibi. She can't have killed Christine.*

That's exactly the effect we were going for. At the same time Isabelle is at the ballet, Christine is being murdered. On one half of the screen is a close-up on Isabelle's eyes as she watches the dancers, so she can't be in Christine's house at the same time – can she? Then we move to the house, to a subjective camera shot, and never return to that close-up on the eyes. Audiences these days are so conditioned to being taken by the hand, from point A to point B, that they don't question this correlation. They have most likely taken on board the implication that Isabelle has an alibi for the murder, while the split screen actually suggests that the connection is not as solid as they assume. In *Carrie* and *Blow Out* I used split screen to question the viewer's perception. When two images coexist on the screen in this way, it's essential for the camera movements to be harmonious, so as not to confuse audiences. The viewer has to be able to watch the two sequences together and make the necessary connections between them. Storyboarding is often necessary for this.

Precision camerawork and utmost attention paid to blocking and framing – it all harkens back to the kind of filmmaking that seems to be vanishing.

I'm sick and tired of realism in cinema, and find handheld camerawork really dull, even in the hands of someone like Lars von Trier, whose film *Melancholia* I really like, especially its glorious opening shots. But that banquet sequence he inflicts on us in the middle of the film, shot in ersatz cinéma vérité, with a camera wiggling about in all directions, is so ridiculous. There's always a strong sense of a framing, of solid composition, in every shot in my favourite films – *The Red Shoes*, *Rebecca*, *Vertigo*, *Lawrence of Arabia*. I miss that kind of cinema.

Redacted was made on video but Passion *was shot on 35mm. Why?*

Because I wanted glamorous actresses, and there's nothing like 35mm film to make women look sublime. I wanted *Redacted* to look different, like a documentary. When you're dealing with beautiful women in sensational locations and you want to light them properly, film is essential. Digital doesn't come close to what 35mm has to offer. I found it almost odd to go back to film after *Redacted*, if only because digital allows you much longer takes and with film you have to change reels. But I missed the stylised lighting, which I couldn't get with digital – though that will surely change. My director of photography, José Luis Alcaine, worked with Pedro Almodóvar and knows how to light actresses. He's two years older than me, and works in slightly antiquated ways that suit me perfectly. But let's face it, not only is digital technology improving every day, but *Passion*, which was shot on film, will be transferred to digital to be shown in theatres. Film is a thing of the past.

Why did you shoot Passion *in Berlin?*

The original idea was to shoot in London, but as most of the financing came from Germany, Berlin quickly became an option. We thought of shooting there and pretending it was London, but that clearly wasn't going to work. Nothing looked real enough. I like the idea that audiences realise only halfway through the film, when some of the characters start speaking German, that we're in Berlin. It's an odd moment, as if the story is playing out in a neutral, indefinable space.

You like Berlin and even considered shooting sequences of Mission: Impossible *there, and yet you don't show much of the city in* Passion.

We don't see many exteriors because most of the story takes place in offices. Back in the day, I explored Europe on a scooter, but by the time I hit Berlin I was too old, and didn't take the subway or buses, or even do much walking, as I had done in Rome when we were thinking of shooting *The Black Dahlia* there. I ended up realising that Rome is one of the most complicated cities in the world; you're constantly going round in circles. I also had trouble finding my way around London, even after living there for almost a year during production on *Mission: Impossible*.

In Paris, on the other hand, I always know where I am, which is why I like it so much. In fact, one of my first experiences in a foreign city was riding a scooter through Paris after I finished college. New York is also very clearly delineated, with its uptown and downtown.

We sense that you're more inspired by specific places in a city rather than the broad outlines. When you were working on Toyer, *for example, which was never made, you wanted to shoot a murder scene in the Pompidou Centre because you found the place so interesting. But* Passion *never hones in on a specific, prominent spot in Berlin.*

Again, it's because of old age. I like to breathe a city and walk around it. I need that to be able to visualise it. But these days I'm not as able to do that.

You told us a few years ago that you no longer wanted to work with Pino Donaggio because your collaboration with him was getting repetitive, and yet you asked him to write the music for Passion.

You know I like to work with a variety of composers, as well as writers; I collaborated with several musicians throughout the Nineties and 2000s. But I needed Pino for my erotic thriller comeback. With him, I'm used to preparing temp tracks. For several scenes in *Passion* I suggested the score from Godard's *Contempt* to him and he wrote some music inspired by it. Sometimes that kind of thing works, sometimes it doesn't. The most difficult piece to get right was for the scene where Noomi is humiliated, goes down to the garage of the building, takes her car, and smashes it against a pillar. We had to convey that she was absolutely devastated while keeping it from being corny. It wasn't easy.

You deliberately quote some of your old films, including Dressed to Kill, *which the ending of* Passion *is reminiscent of.*

In hindsight, I can see what you're talking about. *Passion* took a long time to prepare and I spent a lot of time when I was living in Paris thinking about the visuals and working on storyboards.

I was also studying Corneau's film, the ending of which always bothered me, when that character, the assistant, says to Ludivine Sagnier that he knows what she did. "You belong to me now." I wanted something other than that at the end of *Passion*. As you know, I like dream sequences and twins. I wanted to leave audiences wondering whether Isabelle really killed Christine or not. The ending came to me rather late, and yes – it does evoke *Dressed to Kill* and *Carrie*. I just can't help that. Rachel had a lot of fun playing the twin sister; she really went all out.

As I told you, there were problems with Noomi during filming. She kept arguing about my choices and sent me notes every night to the point of refusing to do anything I asked her to do if I didn't use her ideas. Usually when we disagree, an actor does one take my way and another their way, but here she simply refused to follow my directions. That hadn't happened to me since working on *Obsession* with Cliff Robertson, who did everything he could to undermine Geneviève Bujold so that she wouldn't steal the spotlight.

Do you find yourself with fewer resources today, without Hollywood behind you?

I made *Passion* in Germany with a French producer, American and Swedish actresses, and a Spanish director of photography. When you have so many different nationalities on a team, there's less chatter on set and it's easier for me to concentrate. I don't really miss the Hollywood machine. I remember the *Mission to Mars* days when I spent my time in the company of programmers staring at computer screens. If you only knew how long it took to get those effects, and at what cost… It isn't anything I want to do again. At my age, I prefer to let other generations make that kind of cinema. For every Christopher Nolan, who masterfully utilized digital technology in *Inception*, how many mediocre movies are produced? Superhero movies never interested me when I was younger, so you can imagine what I think of them today. I haven't actually seen that many, and was even asked to direct the first *Spider-Man*. I remember the producer bringing me a huge stack of *Spider-Man* comics. I ended up giving them to Nicolas Cage, who collects them.

At 76, I watch Michael Haneke directing a dying couple in *Amour*, which is much closer to what I'm going through today than guys in tights saving New York from destruction. There has to be some kind of balance between the life you live and the kind of films you make. If it were up to me I would make a silent film. I can't stand films full of dialogue that's so carefully filmed, punctuated with close-ups. That being said, take a look at the opening sequence of *The Social Network*, where David Fincher shows just how good he is at filming dialogue. That's an exception, of course. Today, most directors come from television and think only of making films full of people talking to each other that audiences will watch on ever-shrinking screens. I remember discovering *Vertigo* in VistaVision and *Lawrence of Arabia* in 70mm – with an intermission! Nobody knows what I'm talking about anymore because these days everyone watches films on iPads.

What do you think of 3-D, which aims to bring cinemas back to their central place in watching films.

Who really knows how to use 3-D? James Cameron, for sure. I'm thinking of one of the opening shots in *Avatar* where Sam Worthington looks like he's come from a morgue. It's like you're wrapped up in the shot; an absolutely extraordinary image. I'm also thinking of the murder scene in *Dial M for Murder* and the way Hitchcock uses scissors. But in other 3-D films, all you get are objects thrown in your face. My older brother Bruce and I thought up a 3-D technique with Polaroids in the 1950s, and we came to the conclusion that some things work well in 3-D and other things absolutely don't. It's just like with close-ups, Steadicam and split screen. Directors today rely too much on special effects. But actors don't act the same way in front of a blue screen as they do on location. Those kinds of techniques should be used only when they really add value. I'm curious to see what will become possible with motion capture; I'm certainly impressed with the results in video games. I'm not saying we're going to get performances like Al Pacino's in *The Godfather*, but it's certainly intriguing.

Visual creativity is in the hands of the people at ILM, George Lucas' special effects studio. Every action scene is now digitised and stored on hard drives to be used in other films, which explains why everything looks the same. It's always the same car crash, the same monster crossing the screen from right to left. The obsession with technology, the need to make your equipment cost-effective, forces directors to ask actors to behave like machines or puppets. When you see one of the best American actors, Robert Downey Jr., playing a clown in *The Avengers*, you say to yourself, "This is all wrong." You have to have spent time in Hollywood to understand their mentality. These days a movie that makes $600 million worldwide isn't enough – you have to aim for a billion dollars.

I spent twelve years in a Quaker school. I'll never forget the sermons at Christmas where we were warned about greed. The idea was to earn a living and earn it well, but never scramble for more than you really needed. It's a dignified response that to this day I very much believe in, something everyone – especially artists – should heed. And yet these days everyone in Hollywood wants their own yacht. Spielberg showed me the boat that was designed for him; it must have cost $100 million, though it's still smaller than Paul Allen's, the co-founder of Microsoft. When David Geffen goes to Cannes he never leaves his yacht. The idea is that you have to make a trip out to the boat the way you used to go to the king's court. Once you've made $100 million, how much more do you need? Fortunately young directors don't have that much money because their films don't make much.

Your last four films were shot outside America: Femme Fatale *in France,* Black Dahlia *in Bulgaria,* Redacted *in Jordan and* Passion *in Germany. Were those good experiences?*

I liked all of them because I like living abroad. Those four films are certainly outside of mainstream Hollywood, but it meant I had total control, something that would never have happened if I had filmed in America. Of the four, *Femme Fatale* is probably my favourite. I also had a lot of fun making *Redacted*. I don't enjoy making big Hollywood studio films anymore. When you're over sixty, as I was when I made those four films, you don't want to be told what to do. As Orson Welles said, it's great to be able to play with this big electric train that Hollywood puts at your disposal, but in order to get something really worthwhile out of it, you need to be in control, and that requires enormous energy.

It's time to move on. Cinematic forms are changing. In the Seventies, Eighties and Nineties we didn't make movies the same way we made them in the Thirties, Forties or Fifties. Today, we have to get used to the fact that we can't make films the way we did in the Seventies and Eighties. Digital technology, the fact of being able to shoot an entire film on an iPhone, allows us to explore a lot of new narrative forms. As a former scientist, I find it all very exciting. Alain Corneau's *Crime d'amour* doesn't make any reference to new technology, but I decided that the two lead characters in my remake should work in the smartphone industry, and because you can use them to film at important moments, phones play a crucial role in *Passion*. After all, these days everyone has their noses permanently buried in their phones.

How did the documentary that Noah Baumbach and Jake Paltrow made about you happen?

The three of us live in New York. We're friendly; I've known Noah for twenty years, Jake for ten. We go out a lot, sometimes with Wes Anderson when he's in town. The idea came about at one of our weekly dinners. Jake and Noah were interested in new digital cameras and wanted to try one out. Long before he shot *Frances Ha*, Noah said to me, "Why don't we film you talking about your career?" They wanted to record all the stories I had told them. We went to Jake's house; he filmed and Noah did the sound. It was just the three of us in a room. We shot six or seven hours a day for a week.

Six or seven hours a day? You would have killed us if we took that much of your time for this book.

They kept coming back for more. I ended up wearing the same clothes for a week. They went off to make other movies, then two years later, when they had time on their hands, they edited the footage.

It was a good idea for you to talk about your career in an uninterrupted flow, without questions.

During editing they decided to remove their voices from the soundtrack.

There was something of a critical re-evaluation of your films when the documentary was released.

Noah and Jake did a great job, considering I'm not used to talking for so long in front of a camera. Orson Welles could do that kind of thing really well, but unlike me he was an actor. He was a great talker and an incredible storyteller. A man of culture with an incomparable sense of humour, he knew how to express himself better than anyone. He was my reference when we shot the interviews, and while I'm certainly not as brilliant, I did pretty well. I was comfortable doing it because I was in the company of two friends that I've known for a long time. My sense of humour comes across. Every story I tell in the film is one they had heard at our dinners.

The way they use excerpts reminds us of the great diversity of your films, as well as the spectacular visuals.

They're directors and know how to use images. I'm sorry to tell you guys this, but the best interviewer of a film director is another film director.

That depends. A lot of directors are unable to talk analytically about a colleague's films. Everything you say in the documentary also appears in this book. That plus lots more.

I can't wait for your book to be translated into English so I can finally read it.

We discovered your films when we were teenagers, which is one reason why they're so resonant for us, even today. Was that the case with Baumbach and Paltrow?

They made references to scenes from my films that they'd had in mind for decades, but their films are very different from mine.

You were supposed to make a thriller called Lights Out in China. *Is that ever going to happen?*

No. The financing was from China, and I auditioned a lot of Chinese actresses for the lead role to see how they did in English, but the person I selected wasn't available at the time we needed her so we continued casting. There were lots of very commercial Chinese actresses who could play the part, but I didn't like how they acted in English. In the end I abandoned the project because I had the impression that the story actually wasn't that original. There are already a few thrillers about a blind girl, some of them quite good.

Like Wait Until Dark?

Yes. A few films about blind people being attacked in their homes were released last summer, like *Don't Breathe*, so I decided that we had missed that boat and left the project.

Are you working on another film at the moment?

I have one or two projects in motion. The one making the most progress is based on a book called *The Truth and Other Lies* by a German author called Sascha Arango, who worked with me on the script. We're looking for the right actor, someone who can get the film off the ground. There's also a very low-budget project that might be financed by a Brazilian producer based on an original script of mine, *Sweet Vengeance*, which is a kind of film version of a true crime television show.

There's a series in the US called *48 Hours*, where they interview police officers, show you the crime scenes, and interview witnesses. There are different levels of reality. Sometimes the crime is staged; other times it's the witnesses speaking. I'm really fascinated by it all. My film is based on very famous cases, including the "mall murderer," who grabbed women from shopping malls. He waited for them in the parking lot, pointed his gun at the children, and told the woman to do what he asked her. He would take the women to his house and rape them. The other case that always fascinated me was of a woman who worked in a bank. Burglars broke into her house, tied dynamite around her, and told her to go into the bank to get some money. If she refused, they said, they would detonate the explosives. She did what she was told, but when the police questioned her it turned out there was no dynamite. There are also lots of things on the web that interest me, like girls who are interviewed about their sex lives. I'm fascinated by pornography filmed from the point of view of the girls. I saw one where a girl is being interviewed by a guy. She gets undressed and sucks him off. I was convinced she was an amateur, but a producer friend told me that she's a very talented professional.

Amateur porn has always fascinated you.

Subjective camera porn is incredible; it's a genre unto itself. I would put it all into my script, which includes a split-screen scene.

A film like that would be X-rated.

We wouldn't show the girl actually doing anything, though we would get close. The problem is that it's become impossible to include real eroticism in films. You hardly ever see sex in films anymore. Pornography has been cannibalised by cable and the Internet.

What do you think about the omnipresence of pornography on the Internet today?

I have no idea where it will lead. Probably to 3-D porn.

What happened with the remake of Heat, *based on William Goldman's novel, which was filmed in 1986 by Dick Richards starring Burt Reynolds? In the end it was made without you, with Jason Statham in the main role.*

The producers rejected the script I rewrote with Natalie Carter; they preferred William Goldman's version, which I didn't think was very good. The movie they made also wasn't great. The original story took place in Las Vegas, but I wanted to set it in France. In Nice, to be exact, because that's where the casinos are.

You also had a film project in the works for HBO starring Al Pacino called Happy Valley.

I cast it and found the locations, but it was a touchy subject, inspired by an infamous child abuse case in the United States, the Penn State University scandal which ended the career of football coach Joe Paterno, whose assistant was also implicated. The question was, what exactly did Paterno know? Did he have any idea what was going on? It had to be handled very delicately. HBO was interfering too much; I spent too much of my time arguing with them. They kept asking for rewrites and overwhelming me with notes, so I quit.

It sounds as though a network like HBO is even more controlling than a studio. That's not their reputation though.

HBO is supposed to be the best place on television for writers and artists, but that wasn't my experience at all. I found it unbearable. You have to understand that television is a medium where the director is relatively powerless. Writers and producers have much more influence. Of course, they don't tell you that up front, but in the end you're just a hired gun, no different from any ordinary TV director. What's the point of getting big names from the movies if you're not going to give them any freedom? And anyway, every episode of a show looks the same. For a stylist like me, who prizes visuals above all else, working in TV is a waste of time.

Are there any series that stand out for you when it comes to directing?

I liked Steven Zaillian's mini-series *The Night Of*. The cinematography and acting were excellent. The writing kept me on the edge of my seat until the final moments.

Have there been any other TV offers?

Plenty, but my experience with HBO was so bad I don't want to go down that road again. It's like working in the old studio system.

What do you think of Vinyl, *Martin Scorsese's television series? Have you talked with him about what it was like working with HBO?*

Marty had a bad time on *Vinyl*. We had a long discussion about it when we met a couple of weeks ago, and he wasn't at all happy. But unlike me he'd already had experience working on television – with his series *Boardwalk Empire* – so he knew how to adapt. *Vinyl* took years to develop, and as you know it wasn't renewed.

Do you still see your New Hollywood pals – Scorsese, Spielberg, Coppola, Lucas, Schrader?

Since we're all often on the move around the world, it's not often that we're in the same place at the same time, even if we wanted to be. I spent time with Marty recently because he gave a moving and sincere introduction to Noah and Jake's documentary at a screening. I was very touched. He talked about how we had met in New York in the Sixties and how our friendship developed. As for Spielberg, he works all the time, but I see him now and then when he's at his house in the East Hamptons because I have one not far away. He comes to New York more often these days because his wife Kate wants to spend more time there. Their children have all left their home in Los Angeles, so they have more free time. George Lucas calls me when he's in town, but I'm not always there. He lives in a bit of a parallel universe, like Francis Coppola, who made his fortune in the food business. He and George are two interesting guys who, like Chaplin, could finance any film with their own money, but they never will. Of Francis' last films, I liked *Tetro* quite a bit, but *Youth Without Youth* I couldn't sit through.

Among the directors of your group from the Seventies, Spielberg and Scorsese are the only ones still making films for Hollywood studios. You haven't done that since Mission to Mars.

It makes sense for Steven, the most commercially successful director of any generation. He has created production companies and a studio, he works non-stop and continues to churn out hit after hit. Marty makes less mainstream films, but he has developed an ongoing relationship with Leonardo DiCaprio and Bob De Niro, who help him find financing. I was disappointed by my last experience with a studio seventeen years ago. Films are too expensive these days, and it's more and more difficult to make anything original.

Are you still getting offers from Hollywood?

It's been a long time since I was on the A-list. My last real commercial success was *Mission: Impossible*. I get offers from time to time, but not many.

You say you're no longer a player in Hollywood, but paradoxically Hollywood produces sequels and remakes of your films.

I've never been interested in making sequels or remakes, except for *Passion*, though that was different, because the original was in French. Today I'm interested in new forms of storytelling, which is why I made *Redacted*. Digital technology allows us to tell stories differently. I recently found myself on the jury at the Toronto Film Festival, and realised that because we don't necessarily have to light anymore, the job of lighting technician as we once knew it no longer exists. Digital technology allows us to shoot without extra light. The problem is that every film has the same look to it. That's what I liked about *The Night Of*, which is more like the kind of cinema that existed pre-digital. Every film in Toronto was similar, all with the same Steadicam shots, where the camera just follows the characters around. The technology means that the camera can go wherever it wants, but the whole thing puts me right to sleep. The Steadicam has become a horrible cliché; there's nothing surprising about it anymore. It was disappointing to see.

It strikes us that Kimberly Peirce's remake of Carrie *is very faithful to the novel but lacks any real cinematic treatment of the story, unlike your version.*

Carrie has been adapted several times. There's the version you're talking about as well as a four-hour mini-series, the sequel, *The Rage: Carrie 2*, and the Broadway musical.

Sisters *has also been remade. Were you consulted?*

I had nothing to do with that film. They did what they wanted with the material and the result was awful. When it came to my remake of *Scarface*, I was lucky to have a very good script and a great cast. It's a good movie.

The Mission: Impossible *sequels diverged from your film and became big action movies, like James Bond or Jason Bourne.*

The sequels are more Tom Cruise's doing; he's the one who decides everything. You have to be *very* persuasive to make him change his mind. I know something about that.

Do you still play video games? In our first conversations twenty years ago, you said that they were a new way of telling stories through images. Do they still interest you?

I'm not as on the ball as I was twenty years ago, but it's certainly true that movies and video games are now fully intertwined. They make movies from games because these days video games are more successful than movies, and they both use digital technology, with very similar techniques. It was George Lucas that initiated all this years ago with ILM, his special effects lab. What you see today is the evolution of what George set in motion. As far as I'm concerned, the big revolution in video games came with the POV shooter games and their use of subjective camera to put you in the perspective of a character who's watching. Considering the kind of films I made, I'm obviously interested in that. These POV games have gotten better and better and more and more mesmerising thanks in part to 3D. My daughters absolutely love them.

It's true that visually these games have become more impressive, but narratively, they haven't changed much in twenty years.

That's true, but some games are still quite complex. I was playing *Fallout 4* the other day, and let me tell you, it's very complicated. Basically, you have to wander around looking for hidden clues, and if you don't find them you can't get to the next level; you're stuck. So you spend your time wandering sometimes more than two hours in this artificial space, until you think, "Just what the hell am I doing here?"

Do you know the video game they made from Scarface? *It's a kind of* Grand Theft Auto *with Tony Montana as the main character.*

One of the first *Grand Theft Auto* games, the one set in Miami, was inspired by *Scarface*. I remember playing it back then.

Do you still watch movies from the Fifties? You told us it was your favourite period.

I watch a lot of them on TCM. The crazy thing is that my kids and my girlfriend's kids have never heard of these movies. You say, "Do you know *Red River*?" and they say, "What's that?" They have a hard enough time dealing with movies from the Seventies, so can you imagine the ones from the Thirties or Forties? That's the Stone Age for them.

In 1997 and 1998 you lost your brother Bruce and your mother in quick succession. They were both very important in your formation as an artist and a person, and we wonder if their absence has impacted your work in any way.

By the time they were gone, neither my brother nor my mother were really a part of my life anymore, and I was at peace with both of them. Bruce, who died in New Zealand, had become so eccentric. My brother Bart only learned of his death two weeks after he had been buried. My mother, for whom Bruce meant everything, died shortly after. They were like an old couple, where the husband dies and almost immediately after the wife goes. Bruce continues to influence some of the characters in my films, but I don't think it goes any further than that.

A fan of yours named Peet Gelderblom produced a director's cut of Raising Cain. *Why didn't you re-cut the film yourself?*

As you know, I felt that starting the film with Lolita Davidovich's story would make it too much like a soap opera. I wasn't too happy with the scenes between her and Steven Bauer; I just didn't think they worked, whereas everything about John Lithgow seemed so fascinating to me that I switched the two parts around. But I was wrong. The scenes with Lolita and Steve weren't so bad, and when I saw the new cut I realised that they actually work very well.

The new version begins in a clock store, where Lolita Davidovich meets Steven Bauer. The close-ups on the clock dials introduce the theme of time, which is so decisive in their relationship, since the drama results from the fact that she stays overnight at his place. It's a much more effective beginning.

I know, and it hit me too when I saw it on the Internet. I thought "This is how it should have been done in the first place." Peet did a good job. His only mistake was that when he introduced the John Lithgow part of the film, when the women are talking in the park, he repeated an exterior shot that's actually an objective shot, in which they're not there. He pasted in off-camera dialogue between Lolita and her friend to create an illusion, which isn't something I would have done. He should have started with the subjective shot of Steven Bauer walking towards her with the girlfriend saying, "Don't do what I would do." I don't know why he used the exterior shot that the women aren't in. I know I'm nitpicking, but it bothered me.

You also made a longer version of Casualties of War *for a special DVD edition.*

I added interrogation scenes during the trial of Meserve and his men.

Do you plan on doing that with any of your other films? Ridley Scott does it with almost every film.

No. I originally removed those scenes so that the story had a better flow, but it was a mistake. In fact, I came to see that those scenes were vital to drive home the point that these guys had attacked Ericksson's character.

What films have made an impact on you in the last ten years?

Caché by Michael Haneke. *A History of Violence* by Cronenberg. I liked Tom Tykwer's last film with Tom Hanks, *A Hologram for the King*; I've never seen anything like it. Apparently nobody understood it and it did poorly in America, but he did a very good job. Tom is a visual stylist like me; I love what he does. I've read several books by Dave Eggers, the author of the novel the film is based on, and I'm a big fan of his work.

Did you like Cloud Atlas, *which Tykwer co-directed with the Wachowski sisters?*

No, but I also didn't like the book. I thought *Jackie* by Pablo Larraín was very good. I saw it in Toronto, where it won an award.

Do you often go see new films?

I go quite a lot with Noah, Jake and Wes Anderson. We saw *Star Wars: The Force Awakens* together, and we also go to the New York Film Festival because Wes always has tickets. He's the one who organises the outings.

We've never understood Wes Anderson's popularity in America.

He's a wonderful stylist. Visually his films are very elaborate; I like them a lot. They have nothing to do with what I do, like Noah Baumbach's *Frances Ha*, but that doesn't stop me from appreciating them. I watch more movies on TCM nowadays. I recently saw Rouben Mamoulian's *Dr. Jekyll and Mr. Hyde*, which I had never seen. It's great, full of elaborate, subjective camera shots. I also love rewatching Westerns because they were the first films I saw as a teenager in the Fifties. Mann, Hawks, Ford.

And Hitchcock?

These days I mostly watch them with my daughters, who are seeing them for the first time. The crop duster scene in *North by Northwest* always keeps me on the edge of my seat; it's a great example of perfectly choreographed suspense, because Hitchcock takes his time to set the scene and situate the characters in the space. It's the slow progression that makes the outcome that much more powerful, which is something no one knows how to do these days. Filmmakers today just cut straight to the explosion. Look at the staircase scene in *Battleship Potemkin*. You have to slow down the action so that the audience has time to register everything, which is what I did in *Carrie*. It's the same thing with Westerns, with that final gunfight on Main Street, where you take your time to show the first guy, then establish where he's standing in relation to the second guy. Making a Western is like architecture; it's like building a space. It's a genre I absolutely adore. No one who makes science fiction or superhero movies knows how to do this anymore, which is why action scenes are so confusing – though to be fair to those directors, so much of it is computer generated, and the same special effects software is used in film after film. The director gives his script to the special effects guys, who turn it into CGI and pre-visualise the scene. Those kinds of shots are so expensive that they have to be done like that. But it's also why they all look the same.

Are you aware of any new film composers?

Absolutely. I think Alexandre Desplat, from France, is brilliant. There's also an Italian, Dario Marianelli, who I like a lot.

Have you written other scripts in recent years?

Plenty. When RKO gave me a list of their films that they were looking to remake, *His Kind of Woman*, a John Farrow film with Robert Mitchum and Jane Russell, produced by Howard Hughes, caught my attention, and I wrote a new version. The problem was that I couldn't convince the head of RKO, Ted Hartley, to give me the rights.

The world is looking more and more like one of your paranoid thrillers.

Let me tell you my theory. You know all the talk about the NSA listening and reading everything we do? Every single Skype conversation, every single email, is stored on a server somewhere. Everything you type on your computer, your smartphone, everything is archived somewhere underground – in Utah most likely. The trick is to find the right algorithm to go fishing for information in that huge database. It's the kind of thing that can wield real power over a presidential election. Remember the hacking of Hillary Clinton's email account? Imagine that everything you said or wrote in your youth, in an email, is stored somewhere; it's just a matter of knowing how to access it. It can become a powerful weapon against any politician who might find themselves exposed overnight on WikiLeaks, who will then say it was the Russians who released this information. But I don't believe that at all. What happened is similar to Watergate, except that nowadays you don't need to hire burglars to bug the offices of the Democratic Committee; you just need to hack into the candidate's mailbox, because all the information you're looking for is there. That's what's happening today and that's what turned the last election around.

As soon as it was announced that the NSA could tap into the AT&T phone network to supposedly listen in on terrorist conversations, I knew it was going to go way beyond that. Otherwise, one of the big differences between today's world and the one I grew up in is that when someone said white one day and black the next, you could say, "That guy's a liar!" Today when someone contradicts themselves from one day to the next on the air, it's called "re-examination," and because of reality TV, which everyone takes at face value, people have come to accept a version of reality that can be completely fabricated. Donald Trump does this all the time on TV, but people think it's reality TV and don't take his contradictions seriously, whereas before he would have been exposed as a liar. The rise of reality TV has plunged us into a world where the fake is the real thing.

Donald Trump is himself a pure product of reality TV with his show The Apprentice.

Yes, which makes it all the more perverse. Do you have reality TV in France?

Of course. Our television is becoming more and more American. We watch the same kind of shows, and our presidential candidates are increasingly similar to yours.

What our last presidential election demonstrated was the power that reality TV can hand to even the most ridiculous candidate. No matter what he says, it's considered first and foremost as entertainment.

Would you like to make a film about the last presidential election?

I'd like to make a film about a character hired to find information to smear a presidential candidate. That kind of guy fascinates me. Orson Welles dealt with this in *Mr. Arkadin*: "If I want to run for office, I should research myself to see which of my most unmentionable secrets might fall into the hands of my opponents." That's a great idea.

Some of your films, like Dressed to Kill *and* Body Double, *and others like William Friedkin's* Cruising, *generated enormous protests from feminists. This is something we see less and less, because films are becoming more and more sterile. Are you nostalgic for that era?*

For me it never really stopped. *Redacted* was dragged through the mud and people protested in front of the theatres that were screening it. But that didn't last very long. As far as sex is concerned, we don't see that much of it in theatres anymore. There's more of it, and more explicit sex too, on cable and the Internet.

You wanted to make a film with Michael J. Fox about his Parkinson's condition.

That wasn't a great experience. I had an idea that I presented to a screenwriter friend who worked on it for a while, but then dropped the project before finishing, which ended our friendship. When I told Michael J. Fox that we needed to hire a new writer, he lost interest, and that was the end of that.

You have been working for a long time on a film project about Howard Hughes. What did you think of Rules Don't Apply, *Warren Beatty's film about Hughes?*

What surprised me is that Beatty, who was almost eighty years old when he made the film, couldn't help himself and included a sex scene between his character and the girl played by Lily Collins – which is, of course, absolutely impossible. Even Woody Allen wouldn't dare go that far.

The character of Hughes that Beatty plays is in his fifties.

Yes. He's twenty-five years older than that! He filmed in the dark so the age difference didn't show. Apart from that, I thought the film was pretty amusing at the beginning, but I lost interest when he sleeps with the young actress. I was listening to an interview with Beatty not long ago in which he was asked why he hadn't made a film for fifteen years. He said it was because he wanted to watch his children grow up. It's the same with me. My daughters grew up in the 2000s. I spent time with them, managing family affairs, which is why I've made so few films recently.

If you were a young director starting out in the United States today, what would you do?

The same thing all beginners do: make a film by any means necessary and send it to the Sundance Film Festival.

What do you see happening for you in the next few years?

I'm optimistic and my health is good. I have two wonderful children who I have a lot of fun with. I'm still thinking about the films I want to make and the ones I can't make. There are projects we can't get done, so every now and then I have to go back and work for the system. If I have a big success by making a "mainstream" film for them, it gives me the possibility to set up a more personal project. But as time moves on I have to be more careful about the jobs I say yes to. They absolutely have to be worth my time. At the same time, no one's asking me to write a symphony or an *In Remembrance of Things Past*, but to make use of my skill and experience.

How would you like to be remembered?

I would like to make as big an impact on the next generation of directors and audiences as Orson Welles did on me. I'm at peace with myself. People often tell me how much they like my films. I'm rarely on TV, so I can still walk down the street and people don't throw themselves at me. When you're on television too much, people recognise you all the time, which makes it harder to get around. I like to be able to walk around incognito. But I also like it when someone comes up to me and tells me that one of my films made an impression on them. I realise that I've made something of an impact. The films will outlive me.

AFTERWORD

BY BRUCE JOEL RUBIN

I met Brian in the fall of 1963, when we both entered the New York University film programme. There were two students who stuck out in that incoming group – Marty Scorsese and De Palma. Both had an impact on my life, but Brian would prove to have an enduring effect in subtle but real ways. In a certain sense I am a footnote in Brian's career, but the intermingling of our lives continues to this day.

Brian entered NYU as a celebrated director. He had already made a notable film, *Wotan's Wake*, which became part of the Cinema 16 program, founded by Amos Vogel. He was also the only male student at Sarah Lawrence College and his reputation as a ladies' man preceded him. I was somewhat in awe of him and shocked when the first film he wanted to direct was one I had written, called *Hide and Seek*, later retitled *Jennifer*. Watching him direct was my introduction to his skills and a tutorial in directing itself. But then watching him destroy my script was an unexpected and disturbing introduction to what would later become a lesson in making movies in Hollywood. Brian, it seems, felt that our finished film was too linear, too traditional, and decided, unilaterally, to cut the film into pieces, re-assemble it willy-nilly, and let it find a new, more experimental, voice. It found no voice at all. It was a total mess and the head of the film department removed Brian from the program after viewing it. I was devastated by the destruction of my work but couldn't discount the power of Brian's presence in my life. He had a personality like no other and seemed to be fearless in ways I aspired to. We stayed friends.

After graduation, I co-directed and edited Brian's split-screen epic, *Dionysus in 69*. A mutual NYU friend, Bob Fiore, joined us on *Dionysus* and the three of us share onscreen directorial credit. When the film received a rave review in *The New York Times* and claimed Brian as its sole creator, Bob and I wrote a letter to the *Times*' critic correcting his error. We asked Brian to sign it. He refused. This was another opportunity to end my relationship with Brian, but he wasn't so easy to quit. Bob went on to become Brian's cameraman on his next film, *Greetings*, and I was his assistant director on *Hi, Mom!* and the Museum of Modern Art documentary *The Responsive Eye*.

Brian's basement apartment at 65 Bank Street was as underground and cool as any apartment I had ever seen. When he decided to move, he bequeathed it to me and I suddenly became cool as well – at least in my own eyes. My life changed in that apartment. I became a bohemian. I smoked grass and took LSD there. I became myself. I am grateful to Brian to this day for that transformative opportunity.

After a year and a half of hitchhiking around the world in search of a mystical teacher who might be able to explain the deeper secrets of my LSD trip, I returned to New York and found a teacher just four blocks from my Bank Street apartment, and began a meditative practice that I continue to this day. Brian would visit me at the Whitney Museum, where I worked as a curator in the film department. We would go for walks in Central Park. I would try to picnic with him on the grass, but he would only sit on the rocks. We talked about our Hollywood dreams. In the end, I moved to Indiana to live in a yoga ashram and Brian made the move to Los Angeles. Several years later he called me and said I should join him. Scorsese was there, George Lucas and Spielberg too. They were living on the beach in Santa Monica. I couldn't imagine Brian walking on sand any more than I could see him sitting on grass. It just didn't fit. I declined his offer.

Several years later, a film I had written, *Brainstorm*, was made, and my wife Blanche and I went to Hollywood for the premiere. The film had taken years to get produced, and the story behind it was full of strife and tragedy. While we were there we had lunch at Brian's home, and he said something that changed our lives completely. "If you want a career in Hollywood, you have to move here." To my amazement, Blanche went back to our home in the Midwest, quit her job as a professor, put our house on the market, and told me, "We're moving to Hollywood." I don't know where she got the courage to uproot our lives, but it was the beginning of what proved to be a successful, Oscar-winning Hollywood career for me. I really do owe it all to Brian. I would never have had the courage to move without that exchange, his affirmation.

I never regretted not moving to Los Angeles when Brian first offered me the possibility. My spiritual journey was a core part of my life and a defining part of my storytelling career. If I had joined the Movie Brats back then, I suspect I wouldn't have lasted long. They were all gifted directors. I was just a writer. As it turns out, I won an Oscar before any of them for my film *Ghost* and had a long and satisfying career.

I still talk to Brian. At one point, two movies we had directed opened the same weekend. My film *My Life* was a bit of a commercial disaster. Brian's *Carlito's Way* fared better. What was most affecting to me was that we had films opening at the same time. Who would have guessed, back at NYU, that such a thing might happen? Even more amazing is that Brian told me he listened to recordings of my spiritual talks, something I would never have imagined in a thousand years. He also became an encouraging supporter of my turning *Ghost* into a musical, which has played in London, on Broadway, and around the world.

Brian's lasting impact on my journey can't be overstated, and remains central to my life. I am clearly one of many whom have been touched by him, and there are certainly others who could have written this afterword with as much gratitude as I. Knowing Brian has been a true and defining gift. I hope this book has been a gift to you as well.

INDEX

8½ (Fellini), 32
20th Century Fox, 61
48 Hours (TV), 267, 282
1941 (Spielberg), 182
2001: A Space Odyssey (Kubrick), 50, 73, 184, 204, 234
660124: The Story of an IBM Card (De Palma), 13, 31

Abraham, F. Murray, 127
Ace in the Hole (Wilder), 91, 127
Act of Vengeance (Mackenzie), 199
Actors Studio, 138
Adler, Gil, 100
Adjani, Isabelle, 207
A French Woman (Wargnier), 3
A History of Violence (Cronenberg), 289
A Hologram for the King (Tykwer), 289
Alcaine, José Luis, 20, 275
Allen, Nancy, 37, 84, 91, 94-5, 100, 111-12, 115, 120, 123, 141-2, 245
Allen, Paul, 279
Allen, Woody, 199, 293
Almodóvar, Pedro, 275
Alonzo, John A., 15, 17

Altman, Robert, 57, 70, 123
Amadeus (Forman), 202
Amazing Stories (TV), 151
Ambler, Kim, 17
Ambrose Chapel (De Palma), 199
American Beauty (Mendes), 237
American Gangster (Scott), 259
American Graffiti (Lucas), 201
American Psycho (Ellis), 134
Amistad (Spielberg), 104
Ammar, Tarak Ben, 9, 259
Amour (Haneke), 277
Anderson, Paul, 270
Anderson, Paul Thomas, 224
Anderson, Wes, 272, 280, 290
Animals, The, 36
Anne of a Thousand Days (Jarrott), 65
Antonioni, Michelangelo, 29, 122
Apartment, The (Mimouni), 248
Apocalypse Now (Coppola), 167-9
Appointment at Samarra (O'Hara), 265
Apollo 13 (Howard), 230, 234
Arango, Sascha, 282
Arbogast, Thierry, 19, 248
Argento, Dario, 58

Arrangement, The (Kazan), 91
Arrowsmith, William, 15
Ashby, Hal, 85
Ashley, Ted, 46-7
A Star is Born (Pierson), 57
Atlantic City (Malle), 214
Avatar (Cameron), 278
Avengers, The (Whedon), 279
Avrech, Robert J., 17, 135

Bacchae (Euripides), 39, 41
Badalamenti, Angelo, 268
Bad Influence (Hanson), 192
Badlands (Malick), 37, 55, 61, 236
Bach, Steven, 174
Baker, Rick, 92
Barry Lyndon (Kubrick), 50, 265
Bartel, Paul, 37, 272-3
Bartók, Béla, 73
Basic Instinct (Verhoeven), 140
Bauer, Marty, 201
Bauer, Steven, 127-8, 189, 288-9
Baum, Frank L., 27
Baumbach, Noah, 11, 272, 280-1, 290
Battleship Potemkin (Eisenstein), 151, 221, 290
Bay, Michael, 106
Beach Boys, The, 23, 57
Béart, Emmanuelle, 4, 203, 207, 209
Beatles, The, 57
Beatty, Warren, 293
Bee Gees, 198
Bel Geddes, Barbara, 66
Belushi, James, 96
Benitez, Jellybean, 198
Beineix, Jean-Jacques, 247
Bergman, Ingmar, 31-2, 142, 221
Bergman, Ingrid, 207
Berlin Film Festival, 39, 155
Bernstein, Leonard, 24
Bertolucci, Bernardo, 225, 236
Besson, Luc, 72, 208, 248
Bester, Alfred, 27, 87, 228
Big Blue, The (Besson), 208
Big Sky, The (Hawks), 91
Binoche, Juliette, 207
Birds, The (Hitchcock), 94
Biskind, Peter, 104
Black Book (Verhoeven), 271

Black Dahlia, The (De Palma), 9-10, 20, 248-59, 276, 279
Blair Witch Project, The (Myrick/Sánchez), 267
Blood on the Moon (Ellroy), 251
Blow Out (De Palma), 17, 37, 52, 68, 74-5, 89, 93, 95, 115-23, 138, 141, 143, 145, 166, 170-1, 183, 245, 248, 252, 259, 262
Blow-Up (Antonioni), 122
Boardwalk Empire (TV), 284
Bode, Ralf D., 17
Boden, Kristina, 19
Boetticher, Budd, 152
Body Double (De Palma), 17, 52, 74, 89, 93, 96, 115, 134-47, 149, 161, 263, 273, 292
Bogart, Humphrey, 194
Boileau-Narcejac, 259
Bolero (Ravel), 246-7
Bonfire of the Vanities, The (De Palma), 3, 5, 18, 46, 59, 72-3, 88, 127, 143, 145, 172-83, 185, 187-9, 215, 219, 245, 249, 252-3
Boorman, John, 27, 150, 168, 174, 188, 237
Bottin, Rob, 209
Bound for Glory (Ashby), 85
Bourgoin, Stéphane, 257
Bouzereau, Laurent, 2
Boys Don't Cry (Peirce), 251
Branagh, Kenneth, 197
Brando, Marlon, 132, 169, 246
Bregman, Martin, 126, 133, 192, 203, 215
Bridge on the River Kwai, The (Lean), 81, 161
Bringing Out the Dead (Scorsese), 103
Bronson, Charles, 199
Browning, Tod, 54
Brynner, Yul, 47
Buckley, Betty, 85
Bugsy Malone (Parker), 57
Bujold, Geneviève, 26, 65, 67, 209, 277
Bullock, Sandra, 228
Burger, Neil, 271
Burum, Stephen H., 17-19, 122, 209

Burrows, Kenny, 36-7
Burton, Richard, 65
Burton, Tim, 233
Butch Cassidy and the Sundance Kid (Hill), 76

Caché (Haneke), 289
Cage, Nicolas, 200-1, 214-15, 217, 223-4, 226, 260, 277
Cahiers du Cinéma, 199
Caine, Michael, 4, 52, 110-11
Callaghan, Christina, 31
Calley, John, 47
Cameron, James, 93, 198, 278
Campbell, Joseph, 204
Candid Camera (TV), 52-3
Cannes Film Festival, 6, 11, 240, 246, 279
Canton, Mark, 182-3
Capone, Al, 151-2
Capone Rising, 260
Capote, Truman
Carlito's Way (De Palma), 2-3, 19, 72, 75, 93, 119, 143, 145, 171, 175, 183, 191-9, 201, 215, 227, 243-4, 249, 297
Carmen (Bizet), 72
Carnival of the Animals (Saint-Saëns), 246
Carpenter, John, 86
Carpool (De Palma), 199
Carrey, Jim, 200
Carrie (De Palma), 11, 16, 39, 41, 51, 56, 61, 69, 73, 75-87, 89, 92, 94-6, 113-14, 243, 274, 277, 286, 290
Carter, James L., 17,
Carter, Natalie, 272, 283
Casablanca (Curtiz), 194
Casino (Scorsese), 217
Cassavetes, John, 29, 92, 94-5, 253
Cassavetes, Nick, 271
Casualties of War (De Palma), 18, 41, 59, 89-90, 108, 115, 154-73, 175, 177, 193, 225, 249, 260-1, 263, 266, 268, 289
Cheadle, Don, 230, 233
Chamber Brothers, The, 167
Chinatown (Polanski), 72, 134, 215, 237, 253-5, 258

Cimino, Michael, 168, 174, 182
Cinema 16, 32, 295
Citizen Kane (Welles), 45, 146, 203
Clancy, Tom, 72
Clark, Mary Higgins, 90
Clayburgh, Jill, 33, 39, 125, 156
Clemm, Susanna, 111
Cliff, Jonathon, 20
Clinton, Bill, 39
Clinton, Hillary, 291
Clooney, George, 229
Cloud Atlas (Wachowski/Tykwer), 289
Cocks, Jay, 5-6, 36, 53-4, 104, 199-200, 205
Coen brothers, 102, 137
Cohen, Lawrence D., 16, 76
Cohn, Nik, 198
Colbert, Claudette, 207
Colbert, Peter, 15
Colla, Richard A., 47
Collins, Lily, 293
Columbia University, 28-9, 32-3, 102
Comfort of Strangers, The (Schrader), 268
Conan Doyle, Arthur, 27
Congo (Marshall), 200
Connery, Sean, 91, 111, 150, 153, 260
Conrad, Joseph, 169
Conversation, The (Coppola), 106, 122
Cook, Brian W., 161
Cop (Harris), 251
Coppola, Francis, 1, 11-12, 46, 101-2, 106-7, 122, 169, 182, 284
Corneau, Alain, 269-71, 277, 280
Costner, Kevin, 151, 182
Cox, Courtney, 146
Creative Artists Agency, 201
Crichton, Douglas, 55
Crichton, Michael, 55, 200
Crime d'amour (Corneau), 269, 272, 280
Cristofer, Michael, 18, 175, 215
Crittenden, Jordan, 15
Cronenberg, David, 86, 140, 187, 289
Cruise, Tom, 1, 3-4, 132, 183, 201-10, 225, 286
Cruising (Friedkin), 109, 292
Cuarón, Alfonso, 229-30

Cuban, Mark, 260, 262

Daft Punk, 86
Dalva, Robert, 18
Daly, Bob, 181-2
Dante, Joe, 86
Dargis, Manohla, 268
Dassin, Jules, 205
Davenport, Mary, 100
Davidovich, Lolita, 141, 189, 288-9
Days of Heaven (Malick), 236
Dead Presidents (Hughes brothers), 169
Dealing (Williams), 55, 70
Death Becomes Her (Zemeckis), 192
Death Proof (Tarantino), 248
Debussy, Claude, 274
Deer Hunter, The (Cimino), 167-8
Delerue, Georges, 72
Deliverance (Boorman), 168
Del Toro, Benicio, 10
DeMille, Cecil B., 86, 132
Demolished Man, The (Bester), 27, 87, 139, 228
Deneuve, Catherine, 207
De Niro, Robert, 33, 38, 41, 43, 104, 138, 151, 178, 207, 252-3, 257
De Palma Cut, The (Bouzereau), 2
Depardieu, Gérard, 131
Dernier Combat, Le (Besson), 208
Desplat, Alexandre, 291
DeVito, Danny, 149
Devil's Candy, The (Salamon), 3, 173
Dial M for Murder (Hitchcock), 278
DiCaprio, Leonardo, 285
Dickinson, Angie, 91, 109-13, 221
Dionysus in 69 (De Palma), 6, 15, 31, 39-41, 52, 60, 223
Dirty Dozen, The (Aldrich), 202
Dirty Grandpa (Mazer), 252
Disney, Walt, 12, 60, 106, 200, 232
Dog Day Afternoon (Lumet), 110
Dolgen, Jonathan, 211
Domino (De Palma), 20
Donaggio, Pino, 16-18, 20, 74, 85, 123, 276
Donahue Show, The (TV), 110
Don Giovanni (Mozart), 73
Don't Breathe (Álvarez), 282
Don't Look Now (Roeg), 74

Doors, The, 146, 201
Dostoyevsky, Fyodor, 64
Double Indemnity (Wilder), 192, 242, 246
Dougherty, Marion, 96
Douglas, Kirk, 91, 96, 100
Downey Jr., Robert, 279
Doyle, Patrick, 3, 19, 197, 246-7
DreamWorks SKG, 106, 212
Dressed to Kill (De Palma), 2, 4, 17, 41, 52, 74, 91, 93, 108-19, 124, 137, 144, 166, 185, 187, 213, 221, 225, 240, 246-7, 273, 276-7, 292
Drew, Robert, 28
Dr. Jekyll and Mr. Hyde (Mamoulian), 290
Dr. Strangelove (Kubrick), 173, 177
Dullea, Keir, 234
Durning, Charles, 54, 91
Dye, Dale, 158-9

Earp, Wyatt, 152
Earthquake (Robson), 128
East/West (Wargnier), 246
Eastwood, Clint, 251
Easy Riders, Raging Bulls (Biskind), 104
Ebert, Roger, 268
Ebouaney, Eriq, 246
Eckhart, Aaron, 251-3
Edelman, Dana, 17
Eggers, Dave, 289
Eisenhower, Dwight, 39
Elfman, Danny, 19, 203, 208
Elfstrom, Robert, 15
Elliott, Jack, 15
Ellis, Bret Easton, 134
Ellroy, James, 249-51, 253-5, 257-8
Empire of the Sun (Spielberg), 170
Euripides, 15, 39, 41
Evans, Robert, 237
Exorcist, The (Friedkin), 58, 85-6, 107
Exorcist II: The Heretic (Boorman), 188
Eyes of a Stranger (Wiederhorn), 134
Eyes Wide Shut (Kubrick), 167, 236

Face/Off (Woo), 223
Fallout 4 (video game), 287

Family Plot (Hitchcock), 11
Family Ties (TV), 159
Fargo (Coen brothers), 102
Farris, John, 16, 87
Farrow, John, 291
Fast Times at Ridgemont High (Heckerling), 196
Fatal Attraction (Lyne), 154
Faust (Goethe), 57
Fedora (Wilder), 101
Fellini, Federico, 28, 32
Femme Fatale (De Palma), 7, 9-10, 19, 239-49, 257, 259, 279
Ferguson, Allyn, 15
Ferretti, Dante, 252
Fight Club (Fincher), 250
Film Comment (magazine), 1
Filmways, 119
Fincher, David, 250-1, 278
Finian's Rainbow (Coppola), 46
Finley, William, 32-3, 37, 39, 41, 53-4, 58, 62, 70, 76, 258
Fiore, Robert, 15, 40, 296
Fire (De Palma), 146
Fire in the Lake (FitzGerald), 171
Fisk, Jack, 61, 77, 83-4
FitzGerald, Frances, 171
Flowers, A.D., 92
Forbidden Planet (Wilcox), 228
Ford, John, 10, 103, 179-80, 193, 236, 290
Forman, Miloš, 202
Four Friends (Penn), 136
Fox, Michael J., 158-60, 163, 166-7, 293
Fox News, 262, 268
Frances Ha (Baumbach), 280, 290
Franz, Dennis, 37, 93, 110, 213
Frankenheimer, John, 199
Frankie Goes to Hollywood, 145-6
Freaks (Browning), 54
Free Cinema, 29, 33
Freeman, David, 76
Freeman, Morgan, 176
French Connection, The (Friedkin), 93
French New Wave, 33
Frenzy (Hitchcock), 11
Friedkin, William, 1, 58, 93, 107, 109, 182, 293

Friedman, Josh, 20, 249-50, 258
Frye, Mia, 247, 257
Fuller, Samuel, 147
Full Metal Jacket (Kubrick), 146, 167, 179
Fury (Lang), 222
Fury, The (De Palma), 2, 16, 41, 72, 75, 87-97, 99, 110, 143
Fuzz (Colla), 47

Gale, Bob, 199
Gallo, George, 18
Gangster Squad (Fleischer), 260
Gardenia, Vincent, 100
Garfield, Allen, 38, 44
Gates, Bill, 239
Gédigier, François, 20
Geffen, David, 107, 279
Gelderblom, Peet, 288
Get to Know Your Rabbit (De Palma), 15, 43-4, 46-7, 55, 76, 253
Ghost (Zucker), 297
Ghost Story (Irvin), 136
Gibson, Mel, 155
Girlfriend Experience, The (TV), 262
Godard, Jean-Luc, 28-9, 52, 72, 187, 203, 276
Godfather, The (Coppola), 46, 106-7, 278
Godfather Part II, The (Coppola), 122
Godfather Part III, The (Coppola), 73
Goldman, William, 283
Goldsmith, Jerry, 72, 258
Goodfellas (Scorsese), 46, 101, 219
Gordin, Alixe, 96, 127
Gordon, Keith, 100-101, 110, 114, 253
Graham, Gerrit, 38, 100
Grand Theft Auto (video game), 287
Grant, Hugh, 175
Gravity (Cuaron), 229
Greenberg, Jerry, 17-18
Greetings (De Palma), 2, 15, 28, 31, 33, 37-9, 41-3, 137, 143, 168, 178, 218, 236, 264, 267, 296
Griffith, Melanie, 127, 135-6, 182, 189, 197, 245

Grosbard, Ulu, 33
Groundhogs, The, 58
Grusin, Dave, 18, 72
Guare, John, 125
Guber, Peter, 173, 181
Gugino, Carla, 221-2

Hackman, Gene, 122
Hancock, John, 33
Handel, 265, 268
Haneke, Michael, 277, 289
Hanks, Tom, 176, 182, 200, 289
Hanson, Curtis, 192, 149
Happy Valley (De Palma), 283
Hardcore (Schrader), 139
Harders, Robert, 17
Harper, Jessica, 58
Harris, James B., 251
Hartnett, Josh, 251-2
Haven, Annette, 135-6
Hawks, Howard, 126-7, 132-3, 179, 290
Hawthorne, Nathaniel, 69
Hayworth, Rita, 246
Heard, John, 214
Heart of Darkness (Conrad), 169
Heaven and Earth (Stone), 161
Heaven's Gate (Cimino), 174
Hecht, Ben, 127
Heckerling, Amy, 196
Hedren, Tippi, 136
Heffner, Richard, 108
Herfurth Karoline, 271, 273
Hefner, Hugh, 60
Hemmings, David, 122
Henry V (Branagh), 197
Herrmann, Bernard, 16, 45, 55-6, 66-7, 71, 73-4, 206, 225, 256
Hi, Mom! (De Palma), 15, 41-3, 57, 109, 115, 143, 218, 256-7, 264, 267, 296
Hinckley, John, 194
Hirsch, Charles, 15, 37
Hirsch, Paul, 15-19, 55-6, 208
His Kind of Woman (Farrow), 291
Hitchcock, Alfred, 2, 10, 11, 28-9, 35, 37, 45, 49-51, 56, 63-7, 69, 73, 94-6, 103, 109, 112, 120, 134, 136-7, 143, 149, 166, 189, 199, 219-22, 235-6, 256, 266, 270, 278, 290

Hoax, The (Irving), 201
Hoffman, Anthony, 234
Holden, William, 254
Home Alone (Columbus), 105
Home Movies (De Palma), 17, 74, 99, 110, 112, 114-15, 137
Hopkins, Anthony, 10
Horner, James, 72, 258
Hoskins, Bob, 151
Howard the Duck (Huyck), 182
Hubbard, L. Ron, 235
Hughes brothers, 169
Hughes, Howard, 12, 60, 106, 200-1, 214, 231, 235, 291, 293
Hugo, Victor, 258
Huppert, Isabelle, 269
Hurd, Gale Anne, 154, 185
Hustler, The (Rossen), 84
Huston, John, 173, 255
Huyck, Willard, 201-2

Icarus (De Palma), 13, 30
Ice Storm, The (Lee), 236
Inception (Nolan), 272, 277
Indecent Proposal (Lyne), 154
Indiana Jones and the Last Crusade (Spielberg), 263
Indochine (Wargnier), 3, 197
Industrial Light & Magic, 232, 278, 287
In Remembrance of Things Past (Proust), 294
Interview with the Vampire (Jordan), 4
Interview with the Vampire (Rice), 82
Irvin, John, 135
Irving, Amy, 77, 79, 83-4, 94-6
Irving, Clifford, 201
Isham, Mark, 20, 258-9

Jackie (Larraín), 290
Jack the Ripper, 117
Jarre, Maurice, 72
Jennifer (De Palma), 14, 295
Johansson, Scarlett, 253
Johnston, Joe, 10
Johnson, Laurie, 70
Johnson, Lyndon, 31
Joubert, Sylvain

Juicy Fruits, The, 58

Kael, Pauline, 53, 108, 171
Karina, Anna, 187
Kasdan, Lawrence, 151
Katz, Gloria, 106, 201-2
Katzenberg, Jeffrey, 107
Kavanagh, John, 255
Kaz, Eric, 15
Kazan, Elia, 155-6, 159, 259
Keitel, Harvey, 104
Kelly, Grace, 246
Kennedy, Edward, 117
Kennedy, John F., 31, 38-9, 116-7, 216, 257
Kershner, Irvin, 210
Kill Bill (Tarantino), 245
Killing, The (Kubrick), 251
King Kong (Cooper/Schoedsack), 32
King of Comedy, The (Scorsese), 128
King, Larry, 175
King Solomon's Mines (Bennett/ Marton), 232
King, Stephen, 75-6, 82, 87
Kidder, Margot, 47, 52, 62, 76, 109
Kirshner, Mia, 251
Kline, Richard H., 16
Koehler, Bonnie, 18
Koepp, David, 5, 19, 192, 201-3, 210, 214-15
Kroeger, Wolf, 161
Kubrick, Stanley, 49-50, 73, 143, 167, 177, 179, 184, 229, 234, 236, 251, 265

L.A. Confidential (Hanson), 245, 249, 253
Ladd, Alan, 153
Ladd Jr., Alan, 61
LaMotta, Jake, 95
Landau, Jon, 146
Lang, Daniel, 155-6
Lang, Fritz, 222, 239
Lansing, Sherry, 110, 154, 211
Lantz, Robbie, 56
Larraín, Pablo, 290
Last Tango in Paris (Bertolucci), 236
Laurie, Piper, 82-4
Lautner, John, 142

Lawrence of Arabia (Lean), 120, 274, 278
Leach, Wilford, 15, 32-3
Leacock, Richard, 28
Lean, David, 29, 72, 199
Lee, Ang, 236
Leguizamo, John, 160
Lehman, Susan, 259
Leigh, Janet, 56, 112, 137
Le May, Stephen, 17
Le Mépris (Godard), 72
Leone, Sergio, 166
Lester, Richard, 33
Le, Thuy Thu, 158, 266
Leuci, Bob, 118-19
Life (magazine), 51, 242
Light Sleeper (Schrader), 63
Lights Out in China (De Palma), 281
Linson, Art, 150-2, 159, 249-50
Lithgow, John, 52, 68-70, 189, 288-9
Litto, George, 56-7, 65, 70, 76, 110
Little Buddha (Bertolucci), 225
Lolita (Nabokov), 173
Lopez, Jennifer, 244
Loren, Sophia, 207
Los Angeles Times (newspaper), 268
Lost World: Jurassic Park (Spielberg), 104
Love at Twenty (Rossellini), 33
Loventhal, Charlie, 17
Lucas, Frank, 259
  Lucas, George, 1, 12, 46, 84, 86, 100-7, 169, 182, 204, 210, 213, 229, 232-33, 278, 284-5, 287, 296
Lucky Ones, The (Burger), 271
Lumet, Sidney, 118-19, 126-7
Lynch, David, 27, 86, 240, 243-4
Lynch, Jessica, 269

Mackendrick, Alexander, 171, 176
Mackenzie, John, 199
Magnificent Seven, The (Sturges), 127
Magnolia (Anderson), 224, 237
Mahler, Gustav, 197
Malden, Karl, 136
Malick, Terrence, 37, 54, 61, 236
Malle, Louis, 214
Malloy, Merrit, 85

Mamet, David, 18, 75, 127, 150-2, 154, 215
Mamoulian, Rouben, 290
Manchurian Candidate, The (Frankenheimer), 199
Mankiewicz, Herman, 203
Mann, Anthony, 290
Man Who Knew Too Much, The (Hitchcock), 199, 266
Man Who Laughs, The (Leni), 257
Man Who Shot Liberty Valance, The (Ford), 103, 193
Marianelli, Dario, 291
Marnie (Hitchcock), 96, 221
Marner, Eugene, 29-30
Mars Attacks! (Burton), 233
Martin, Jared, 31, 33
M*A*S*H (Altman), 47
Massachusetts Institute of Technology, 23
Mastrantonio, Mary Elizabeth, 127
McAdams, Rachel, 269-71
McBride, Jim, 28
McCambridge, Mercedes, 271
McConkey, Larry, 246
McDowell, John Herbert, 14-15
McKay, Gardner, 259
McNally, Terrence, 30
Mean Girls (Waters), 271
Mean Streets (Scorsese), 46, 64, 95, 104
Medavoy, Mike, 76, 84, 119
Medeiros, Elli, 240, 246
Medicine Ball Caravan (Reichenbach), 46
Melancholia (von Trier), 274
Merry Christmas, Mr. Lawrence (Oshima), 225
Metropolitan Museum of Art, 114
Midnight Express (Parker), 132
Michelangelo, 70
Midler, Bette, 109
Miles from Home (Sinise), 226
Miles, Vera, 66
Millennium trilogy (Oplev/Alfredson), 270-1
Miller, George, 181
Miller, Penelope Ann, 197
Million Dollar Baby (Eastwood), 251
Mimouni, Gilles, 248

Mission: Impossible (De Palma), 1, 3-5, 19, 52, 72, 75, 103, 105, 121, 131, 143, 201-11, 214, 216, 225, 227, 230-2, 246, 254, 262, 275-6, 285-6
Mission to Mars (De Palma), 6-7, 9, 11, 19, 52, 96, 225-35, 240, 285
Mitchum, Robert, 291
Mod (De Palma), 14
Memento (Nolan), 240
Miami Vice (TV), 130
Moment by Moment (Wagner), 116
Monash, Paul, 76
Monroe, Marilyn, 221
Montoute, Edouard, 246
Moroder, Giorgio, 17, 131-2
Morricone, Ennio, 18-19, 154, 170, 197, 233
Morrison, Jim, 146
Mortal Transfer (Beineix), 247
Mozart, Wolfgang Amadeus, 73
Motion Picture Association of America, 133
Mr. Arkadin (Welles), 292
Mr. Hughes (De Palma), 200, 227
MTV, 146, 184
Mueller-Stahl, Armin, 233
Mulholland Drive (Lynch), 240, 243-4
Mulligan, Robert, 62
Muni, Paul, 126, 182
Munroe, Cynthia, 15, 32
Museum of Modern Art, 36, 296
Murder a la Mod (De Palma), 6, 14, 37, 42
Musso & Frank, 64
My Life (Rubin), 297
Myst (video game), 211

Nabokov, Vladimir, 173
NASA, 228-9
National Association for the Advancement of Colored People, 36
Nazi Gold (De Palma), 6, 36, 200, 227, 231
Neon Demon, The (Refn), 263
Netflix, 263
Newborn, Ira, 18
New York Film Festival, 290

New York (magazine), 198
New York, New York (Scorsese), 182
New York University, 29, 213
New Yorker, The (magazine), 104, 155, 171
New York Times, The (newspaper), 296
Nicholson, Jack, 215, 237, 253-4
Nichols, Mike, 156
Nielsen, Connie, 233
Nikita (Besson), 72
Nixon, Richard, 157
Nolan, Christopher, 240, 272, 277
Norris, Gloria, 17
North by Northwest (Hitchcock), 290
Notebook, The (Cassavetes), 271
Notorious (Hitchcock), 120
Novak, Kim, 63-6, 220, 256

Obsession (De Palma), 16, 26, 62-71, 75-6, 78, 90, 109, 122, 143, 170-1, 209, 214, 241-2, 252, 253, 266, 277
O'Connell, Jerry, 233
Of Mice and Men (Sinise), 226
O'Hara, Corky, 17
O'Hara, John, 47, 265
o.k. (Verhoeven), 155
Olmos, Edward James, 176
Omen, The (Donner), 85
Once Upon a Time in America (Leone), 166
Once Upon a Time in the West (Leone), 166
One from the Heart (Coppola), 182
On the Waterfront (Kazan), 132, 159
Oshima, Nagisa, 225
Oswald, Lee Harvey, 117, 194
Orion Pictures, 119
Other, The (Mulligan), 62
Out of It (Williams), 55
Out of Sight (Soderbergh), 244
Ovitz, Michael, 201

Pacific Heights (Schlesinger), 127
Pacino, Al, 109, 125-7, 131, 152, 164, 192, 195, 207, 215, 226, 253, 278
Palance, Jack, 271
Paltrow, Jake, 11, 272,
Pankow, Bill, 17-20

Papp, Joe, 156
Parallax View, The (Pakula), 119
Paramount Pictures, 5, 150, 152, 154, 156-7, 171, 210, 211, 223
Paranormal Activity (Peli), 267
Paris vu par... (Godard), 187
Parker, Alan, 57
Party Girl (Ray), 152
Passion (De Palma), 10-11, 20, 269-80, 286
Paterno, Joe, 284
Paths of Glory (Kubrick), 251
Patriot Games (Noyce), 72
Peck, Gregory, 64
Peckinpah, Sam, 81, 94, 130
Peeping Tom (Powell), 52, 185
Peirce, Kimberly, 286
Penn, Arthur, 136
Penn, Sean, 158-60, 166, 193, 196, 253, 260
Pennebaker, D.A., 28
Performance Group, The, 39, 41
Perfume: The Story of a Murderer (Tykwer), 271
Perkins, Anthony, 95, 137
Perry, Frank, 136
Pfeiffer, Michelle, 127
Pfluger, Charlie, 33
Phantom of the Opera, The (Leroux), 57, 61
Phantom of the Paradise (De Palma), 11, 16, 39, 41, 55, 57-62, 69, 86, 88, 90, 120, 128, 205, 213, 219, 258, 273
Phillips, Julia, 62, 174
Phillips, Michael, 62
Picture (Ross), 173
Pizer, Larry, 16
Platoon (Stone), 156, 158, 167, 171
Playboy (magazine), 60
Poe, Edgar Allan, 69
Polanski, Roman, 215, 237, 253
Pollack, Sydney, 201
Picture of Dorian Gray, The (Wilde), 57
Postman, The (Costner), 182
Potter, Monica, 233
Powell, Michael, 28-9, 52, 59, 68, 185
Powell, Peter, 15, 33
Predator (McTiernan), 228

Preminger, Otto, 256
Pressburger, Emeric, 29, 68
Pressman, Edward, 54-5, 57, 61, 203
Prince of the City (Lumet), 110, 118-19, 156, 260
Pritchard, Anne, 214
Projections (Boorman/Donohue), 174
Puccini, Giacomo, 268
Pulp Fiction (Tarantino), 116, 184
Psycho (Hitchcock), 56, 73, 86, 95, 109, 111-12, 114-15, 137, 270
Ptak, John, 65
Pyne, Daniel, 127

Quiet Man, The (Ford), 153

Rabe, David, 18, 110, 119, 126, 156-7, 170, 215, 260
Rage: Carrie 2, The (Shea), 286
Raging Bull (Scorsese), 219
Raising Cain (De Palma), 18, 74-5, 90, 97, 141, 185-90, 210, 219, 288
Ransohoff, Martin, 41, 47, 53-4, 56-7
Rapace, Noomi, 269-73, 276-7
Rashomon (Kurosawa), 214-15
Rasmussen, Rie, 247
Ravel, Maurice, 246
Raven, The (Poe), 69
Ray, David, 17-18
Ray, Nicholas, 152
Rear Window (Hitchcock), 134, 137, 199
Rebecca (Hitchcock), 274
Redacted (De Palma), 10, 20, 260-9, 274, 279, 286, 293
Red and the Black, The (Stendhal), 27
Red Badge of Courage, The (Huston), 173
Redgrave, Vanessa, 122, 207, 255
Red Planet (Hoffman), 234
Red River (Hawks), 288
Red Shoes, The (Powell/Pressburger), 28, 59, 68, 146, 274
Refn, Nicolas Winding, 263
Reichenbach, François, 46
Reisz, Karel, 29
Reno, Jean, 4, 202

Reservoir Dogs (Tarantino), 116, 128, 146, 184
Responsive Eye, The (De Palma), 14, 296
Revolutionary, The (Williams), 55
Reynolds, Burt, 47, 283
Reynolds, Norman, 204
Rhames, Ving, 202, 206
Rice, Anne, 82
Richard III (Shakespeare), 125, 193
Richards, Dick, 283
Richardson, Tony, 29
Rio Bravo (Hawks), 116
Rise and Fall of Legs Diamond, The (Boetticher), 152
Riven (video game), 211
Robbins, Tim, 233, 253
Roberts, Eric, 61
Robertson, Cliff, 26, 65, 68-9, 209, 253, 277
Robson, Mark, 128
Rock, The (Bay), 223
Rockwell, Norman, 152
Rocky (Avildsen), 85
Roeg, Nicolas, 74
Rollerball (McTiernan), 247
Rolling Stones, The, 36
Romancing the Stone (Zemeckis), 200
Romijn-Stamos, Rebecca, 7, 243, 245
Rose, Louisa, 16, 52, 57
Rosemary's Baby (Polanski), 237
Rosen, Ned, 4
Ross, Lillian, 173
Rossen, Robert, 30, 84
Rossen, Steve, 30
Rózsa, Miklós, 246
Rubin, Bruce Joel, 14-15, 163
Rules Don't Apply (Beatty), 293
Run Lola Run (Tywker), 236
Russell, Jane, 291
Russo, Aaron, 149

Sabrina (Pollack), 201
Sagnier, Ludivine, 269-70, 277
Sakamoto, Ryuichi, 19, 225-6, 246-7
Saïd, Saïd Ben, 269-70, 272
Saint-Saëns, Camille, 246
Salamon, Julie, 3, 173-4, 180
Salazar, Angel, 264-5

Salles, Walter, 6
Salt, Jennifer, 47, 53, 56, 62, 100
Salt, Waldo, 56
Sandor, Gregory, 16
Sarah Lawrence (college), 31-2, 36-7, 54, 58, 99-100, 102, 154, 204, 295
Sarris, Andrew, 108
Saturday Night Fever (Badham), 198
Saving Private Ryan (Spielberg), 104, 172
Scarface (De Palma), 11, 17, 59, 75, 88, 95, 119, 125-34, 143, 152, 176, 183, 189, 192-3, 196, 198, 200, 215, 253, 286-7
Scarface (Hawks), 133
Scarlet Letter, The (Hawthorne), 69
Scent of a Woman (Brest), 196
Schechner, Richard, 39-40, 60
Schickel, Richard, 53
Schifrin, Lalo, 208
Schindler's List (Spielberg), 172, 202
Schlesinger, John, 27, 127
Schrader, Leonard, 63
Schrader, Paul, 16, 43, 62-6, 139, 153, 215, 240, 268, 284
Schreiber, Flora Rheta, 186
Schwab, Eric, 161, 179, 230, 263
Schuler, Fred, 18
Scorsese, Martin, 1, 5, 11-12, 22, 27, 29, 32, 46-7, 59, 62-4, 89, 95, 101-5, 107, 126, 128, 150, 182-3, 210, 213, 217, 219, 284-5, 295-6
Scott, Ridley, 259, 289
Scott Thomas, Kristin, 269
Scream (Craven), 86
Secret Cinema, The (Bartel), 272-3
Selznick, David O., 189
Semel, Terry, 182-3
Serling, Rod, 59
Serra, Eric, 72, 247
Seventh Seal, The (Bergman), 32, 221
Shainberg, Steven, 270
Shane (Stevens), 153
Shaw, Fiona, 254-5
Shelton, Deborah, 95, 144, 147
Shepherd, William, 41, 60
Sherlock Holmes: A Game of Shadows (Ritchie), 270
Shining, The (Kubrick), 50, 73

Short, Elizabeth, 250-1, 255, 257-8
Show Me a Strong Town and I'll Show You a Strong Bank (De Palma), 14, 36
Silverado (Kasdan), 151
Silvestri, Alan, 208
Simpson, O.J., 188
Sinise, Gary, 53, 91, 96, 218, 220, 222, 224, 226, 229-30, 233, 253, 268
Sirens of Titan (Vonnegut), 27
Sisters (De Palma), 2, 11, 16, 41, 47, 50-57, 62-3, 69, 75-6, 91-2, 102, 110, 139, 143, 185, 237, 241-2, 258, 286
Sixth Sense, The (Shyamalan), 237
Skavlan, Petter, 20
Skywalker Ranch, 105, 232
Smith, Steven C., 67
Smothers, Tommy, 44, 253
Snodgress, Carrie, 95-6
Social Network, The (Fincher), 278
Soderbergh, Steven, 244, 262
Solaris (Soderbergh), 228
Soldo, Chris, 54, 195
Soles, P.J., 84
Soles, Steven, 15
Sorcerer (Friedkin), 182
Spacek, Sissy, 61, 78-81, 83-4, 94-5, 271
Spencer, Scott, 199
Spider-Man (Raimi), 277
Spielberg, Steven, 1, 11-12, 27, 46, 70, 86, 100-107, 109, 143, 151, 170, 172, 182, 200-1, 212, 223, 229, 263, 279, 284-5, 296
Sphere (Levinson), 228
Springsteen, Bruce, 145-6
Stalmaster, Lynn, 96
Stanislavski, Constantin, 138-9
Stark, Ray, 110
Star Wars (Lucas), 12, 84, 106, 204, 212, 232
Star Wars: The Force Awakens (Abrams), 290
Star Wars: The Phantom Menace (Lucas), 103, 232-4
Starkweather, Charlie, 37

Statham, Jason, 283
Steel, Dawn, 150, 154, 157, 159
Steinberg, Norman, 18
Stendhal, 27
Stevens, Andrew, 88, 95-6
Stevenson, Michael, 161-2
Stevenson, Robert Louis, 27
Stewart, James, 63-5, 67, 69, 141, 147, 159, 170, 199
Stone, Oliver, 17, 31, 117, 125-6, 128, 132, 143, 158, 161, 167, 215, 253
Strange Case of Doctor Jekyll and Mister Hyde (Stevenson), 185
Strangers on a Train (Hitchcock), 95-6, 134
Streamers (Altman), 156
Streisand, Barbra, 57
Sturges, John, 127
Sugarland Express, The (Spielberg), 70, 109
Summer, Donna, 132
Sundance Film Festival, 294
Sunset Boulevard (Wilder), 132, 192, 237, 254
Survivor (TV), 272
Suspiria (Argento), 58
Swank, Hilary, 251, 254
Sweet Smell of Success (Mackendrick), 171, 176-7
Sweet Vengeance (De Palma), 282
Sybil (Schreiber), 187

Take One (magazine), 117
Tandy, Jessica, 94
Tanen, Ned, 150, 156-7, 171
Tarantino, Quentin, 102, 106, 116, 128, 146, 184, 237, 245, 248
Taxi Driver (Scorsese), 43, 62, 64, 71, 89, 95, 116, 141, 153
Taylor, Elizabeth, 56
Temchin, Jack, 100
Terminator, The (Cameron), 154
Terminator 2 (Cameron), 198
Tetro (Coppola), 285
The Night Of (TV), 284, 286
Thief of Baghdad, The (Powell), 28
Thin Red Line, The (Malick), 236
Thomas, D.M., 87
Thomas, Jim, 19
Thomas, John, 19

Thomas, Melody, 96
Three Days of the Condor (Pollack), 119
THX 1138 (Lucas), 46
Thurman, Uma, 245
Time (magazine), 53-4
Titanic (Cameron), 86
To Bridge This Gap (De Palma), 14
To Catch a Thief (Hitchcock), 28
Topaz (Hitchcock), 11
Topkapi (Dassin), 205
Torbet, Bruce, 14
Toronto Film Festival, 260, 286
Torres, Edwin, 192
Tosca (Puccini), 260, 268
Tosi, Mario, 16
Touch of Evil (Welles), 45, 76, 112, 219
Towne, Robert, 19, 202-3, 209, 215-6, 237
Toyer (De Palma), 258, 276
Traum, Artie, 15
Travolta, John, 83-4, 94-5, 115-16, 118-21, 123, 127, 131, 146, 198, 245
Treasure of the Sierra Madre, The (Huston), 200
Truffaut, François, 28, 180, 203
Truman Show, The (Weir), 200
Trump, Donald, 292
Truth and Other Lies, The (Arango), 282
Tunnels of Cu Chi, The (Mangold/Penycate), 163
Twilight Zone, The (TV), 59
Tykwer, Tom, 271, 289

UCLA, 102
United Artists, 76, 84-5, 119, 174
Universal Studios, 37, 61, 112, 199, 254-5
Unforgiven (Eastwood), 153
Untouchables, The (De Palma), 6, 18, 73, 92-3, 111, 121, 143, 149-54, 161, 166, 170, 189, 193, 201, 210, 221, 249, 252-3, 260
Urioste, Frank J., 15
Ustinov, Peter, 208

Van Houten, Carice, 271
Vanity Fair (magazine), 110
Variety (newspaper), 5
Veidt, Conrad, 258
Verbinski, Gore, 227
Verhoeven, Michael, 155
Verhoeven, Paul, 140, 271
Vertigo (Hitchcock), 28, 63-7, 69, 122, 134-5, 141, 147, 170, 220, 256, 259, 274, 278
Videodrome (Cronenberg), 140
Village Voice, The (newspaper), 171
Vinyl (TV), 284
Visconti, Luchino, 28-9
Visitors, The (Kazan), 155-6
VistaVision, 28, 64, 278
Vogel, Amos, 32, 295
Voight, Jon, 55, 203-7, 209, 225
Vonnegut, Kurt, 27, 121, 245
von Stroheim, Erich, 236
von Trier, Lars, 274

Wachowski sisters, 290
Wahlberg, Mark, 251
Wait Until Dark (Young), 282
Walbrook, Anton, 59
Wall Street Journal (newspaper), 3, 178
Wargnier, Régis, 3-4, 197, 240, 244, 246
Warner Bros., 43-4, 46-7, 55, 125, 134, 173-5, 177, 180-3, 252
Wasson, Craig, 95, 135-6, 139, 144, 147
Waters, Mark, 271
Wayne, John, 153
Weaver, Dennis, 112
Wedding Party, The (De Palma), 15, 32-3, 41
Weintraub, Fred, 46
Weisz, Rachel, 271
Welch, Raquel, 47
Wells, H.G., 27
Welles, Orson, 40, 44, 45, 76, 106, 112, 179, 203, 219, 253, 279, 281, 292, 294
White Hotel, The (Thomas), 87
Whitney Museum, 296
Wiederhorn, Ken, 134
Wilcox, Fred M., 228

Wild Bunch, The (Peckinpah), 81, 130
Wilde, Oscar, 27
Wilder, Billy, 101, 127, 192, 237, 246, 254
Wild One, The (Benedek), 132
Williams, John, 72, 170
Williams, Paul (musician), 16, 57, 86
Williams, Paul (producer), 55, 70
Williams, Treat, 119
Willis, Bruce, 132, 178, 180, 182, 253
Wilson, Lisle, 53
Wilson, Michael, 3
Wilson, Rita, 178
Winslet, Kate, 271
Wise Guys (De Palma), 6, 18, 72, 103, 149, 150
Witches of Eastwick, The (Miller), 181
Wizard of Oz, The (Fleming), 27
Wolfe, Tom, 5, 172-3, 175-7, 183
Woman in the Window, The (Lang), 239
Woo, John, 204
Wood, Robin, 112
Woods, James, 251
Worthington, Sam, 278
Woton's Wake (De Palma), 13, 32
Wright, Frank Lloyd, 142

Yablans, Frank, 87, 96, 203
Yablonski, Joseph, 199
Yakuza, The (Pollack), 64
Yost, Graham, 19
Youth Without Youth (Coppola), 285
You'll Never Eat Lunch in This Town Again (Phillips), 174

Zaillian, Steven, 202, 259, 284
Zapruder, Abraham, 216
Zemeckis, Robert, 192, 199, 208
Zodiac (Fincher), 250
Zoetrope, 46
Zsigmond, Vilmos, 16-18, 20, 70, 122, 252, 257
Zubaidi, Zahra, 263

Milton Keynes UK
Ingram Content Group UK Ltd.
UKHW020357021124
450424UK00014B/1361